DSK

DSK

The Scandal That Brought Down DOMINIQUE STRAUSS-KAHN

JOHN SOLOMON

THOMAS DUNNE BOOKS ST. MARTIN'S PRESS
NEW YORK

THOMAS DUNNE BOOKS.
An imprint of St. Martin's Press.

www.thomasdunnebooks.com
www.stmartins.com

Design by Steven Seighman

ISBN 978-1-250-01263-0

First Edition: June 2012

10 9 8 7 6 5 4 3 2 1

To Judy and Josh, your love, support, and courage inspire everyone around you, starting with me.

To my dad, Jack, who in forty-six years of law enforcement taught me investigations could be tough and courageous without ever losing their fairness.

CONTENTS

ACKNOWLEDGMENTS

There's a reason good sporting coaches require their teams to watch game films the morning after a big contest. It's because watching a competition in slow motion almost always reveals lessons and details—and sometimes even entire new subplots—that weren't visible to the human eye when a game was playing out at full speed.

The Dominique Strauss-Kahn scandal was an epic contest that played out at lightning speed in the courts of public opinion and law under the glare of a relentless and, at times, blinding media spotlight. As a result, almost everyone thinks they know what happened: a housekeeper accuses one of the world's most powerful men of sexual assault, and prosecutors think they have a slam-dunk case and secure indictment. But then the investigators become suspicious of the alleged victim, uncover lies, see their case unravel, and recommend dismissal.

But like the Big Game in sports, re-creating the DSK case from start to finish in slow motion unmasks subplots, secret players, and forces behind the scenes that weren't visible to even its most astute observers. That is why I wrote this book, to slow down one of the most rushed legal dramas of the last decade and to explore the behaviors, motives, and suppositions that weren't visible to the public. Yes, it's a classic exercise of armchair quarterbacking, but one that unmasks some troubling questions about the state of jurisprudence in the United States at the dawn of the twenty-first century. It also exposes a breathless, rush-to-judgment media that seemed to inflame, more than inform, the public while failing to dig beyond the surface story contrived by convenient leaks.

In the end, the nuances and hidden agendas that surface in the slow-motion replay of this legal drama are compelling enough that even a seasoned onlooker like that famous appellate lawyer Alan Dershowitz is compelled to reverse his initial call on the case. If Dershowitz ends up believing as a defense lawyer that this case should have been allowed to proceed to trial, then there is reason for all of us to reexamine our last impressions in the case and ask hard questions of ourselves. Was Nafi Diallo a scheming victim who couldn't tell a straight story or a convenient, vulnerable scapegoat for a stumbling investigation and ill-prepared prosecution team? Should we admire or be troubled by a prosecution team that felt compelled to pull the levers of public opinion and emotion with targeted leaks, arranged publicity statements, and even the tapping of an accomplished author to write its legal motions? And does Strauss-Kahn's rehabilitation tour in France burnish his image or provide fresh evidence of a harrowing sexual predator who has repeatedly escaped punishment?

In the end, those are conclusions best left for you, the reader. My goal as a journalist was simply to slow down the high-speed drama and report out the once-invisible details. To do so required re-creating entire scenes and dialogues for which I wasn't present to witness. But I was blessed to have enjoyed the cooperation of so many frontline players on all sides of the case. Each volunteered their best recollections, their documents, and their time to help me flesh out the compelling narrative that they witnessed firsthand. Some were forced to work through intermediaries or required to defer to their bosses as official spokesmen. In the end, all sides of this case offered its own, unblemished account—one that significantly augments the initial draft of history forged by the first media accounts. Like all exercises in journalism, even this account will be subject to revision and differing recollections and interpretations. But it nonetheless provides a more complete factual accounting by which all of us can assess the good, the bad, and the ugly about the Madness in Manhattan. And I'm deeply grateful for the candor and willingness displayed by all sides in this case to reexamine their own actions in a new light in the aftermath of the case.

I would be remiss if I didn't also acknowledge the extraordinary collegiality, professionalism, and commitment to unearthing the truth that engulfed me in the form of my colleagues at *Newsweek*. A big story like the DSK affair requires precision teamwork to cover properly, and I was lucky to be surrounded by so many talented, humble, and endearing teammates. From Bureau Chief Chris Dickey and correspondent Tracy McNicholl in Paris to Howie Kurtz in Washington, Christine Pelisek and Terry Green Sterling out west, and the entire editing team in New York led by Tina Brown, Edward Felsenthal, and Louise Roug, I was surrounded by fantastic journalists who set aside egos, questions of home turf, and other job demands for a relentless pursuit of the truth in this case.

ONE

"NYPD Needs to Speak with You"

WITH HIS BAGS CHECKED and a half hour to kill before his flight to Paris, Dominique Strauss-Kahn fidgeted inside Air France's VIP lounge at New York's John F. Kennedy International Airport. He should have been relaxed. After all, it was a beautiful but cool Saturday afternoon in mid-May and the jet-setting International Monetary Fund director had just finished a quick jaunt to Manhattan, where he had enjoyed a romantic evening with a female friend followed by lunch with his daughter Camille.

The trip was the perfect, and perhaps last, interlude he would have before diving back into a restless summer grappling with Europe's stubborn debt crisis and preparing for his likely run for the French presidency. Back home in Paris, the conservative Nicolas Sarkozy was looking particularly vulnerable after an extended recession and countless missteps. And most of the speculation among France's pundits was that Strauss-Kahn, the dean of the French Socialist Party, was poised to become the country's twenty-fourth president and custodian of the world's third largest nuclear arsenal in 2012. Though not even a declared candidate, he was already ahead in the polls, and he overtly lusted for what he saw as his inevitable "rendezvous with the French," an election that would thrust him to the pinnacle of his political career.

Strauss-Kahn knew there would be plenty of time on the plane to start preparing for his IMF meeting the next day with German chancellor Angela Merkel. But the silver-haired sixty-two-year-old Frenchman—known affectionately back home simply as "DSK"—was too distracted to be at ease. He was obsessed over having lost his BlackBerry earlier in the day. The last time he had used the phone was inside the Sofitel when he called his daughter to let her know he would be a few minutes late for lunch. On the cab ride from the restaurant to JFK, he had noticed the device was missing and phoned Camille on one of his spare cell phones to ask her to return to McCormick & Schmicks in Manhattan where they had just dined to see if he had dropped the phone on the floor or left it on a seat. He hadn't seen the BlackBerry since he checked out of the luxury Sofitel Hotel at around 12:30 p.m.

Strauss-Kahn fretted about the phone being out of his control for so long. The sensitive secrets of the IMF's current negotiations with various players in the European debt crisis were sitting in the phone's email inbox. So, too, were records of some of the calls with his secret lover, a married French businesswoman working in New York's financial industry who had sneaked back to his Sofitel suite in the wee hours of that morning for a few hours of romance.

Even under normal circumstances, there was reason to be concerned about the phone falling into the wrong hands. But shortly before breakfast that morning, Strauss-Kahn had received an unnerving text from a friend who was embedded as a researcher in Sarkozy's Union for a Popular Movement (UMP) party. The friend's text had warned that the rival party had somehow intercepted at least one recent email from Strauss-Kahn's BlackBerry to his wife, the popular French TV journalist and millionaire heiress Anne Sinclair. The IMF boss was instantly worried that someone may have hacked his phone, and he called Anne back in France around 10 a.m., asking her to help arrange for a security expert to sweep both the BlackBerry and his iPad tablet for any malware or tracing devices when he returned to Paris.

But now the phone with the friend's ominous text message warning and its many other tales of international intrigue was gone. And so, too, was any sense of satisfaction from the weekend interlude. As his cab neared the airport, Strauss-Kahn reached into his carry-on bag for one of his backup phones, determined to make one last effort to locate the BlackBerry before the seven-hour flight to Paris.

At 3:29 p.m. on May 14, 2011, he dialed the switchboard of the Sofitel. It was a call that would forever change his life, and the course of history.

After a few transfers and delays, a friendly voice came to the phone.

"Hello, this is Lost and Found," a man who identified himself as a concierge at the Sofitel answered.

"How are you? I am Dominique Strauss-Kahn. I was a guest and I left my phone behind," he explained.

"What room?" the Sofitel employee inquired.

"2806," Strauss-Kahn answered.

"I'll need about ten minutes to go up and search the room for the phone but I have a problem: if your phone is here, how can I call you back?"

"I will give you another number," Strauss-Kahn explained, giving the number from the backup phone he was now calling from.

Strauss-Kahn was relieved to have reached someone willing to search the room. Little did he know at the time that it was a ruse, manufactured by a quick-thinking NYPD detective.

The man who had answered the phone wasn't a Lost and Found concierge, but rather a security official at the Sofitel. And seated alongside him was Detective John Mongiello, coaching him in how to coax information from Strauss-Kahn.

Police had been called to the hotel around 1:30 p.m. to respond to a report that a thirty-two-year-old housekeeper named Nafissatou Diallo, a Guinean immigrant who spoke broken English, had been sexually assaulted by a "man with white hair" who had occupied Suite 2806. The maid had told a convincing and consistent story, first to her hotel colleagues and then to police, that she had been grabbed from behind by a naked, erect man as she entered Strauss-Kahn's suite to clean it shortly after noon that day.

Diallo alleged the man forced the suite's door shut, grabbed her between the legs, and tried to rape her. When unsuccessful in getting her panties off, she said, he pushed her to the ground in a narrow hallway, grabbed her head and forced her to perform oral sex in a rough-and-tumble few minutes that had left her so shaken she still felt like vomiting an hour later.

At first, Diallo was reluctant to report the crime to police, telling her immediate housekeeping supervisor she feared she might lose her job for walking in on a guest in a VIP suite. But she recounted the same story with exacting detail and consistency, first to two housekeeping superiors and then to two hotel security officials. After some coaxing and assurances that she wouldn't be fired, Diallo agreed to report the crime, and the police were called.

It was about two hours since the 911 call. Strauss-Kahn's $3,000-a-night suite—usually a venue for wealthy French guests to sip fine wines and relax in luxury—was now cordoned off as a crime scene. And police had done their initial interviews with Diallo and were taking the woman, still in her housekeeping uniform, to the St. Luke's-Roosevelt Hospital trauma center for the all-important rape kit and checkup. Diallo did not seem to know her alleged attacker, referring to him only as the "man with the white hair." Police did not want to show a picture of Strauss-Kahn to her or let her know he was one of the world's most powerful men, fearful it might taint any future lineup identification. But a hotel security official Googled a photo of Strauss-Kahn and showed it to Diallo. She affirmed it was her attacker. Police records indicate that "accidental" photo ID happened around 2:30 p.m., after police had arrived at the hotel. Hotel workers, however, remember it occurring twice, once before the police arrived and again after detectives were on scene. Either way, it would later create questions among the defense lawyers about whether Diallo's eventual lineup identification a day later was somehow tainted and whether hotel officials were trying to prompt Diallo to file charges against DSK. The concerns became less relevant when forensics proved that DSK was the man in the room and had had a sexual encounter with Diallo. But the mistakes would portend other investigative missteps that would occur later in the case.

Detectives were still trying to ascertain the Frenchman's whereabouts when the IMF director's call came into the switchboard. Hotel security chief John Sheehan, summoned from the golf course earlier in the afternoon, had told the hotel to flag the security office if Strauss-Kahn called.

Now it had happened. Mongiello, the detective, wanted Sheehan to get two pieces of information critical to finding Strauss-Kahn—his whereabouts and a phone number where he could be reached. The detective listened in on the call and coached Sofitel security on what to say.

The first call from the cab elicited a callback number with little effort. Now the Sofitel had to politely press to find out where Strauss-Kahn was currently located without raising suspicions. Nine minutes after the first call, Sofitel security working with police instructions called Strauss-Kahn back to report, falsely, that it had found his lost BlackBerry. By this time, Strauss-Kahn had exited the cab and reached his gate at the airport.

"Mr. Strauss-Kahn, this is the Sofitel. I have your phone. I need to know where you are so I can return it," the hotel security officer opened, following the police script perfectly.

"I'm at JFK Airport," Strauss-Kahn answered.

A knot formed in the throats of the detectives listening in. The main suspect appeared to be on the lam, ready to flee the country. They needed to think quick.

"Okay, I can be there in forty minutes," the Sofitel security official said.

"I have a problem because my flight leaves at 4:26 p.m.," Strauss-Kahn explained.

"No problem. I will take a cab and be there in forty minutes," the hotel employee answered, putting Strauss-Kahn at ease. Maybe the weekend interlude would turn out just fine if he could recover his BlackBerry before the flight left.

"Okay. I am at the Air France terminal, Gate 4, Flight 23," the relieved Frenchman offered.

"Okay I will see you soon."

The ruse had worked and the police now knew Strauss-Kahn's whereabouts. And they had recorded his statements on the phone in writing, eventually disclosing them in an obscure court filing known as the "People's Voluntary Disclosure Form—Bill of Particulars."

But at that critical moment, detectives knew there was no way they could get to JFK in time from the hotel in midtown Manhattan. The only chance NYPD had to detain Strauss-Kahn and avoid a costly extradition battle in France was to summon the help of the Port Authority police, which controls security at all of New York's airports.

The race was on. Port Authority police needed to work with Air France to ensure the jet did not leave the tarmac and then dispatch two detectives to do the unthinkable—arrest the powerful leader of the International Monetary Fund.

For his part, Strauss-Kahn could take a deep breath and relax momentarily inside the Air France lounge. But perhaps used to instant satisfaction, or still in disbelief that his BlackBerry had been found so conveniently, he began to fidget in his chair. So he called the Sofitel back about twenty minutes later, to leave a prodding message. The flight was about to board.

"I want to speak to the person who is bringing back my phone. When will they arrive?" Strauss-Kahn inquired in his near-perfect English, with just a touch of a French accent. "I am in the Air France lounge. Please call me back at this number."

Another half hour elapsed and Strauss-Kahn boarded Flight 23 as its engines idled at the gate. Soon a flight attendant escorted him from his seat to the accordion-like, retractable hallway that leads from the International Terminal's Gate 4. He was met by two Port Authority detectives in plainclothes, and Strauss-Kahn thought for an instant that they were Sofitel workers who had managed to get there in time to return his BlackBerry.

"Do you have my cell phone?" the Frenchman inquired.

"Mr. Dominique Strauss-Kahn?" Port Authority detective Dewan Maharaj inquired in a voice far too serious for a cell phone delivery.

"Yes."

"May I see your passport? We would like you to come with us," the detective said in an ominous but polite tone, showing a badge.

"What for?" the diplomat inquired.

The detectives knew they were dealing with a world leader and tried to navigate politely around the obvious. Dominique Strauss-Kahn, was about to be yanked from his flight and detained. The police detectives wanted it to be dignified, and out of earshot of the Air France passengers.

"Now is not the time or place to discuss," Maharaj said diplomatically. "Do you have any baggage?"

"Yes," Strauss-Kahn nodded. The detectives grabbed his carry-on bag and escorted him back to the terminal, where he was met by a New York Port Authority police supervisor, Sergeant Raymond DiLena. The seats at the gate were now almost empty and Flight 23 was about to depart without its famous passenger.

"Mr. Dominique Strauss-Kahn. I am Sergeant DiLena," the officer greeted.

Strauss-Kahn's mind was racing. Could his lover from the night before have turned on him? Or maybe those rumors he had been hearing in France that he was about to be set up had manifested themselves in some sort of Sarkozy-led conspiracy? Could something embarrassing have been found on his BlackBerry or had it been used in a crime since he lost it?

"What is this about?" Strauss-Kahn pressed.

"The NYPD needs to speak with you about an incident in the city at a hotel," the sergeant explained.

Strauss-Kahn did not answer, his face suddenly pale. Could it be that seven minutes of fellatio with a housekeeper—to him a consenting sexual send-off to France—was coming back to haunt him?

It was now 4:45 p.m. on Saturday, May 14, about four and a half hours after the incident—described by the housekeeper as a violent sexual attack—had ended in Suite 2806. The world was about to be exposed to a grotesque sexual scandal that would titillate the media with sensational headlines and tawdry half-truths, rob the IMF of its brilliant yet sexually reckless leader, and test the capabilities of a young, inexperienced Manhattan district attorney.

Strauss-Kahn did not speak as he walked alongside the detectives and their sergeant down the long hallways of the terminal and to the Port Authority precinct at JFK Airport. He was about to be introduced to a new world far removed from the elegant diplomatic circles that had dominated his life for years. In fact, he would not set foot in his IMF office in Washington for months or experience spring in Paris as he had planned.

The dingy gray confines of American police stations and prison cells would become his surroundings for the foreseeable future.

"Please empty the contents of your pockets. Place everything on the table," Detective Maharaj commanded politely after they arrived at the airport's police office. "Would you like water?"

"No. But I would like to use the bathroom," he answered.

"Please, have a seat," the detective instructed.

Strauss-Kahn wasn't ready for the humiliation that would ensue. "Is that necessary?" he asked indignantly as the police detective grabbed his hands and placed them in handcuffs.

"Yes, it is."

"I have diplomatic immunity," Strauss-Kahn protested, a claim that would prove untrue. The detectives were already dubious. They had seen his passport upon exiting the plane and it did not contain the customary markings and declarations of those afforded diplomatic immunity in the United States.

"Where is your passport?" the detective inquired.

"It's not in this passport. I have a second passport," Strauss-Kahn offered.

In fact, back at his IMF office in Washington, D.C., Strauss-Kahn had left a type of diplomatic identification known as a laissez-passer, a special travel document issued by the United Nations for representatives of international organizations like the IMF. It does not afford automatic diplomatic immunity, though it can be used like a passport for travel identification.

The detectives weren't persuaded.

"Can I speak with someone from the French consulate?" Strauss-Kahn persisted. "What is this about?"

Maharaj, the detective, had little to offer. "I work for the Port Authority police. I can't answer these questions for you. NYPD will answer these questions. Would you like some water?"

Strauss-Kahn accepted.

John Mongiello, the NYPD detective who had shown up at the Sofitel to interview Diallo and arranged the ruse to catch Strauss-Kahn, arrived at JFK just a few minutes later with a colleague. He took Strauss-Kahn to a squad car to be transported to the Special Victims Squad in Harlem, the NYPD unit that investigates sex crimes and had been made famous by the popular TV show *Law & Order: SVU.*

Strauss-Kahn requested that he be handcuffed in the front to make it easier to walk. In the squad car, the Frenchman inquired anew about what police wanted.

"Manhattan detectives need to speak with you about an incident in a hotel room," Mongiello answered. By this time, DSK knew the matter must have involved the housekeeper, and he was envisioning an extended stay with police. His thoughts immediately turned to the Merkel meeting, and the need to postpone it.

"I need to make a call and let them know I won't be at my meeting tomorrow," he said, asking also that his handcuffs be loosened a bit. They obliged.

For the next four-plus hours, amazingly, Strauss-Kahn was not questioned by detectives and he did not ask to speak to a lawyer, instead sitting mostly quietly in the Harlem SVS detective bureau. It would be the first of several jarring decisions by the authorities that would later raise controversy and questions on all sides of the case.

Strauss-Kahn had had his share of legal troubles recently, stemming from a short affair he had with a subordinate at the IMF that resulted in a lengthy internal investigation. The final IMF report concluded that Strauss-Kahn had exhibited poor judgment in having the affair and trying to help the woman afterward find a job, but that he had not violated any laws or IMF standards of conduct. He had reached out to one of Washington's most respected defense attorneys, Bill Taylor, for that matter and the two had developed a bond of trust while weathering the investigation.

As he sat in the detectives' office in Harlem, Strauss-Kahn knew he'd most likely need Taylor's services again and began contemplating when to ask to make his call. Doing it too soon might signal to police that he had a guilty conscience. And so far no one had asked him any substantive questions about what had happened back at the hotel. So he waited patiently for police to make the next move.

As the hours passed, the Frenchman probably wondered why police had not come in to interrogate him. His mind alternated between two extremes. Perhaps the whole matter was a misunderstanding and police would soon free him. Or they were preparing to book him, essentially ending his political career.

In fact, a prosecutor was already on the scene and the Manhattan District Attorney's Office was fully in charge. The lead detectives in the case had been waiting for Diallo to finish her hospital exam, and then they took her back to the scene of the alleged attack so she could walk them through everything that happened at the Sofitel that day. She recounted in exacting detail where she was allegedly attacked, where she went to hide afterward, and where she had spit Strauss-Kahn's semen after he had ejaculated into her mouth. Crime scene technicians began swabbing walls and cutting up sections of the carpet to capture any DNA evidence.

As the hours passed, Strauss-Kahn remained unquestioned and mostly unbothered back at the Harlem station house.

Around 8:45 p.m., four hours after he was pulled from the plane and a full three hours after he arrived at the NYPD precinct in Harlem, a detective popped in to check on him and ask if he needed anything. "I would like to use the bathroom. I don't want any food but I'll have some coffee," Strauss-Kahn said.

When he got back from the bathroom, Strauss-Kahn decided it was time to make the play for his lawyer.

"I would like to call my lawyer, Bill Taylor," he told the detective who was watching him as the lead detectives in the case worked the crime scene elsewhere. "I need my cell phone."

"We're going to have to wait for the detectives to come back," explained the detective who had stayed behind. "I don't have access to your phone."

"Do I need a lawyer?" the Frenchman inquired coyly.

"It is your right to have one in this country if you want," the detective answered. "I don't know if you have some kind of diplomatic status."

"No, no, no. I'm not trying to use that," Strauss-Kahn responded. "I just want to know if I need a lawyer."

"That is up to you," the detective answered.

If the NYPD had any plans to interrogate DSK—"putting him on the box" as they say in the business—they essentially ended around 9 p.m. when Strauss-Kahn asked to call William Taylor.

More than a dozen officials in New York City law enforcement were working various aspects of the case Saturday evening. Airline passengers had seen Strauss-Kahn pulled from the plane. The Sofitel was abuzz about the incident involving one of its employees, and the District Attorney's Office was in contact with federal officials inside the State, Justice, and Treasury Departments to pass information back and forth with French authorities. They were also trying to resolve thorny questions of immunity and extradition. So it was just a matter of time before word leaked out that the powerful Frenchmen was in some sort of legal trouble involving the possible sexual assault of a housekeeper.

For a while, Taylor was blissfully ignorant of his client's sudden misfortune. He and his wife were in Washington at the Corcoran Gallery of Art, attending the wedding of his law school roommate's daughter. He and his wife had just finished a dance together sometime between 9 and 10 p.m. when Taylor's cell phone vibrated in his pocket. It was a reporter from the Agence France-Presse wire service who had kept his cell number from the earlier IMF case. The reporter relayed the rumors rocketing through France that DSK had apparently been arrested for sexual assault somewhere in New York City. The specifics were sketchy and Taylor had a hard time hearing over the din of the wedding celebration. But he immediately began calling around to locate his client.

Finding a potential suspect in the NYPD system, especially one who wasn't charged yet, on a Saturday night can be nearly impossible. Taylor reached out to a friend in New York, the respected attorney Benjamin Brafman, who as a former prosecutor and successful defense lawyer could navigate the system as well as anyone in the business. Over the years, Brafman had won accolades for winning the acquittal of rapper and record producer Sean "P. Diddy" Combs on charges related to a high-profile bar brawl, and arranging plea deals for NFL player Plaxico Burress and rapper Jay-Z. Shortly before 11 p.m., Brafman's team located Strauss-Kahn at the Harlem precinct. One of Brafman's colleagues, Marc Agnifilo, who was married to one of Vance's top deputies, had an initial discussion with prosecutors. Shortly thereafter, Strauss-Kahn was allowed to talk to Taylor.

"How you doing?" Taylor asked.

DSK was fine, though smart enough not to say too much on the phone. Taylor gave adamant instructions: "Do not talk to police until I get there." He planned to catch an early train to New York City on Sunday morning, where he and Brafman would form a high-powered legal duo aiding Strauss-Kahn's defense.

Now more than six hours into Strauss-Kahn's detention and his call with his lawyer complete, one of the lead detectives in the case, Steven Lane, finally asked Strauss-Kahn if he was willing to talk to authorities. There was no explanation for the long delay, the hours of sitting without interaction. It would prove a costly mistake.

"I was ready to talk," Strauss-Kahn said tantalizingly. "But my attorney has told me not to talk."

The interrogation possibilities were officially dead. There also was no apparent effort that first night to get a warrant to search Strauss-Kahn from head to toe for any forensic evidence, even though police long since knew Diallo's story and had confirming evidence already from her hospital visit. Many crucial hours would pass with little interaction between DSK and his captors, save for the occasional light banter.

About twenty minutes later, Lane asked Strauss-Kahn if he wanted some food. "I'm not hungry," Strauss-Kahn responded politely.

The Frenchman, a respected economist comfortable on the front lines of world crisis or walking the corridors of global power, settled in for an unfamiliar night at the police station, surrounded by sex perps and grizzled detectives. Mostly alone in a police interrogation room, he would nod off periodically through the night, never quite able to fall into deep sleep as he waited for Taylor's friendly, familiar face to arrive in the morning.

The loneliness and the isolation were good conditioning for what would follow.

TWO

The Rush to Judgment

THE MANHATTAN DISTRICT ATTORNEY'S OFFICE at One Hogan Place—near New York City's Chinatown—was buzzing the Saturday and Sunday nights after Nafissatou Diallo came forward with her allegations, its dour gray walls and air-conditioner-filled windows lit by the unfamiliar glow of a full staff on unexpected weekend duty. As soon as police had determined the suspect was a world leader of Strauss-Kahn's stature, a full complement of supervisors, prosecutors, and sex crimes detectives was summoned to work. It was not an ordinary team. This one was going to be supervised by the "eighth floor," the term that line prosecutors and detectives use to refer to the boss.

Everyone on the law enforcement side knew this was the biggest case since the bespectacled, well-coiffed, son of a diplomat named Cyrus Vance Jr. had taken over the Manhattan District Attorney's Office in January 2010 from Robert Morgenthau, the legendary prosecutor who ruled the office for thirty-five years.

Vance had become only the fourth district attorney to serve Manhattan since World War II when he won the Democratic primary to succeed Morgenthau back in September 2009. His path to victory, however, was not inevitable. Despite the name recognition associated with being the son of Jimmy Carter's secretary of state, Vance wasn't the early front-runner. And he faced questions about his decision to escape New York City for a decade to live and work in Seattle. Still, Vance pulled out a plurality election victory—with just 44 percent of the vote—on the strength of a strong endorsement from Morgenthau.

Vance's career, however, has a recurrent theme of escaping long shadows, one that would linger over the DSK case as well. He had left New York City and a job as an assistant district attorney in 1988 to go west, hoping by his own account to escape his father's long shadow on the East Coast. And now like George H. W. Bush succeeding Ronald Reagan, Vance knew that after winning office at the age of fifty-five he would be judged on his ability to carve his own path apart from Morgenthau.

Vance stumbled out of the gate in his efforts to shed the Morgenthau shadow. On the night of his September 2009 primary victory, Morgenthau seized the podium and spoke first, before Vance gave his acceptance speech. It only helped solidify the perception that the victory belonged to Morgenthau and his endorsement, not the victor himself. And a month later, when Vance squeezed himself into a rare photo shoot with the five sitting district attorneys of New York City, he appeared in the background behind Morgenthau. At the time, Vance was still two months from taking office, and Morgenthau was still in charge, but it again reinforced the impression that he was in Morgenthau's wake. And late in the DSK case, Vance would take a step that would leave some inside his office wondering anew whether he was still trapped in the vapor trail of his predecessor.

Once in office, though, Vance had been quick to put his own team and his own stamp on One Hogan Place, bringing in a hard-charging former federal prosecutor named Daniel Alonso to be his number two. Together Team Vance rolled up some early victories, including major busts of a child pornography ring, a cold case indictment against a notorious serial killer, and a crackdown on a major art theft ring. Vance also set out to plow a path as a twenty-first-century prosecutor, creating a major economic crimes unit to deal with the sort of Wall Street finance and mortgage fraud cases that led to the great recession of 2008, and a local cyber-prosecution unit to attack the rapidly rising number of digital crimes.

But Vance's team also had its share of perceived missteps, some outside the courtroom. There were reports in the all-important *New York Times* of low morale in the office as Vance and Alonso removed longtime prosecutors and elevated new leaders, the first revamping of the office in more than three decades. Some inside the NYPD ranks chafed at the perception that prosecutors were seemingly taking the lead on new crime-fighting initiatives, insinuating themselves into what was perceived to be the domain of cops. Boiled down, most concerns seemed to swirl around the political acumen and perceived micromanagement of the new leadership team, not necessarily unexpected after a sea change like the end of the Morgenthau era.

There were also a handful of legal setbacks, too. Vance's prosecutors could not sustain the most serious terrorism charges they had filed against the men they accused of plotting attacks at the city's synagogues. And they failed to secure rape convictions against two NYPD cops accused of attacking a woman in a case that became a tabloid sensation, settling for guilty verdicts on lesser charges.

It was against that backdrop that Vance's office was catapulted onto the international stage with a David vs. Goliath case pitting an immigrant hotel chambermaid against a carousing (he says "sexually liberated") world leader with epic legal and monetary resources at his disposal.

The deputies surrounding Vance were determined from that very first weekend to handle DSK's case with its A-team. No chances, no unturned stones, and no favoritism for a VIP defendant. Just the best prosecutors they had.

But there was a complication. Vance was not comfortable with the longtime chief of the Manhattan District Attorney Office's sex crimes unit who caught the initial case. Assistant District Attorney Lisa Friel had been a prosecutor for nearly three decades and had worked in sex crimes for about twenty-five years, the last decade as the unit chief. That made her one of the office's most experienced at dealing with the sensitivities and complications of sex crimes victims, who often carry lots of baggage.

The reasons for the distrust were many. Friel was viewed as a friend of former judge Leslie Crocker Snyder, who had challenged Vance in the 2009 election and finished second to him. Some inside Vance's inner circle doubted Friel's loyalties, or at least her plans to stay long term on Vance's team. Friel had begun telling people shortly after Vance took over in 2010 that she was looking to depart for the private sector and its higher salaries to help pay the college tuition of her children.

"I have two children who go to college and another who will go soon and I need to earn a little more money," Friel would tell a French interviewer in explaining her departure from the District Attorney's Office in 2011 to take a private sector job at a security and investigations company focused on sexual assaults in the private sector and at college campuses.

Secondly, Friel had acknowledged years ago failing to turn over exculpatory evidence—a single e-mail—to defense lawyers in a sex crimes case she had worked earlier in her career. The case involved a rape victim—a young man who faced his own criminal charges after he was attacked. Given the victim's hardship, Friel agreed to ask the judge in the victim's unrelated criminal case for leniency at sentencing. Friel had disclosed her role to everyone, but failed to turn over an e-mail to the victim's mother in which she made one of the initial promises to argue for leniency. In the big picture, it was a fairly small oversight—known as a Brady violation in lawyers' parlance—and Friel's career had advanced mostly unscathed since. But the Vance team feared DSK's high-powered legal team would stop at nothing to raise questions about the prosecution if the chance arose. They weren't inclined to hand the defense a freebie.

Finally, Friel had become involved in an HBO documentary about her sex crimes unit. The idea for the project had been brought to the office by Friel's predecessor, former sex crimes unit chief Linda Fairstein, and Friel's participation had been approved by Morgenthau before he retired. But Vance's team wasn't as invested in the project and fretted it might open the door for a mistaken quote or misstep that would invite appeals by defendants convicted by the unit. The documentary entitled "Sex Crimes Unit" was set to debut June 21, right in the middle of the Strauss-Kahn case, which only added to the tensions. Vance's fears were quickly realized when in late June his office belatedly turned over HBO footage to the lawyers for the two NYPD cops accused of rape. The footage showed two law enforcement officials who had worked the case talking about specifics, and it opened an immediate door for the defendants' lawyers to seek an appeal. The revelation came after the two officers had already been convicted on lesser charges and were supposed to be sentenced. In the end, a judge concluded that the HBO footage did not contain any exculpatory evidence and would not have swayed the jury, handing a win to the prosecutors. But by that time, Vance's office had already suffered a black eye in public.

Friel, in fact, was at the office helping her team prepare for closing arguments in the "Cop Rape Trial" (as it became known in the New York tabloids) when the call came in that Saturday afternoon from NYPD about the chambermaid's complaint and the plans to detain Strauss-Kahn. She dispatched one of her younger but trusted deputies in the sex crimes unit, John "Artie" McConnell, to be the lead working with the detectives. And she was poising herself to juggle both big cases. But soon it became apparent that she wasn't going to call the shots.

Friel worked to stay in the loop, but soon tasks were being divided above and around her. The chief of the trial division, Karen Friedman Agnifilo, and her deputy, John Irwin, were providing instructions to detectives and gathering information on what was happening and feeding it back to Vance and Alonso that Saturday. Agnifilo's role in those early hours would later raise questions in both the media and with the victim's lawyers because her husband, defense lawyer Marc Agnifilo, was hired to be part of Strauss-Kahn's team. Karen Agnifilo has said she recused herself from the case when she learned of her husband's role, but Diallo's lawyers could never get a satisfactory answer as to exactly when that happened, how much Agnifilo learned about the case before she stepped aside, and how rigid a firewall was constructed between Agnifilo and the prosecutors she still supervised.

In fact, Agnifilo recused herself late that very first night of the case, shortly after she learned her husband had been hired by DSK and her husband's firm had made its first contact with the office. "I am recused from this case. Please substitute Irwin for me on all subsequent e-mails. Thanks," Agnifilo wrote in a short email to colleagues at 10:45 p.m.

With Irwin and Friel directing the front lines that first weekend, Alonso focused on working the phones with Obama administration officials at the Justice Department, the Treasury Department, and the State Department, all who began calling Saturday evening when word spread of Strauss-Kahn's arrest. There were issues of an extradition treaty between the two countries and France's long tradition of refusing to extradite its own citizens that needed to be resolved. And Alonso, a former federal prosecutor, knew France and the United States had bilateral relations on matters of law enforcement, meaning a local authority like New York needed to work through the U.S. Justice Department if it wanted information or cooperation from Paris. There also were the sensitivities of the global economy and how markets might react on Monday morning when word spread that the IMF director, a critical player in European debt negotiations, was detained by police over the weekend and possibly out of action on the global stage. The contacts from federal officials were frequent enough to send an unmistakable message to Alonso: the District Attorney's office couldn't afford to make any mistakes with the entire world watching.

Multiple players inside Vance's office were giving commands in the frenetic first hours, and it was in that environment that NYPD Special Victims Section detectives believe they were instructed not to immediately question Strauss-Kahn after they arrested him at the airport. The detectives apparently were awaiting guidance from Vance's office on the question of whether Strauss-Kahn as IMF director had some sort of diplomatic immunity as he had suggested. And they were waiting for whether there was any new evidence or testimony after Diallo finished her rape kit at the hospital and headed back to the alleged crime scene Saturday night.

Just who gave what instructions to the detectives is a bit murky. Alonso assumed that police were responsible for how they handled the high-profile suspect until he was turned over to the prosecutors for his first court appearance. In fact, Alonso himself inquired Sunday—nearly twenty-four hours after Strauss-Kahn's arrest—why a warrant hadn't been issued to take Strauss-Kahn for a hospital inspection for evidence. Friel simply wanted to learn everything prosecutors could from Nafissatou Diallo, the alleged victim, and from the forensic evidence before detectives interrogated a wily world leader like Dominique Strauss-Kahn.

Whatever the case, Strauss-Kahn sat in police custody for hours without ever being interrogated. It was only after DSK asked and talked to his lawyers around 11 p.m. that Saturday night that detectives first tried to interview him. He says he had been ready to talk until his lawyer instructed him otherwise. We'll never know what he might have said if he had been questioned, even briefly, during the more than six hours that had elapsed since he had been pulled from the plane at JFK International Airport.

About 2:45 a.m. on Sunday morning, the NYPD Special Victims Section detectives officially arrested Strauss-Kahn and filed a notice of charges, according to the police's own records. But they would wait until Sunday afternoon (nearly twenty-four hours after he was detained) to put him in a lineup so the alleged victim could identify him.

By that time, Diallo had already seen photos of the accused four times—twice from a picture given to her by hotel security after police arrived at the scene on Saturday afternoon and twice when she watched television reports of his arrest at the police station and her apartment. Police had failed to shield her from these exposures to the defendant's picture, potentially handing DSK's lawyers the opportunity to argue that her lineup identification was tainted.

After the lineup, a warrant was finally signed to give DSK a head-to-toe body inspection for evidence. Such inspections are standard procedure in sexual assault cases, and the normal rule is the sooner the inspection, the better the chance to find evidence. By the time Strauss-Kahn was finally taken in, he had been sitting in the same clothes for more than a day, gone to the bathroom and washed his hands several times, and had eaten and drunk water. Any marks on his body from a struggle with Diallo, who is taller than him, would have had time to fade or heal. And any DNA under his fingers could have been washed away.

One might wonder why, with so much supervision from the top of Vance's office, the suspect interrogation, photo lineup, and evidence collection would have been so halting and slow. In the weeks that ensued, the lawyers for both Strauss-Kahn and Diallo, the victim, would ask the same questions, never really getting a clear answer. Was Vance's team trying to be too careful? Were there too many bartenders stirring the drink? Were the prosecutors and detectives so consumed with the international intrigue and media attention that they overlooked some of the basics? No one could give, or for that matter get, a satisfactory answer.

The performance, however, would foretell other missteps later in the investigation.

In the meantime, a new schism was forming in the D.A.'s Office over the question of whether Strauss-Kahn should be freed on bail and whether prosecutors needed to rush to secure a grand jury indictment against him within the five-day window mandated by New York State law. As soon as Strauss-Kahn's lawyers arrived at the police station, they made clear to Vance's team that they would be willing to accept a bail package and waive the five-day requirement so that both sides could have more time to review the evidence and better understand the victim and her motives before taking the epic step of formally charging a world leader with attempted rape and sexual assault. They hoped to forestall an unnecessary rush to judgment.

Friel, the sex crimes unit chief, also believed there was no reason to rush to the grand jury, a point she would make to her supervisors. She knew that authorities needed to spend extensive time debriefing the alleged victim and comparing her story to the forensic evidence. And perhaps just as importantly, Friel knew they needed to delve, delicately, into Diallo's potential motives, finances, acquaintances, and honesty. So on Sunday afternoon, prosecutors, and DSK's attorneys, Brafman and Taylor, discussed options for a bail package. Taylor remembers an initial figure of $250,000 and that it may have grown to $1 million later in the day. The amount didn't matter. Strauss-Kahn had the resources to pay, and his lawyers were willing to take what they could get if they could spare him the indignity of being transferred from the police station in Harlem to New York's notorious Rikers Island prison.

The defense lawyers believed they were moving Sunday afternoon toward a bail package when they left the police station around 4:30 p.m. after talking with the prosecutors.

But back at One Hogan Place, a different line of thought was emerging. Vance's top deputy, Alonso, had spent extensive time talking to the Justice Department and the State Department about the complications of getting Strauss-Kahn back to the United States if he ever fled to France. The United States and France had an extradition treaty, but the French government's policy has long been that it will only extradite foreigners from its land to face criminal charges, not its own citizens.

Soon, Vance's top leadership was fretting about a "Roman Polanski scenario," referring to the famed French-Polish movie director who pleaded guilty to having sex with a thirteen-year-old girl in Los Angeles in 1977 only to flee the country before he could be sentenced. Polanski settled in France, taking advantage of his French citizenship and the country's extradition policies, and escaped going to prison in the United States for three decades while continuing to make his movies. In 2009, Polanski was picked up in Switzerland at the urging of U.S. authorities, but that country, too, refused to extradite him.

On Sunday afternoon—informed by his discussions with members of the Barack Obama administration—Alonso and his team did other research on the issue of diplomats in legal trouble who claimed immunity or skipped town. They found a handful of cases dating to the early 1990s, the most relevant being a 1991 case in which an Egyptian-born chief of staff to then U.N. secretary general Boutros Boutros Ghali skipped town before he could be charged in the sexual assault of a Manhattan chambermaid. The case had been handled years earlier by Friel's predecessor as sex crimes chief, Linda Fairstein, now a well-known author and an influential member of Vance's "Kitchen Cabinet" of outside advisers.

While the drama was playing out at One Hogan Place, Fairstein was having her own conversations with Vance. She would prove an influential voice, especially at the end of the case. A frequent media commentator on sexual assault cases, Fairstein began getting calls early Sunday morning from supporters of DSK suggesting his arrest may have been a setup, either by Sarkozy or by a hotel maid seeking to profit from her allegations. Fairstein reached out to Vance to see if she could help. She finally contacted him at a Vance reelection fundraiser the Tuesday morning after the case broke.

Extremely experienced in debriefing sex crime victims, Fairstein stressed to Vance that he would need a skilled interrogator able to question Diallo effectively, pressing her on the obvious issues of motive and financial gain while respecting the likelihood that she was a legitimate victim. Aware that Friel was already talking about leaving the DA's office for the private sector, Fairstein offered her own services to debrief the victim.

"You're going to need someone who can navigate this, ask all the tough questions without putting the victim on trial," she told Vance. "Not everyone can do this. It's not the same as other crime victims. And you can't just put a homicide prosecutor in there who doesn't understand the dynamic and get the right answers."

Vance declined her offer, so Fairstein decided she'd stay on the outside of the case as a media commentator offering expert analysis. But Fairstein's word of caution about choosing an experienced sex crimes prosecutor to debrief the victim would prove prophetic just a few short weeks later. And as the criminal case neared its end in August, Vance would return to Fairstein, giving her a critical role in editing his final court motion.

The immediate concern, however, on Sunday night was how to handle the required court arraignment the next morning that would provide to the world the first glimpse of Strauss-Kahn as a sex crime defendant. All day Sunday, TV news across the globe roared about the developments. Everybody knew the court appearance would be a classic New York media circus.

Vance summoned all the key players to a meeting in his office at 5 p.m. Sunday. Shortly beforehand, Irwin informed Friel that she should remain focused on supervising the Cop Rape Trial as it headed to closing arguments and that one of the office's best investigators, Assistant District Attorney Ann Prunty, was going to handle the initial investigating for the D.A.'s Office. It was the first inkling that Friel would get that she was going to be pushed aside in the case, even though she was among the most experienced at handling sexual assault victims.

A game plan was hatched. The judge would be told Strauss-Kahn was being charged with a long list of crimes: criminal sexual act in the first degree, attempted rape in the first degree, sexual abuse in the first degree, unlawful imprisonment in the second degree, sexual abuse in the third degree, and forcible touching.

McConnell, the junior sex crimes prosecutor, would handle the first court appearance, and Alonso would attend the hearing just to answer any questions about the extradition issues. "I'm going to handle the bail issues," Alonso told Friel firmly in the meeting.

That would spell bad news for DSK and his lawyers. Late Sunday night, they were whipsawed by the news from Alonso that bail was off the table and that Vance's office would ask the judge to remand the powerful leader of the International Monetary Fund to Rikers Island, at least until his indictment. DSK's lawyers pleaded for the decision to be reconsidered but they were told the eighth floor believed Strauss-Kahn was a flight risk and would oppose any bail requests. Alonso, however, began working with DSK's lawyers on a plan to release DSK on bail after the indictment was secured, even suggesting a security firm with an expertise in facilitating house arrest.

The defense lawyers were prepared to surrender his passport as well as retrieve and then turn over his special U.N. identification card in Washington so he'd have no way to legally leave the country. They had arranged for him to stay in Manhattan with his daughter Camille, who was living near Columbia University—where she is working on her Ph.D.—in essentially the equivalent of house arrest. And they saw no reason to put a man with no criminal record behind bars without bail. The idea that Strauss-Kahn would flee the United States and live as a fugitive was preposterous to them. The IMF director believed he could explain what happened in the hotel room, and he had every motive to clear his name. But prosecutors had a few surprises to spring the next morning. In the information they had gathered through traditional research and contacts through the Justice Department liaison in France, they had learned that Strauss-Kahn may have been involved in an earlier forced sexual encounter involving a young, attractive French woman named Tristane Banon.

Banon was the then twenty-two-year-old daughter of one of Strauss-Kahn's friends and an aspiring journalist when she went to interview him in February 2003 for a book she wanted to write. He was then fifty-three and a rising star of the Socialist Party. She alleges Strauss-Kahn jumped her like a "rutting chimpanzee" after she entered the flat where they met, grabbed her breasts, and forced his hands down her pants. She believes he would have raped her had she not fled the room. The details of the attack matched closely with Diallo's own account—two alleged attacks by the same man with a similar MO that were a decade and two continents apart. But the problem was Banon never reported the attack in 2003, apparently dissuaded by her socialite mother from going to police.

After Diallo's case became public in America and the housekeeper began to be criticized by DSK's defenders, Banon belatedly filed a criminal complaint in France against Strauss-Kahn in June 2011. Her lawyer even offered to have her come to America to talk to the prosecutors. DSK sued her for libel in the summer of 2011 but later admitted he had tried to kiss her, though denying there was any sexual attack. French authorities ultimately concluded in October 2011—long after the New York criminal case had ended—that there wasn't enough evidence to charge DSK with attempted rape. They did, however, find evidence to support a lesser charge of sexual aggression but the statute of limitations had long since expired. Both DSK and Banon would declare Pyrrhic victories in the announcement.

But on the weekend of May 14, few in France and almost no one in the United States had ever heard of Banon's allegations. In fact, the only time she had mentioned them publicly was on a 2007 French TV show, and it barely caused a stir. For the most part, Banon's story before spring 2011 was relegated to French social gossip, part of the long lore of Strauss-Kahn's supposed sexual conquests. But somehow, Vance's office was alerted to the Banon allegations on that first weekend.

Strauss-Kahn's supporters have since floated a theory that French judicial officials aligned with Sarkozy called New York authorities and gave them a secret file on his sexual escapades, ranging from trysts with hotel prostitutes to Banon's allegations. But those in New York law enforcement familiar with the case say the actual discovery was much more mundane: Banon's 2007 TV allegation got picked up in an initial sweep of news media clips and research and then police asked France, through the Justice Department liaison, to provide any further information it had. That same weekend, police also obtained a copy of an internal IMF report detailing the affair Strauss-Kahn had in 2008 with a subordinate. Such background digging is common when a new defendant enters the system and the police were fast at work. They were slower, however, to dig into Strauss-Kahn's accuser's background, a delay that would prove consequential.

With a game plan laid for court Monday, prosecutors gave the go-ahead Sunday night to inspect Strauss-Kahn's body for any forensic evidence, bag his underwear as a crime scene exhibit for lab testing, and move him from the precinct where he had been detained for more than a day to jail. That final act—the infamous "perp walk"—gave a ravenous news media both in America and abroad the photo op they wanted—a glum-looking Strauss-Kahn in an overcoat and open business shirt, his hands cuffed behind his back as he was escorted by police detectives to an awaiting squad car.

The iconic photo would be published hundreds of times by TV, Web, and print outlets over the first few weeks, accompanied by a slew of eye-grabbing headlines that all but convicted Strauss-Kahn in the court of public opinion. "SLEAZY MONEY: Head of IMF Arrested for 'Sex Crime' in Midtown Hotel," the *New York Post* blared that first Sunday morning. By the end of the first week, the *Post* had outdone itself with additional headlines like "HE *DID* HAVE SEX WITH THE MAID" and "Shame of Strauss-Kahn Goes Beyond Sex."

The headlines outside America weren't much better. Reuters reported, "IMF Chief to Be Charged over Sex Attack in Hotel." The *Guardian* of London worried: "Debt Talks in Crisis as IMF Chief Held over Sex Assault." And the *Daily Telegraph* noted, "Sarkozy Rival in Court over 'Sex Attack' on Hotel Maid."

In France, where DSK's rise to the presidency was being anticipated, the end of his political career was proclaimed even before his indictment was filed. "Dominique Strauss-Kahn will not be the next president of the French Republic," *Le Figaro* declared. *Libération* added, "The Socialists have lost the only candidate that, in a range of configurations, was a favorite in the polls. The one who could even have beaten Nicolas Sarkozy." Other outlets in America and abroad would brand Strauss-Kahn "Le Perv" or "Le Perp."

When the case began turning in the other direction weeks later, the same media would turn against the hotel maid with little regard for their earlier declarations and pronouncements, with one report in the *New York Post* even accusing Diallo of being a hotel prostitute. (Diallo would later sue for defamation.) Even the vaunted *New York Times* would get stung with an anonymous report that would turn out to be partly inaccurate and significantly misleading. For many who covered the case with a dispassionate eye for the facts, there was a palpable sense of a rush to judgment in the media—both in the beginning and at the end. If prosecutors deserved some of the blame for investigative missteps, blind spots, and shortcuts, the media would need to plead guilty to creating a sensationalized, breathless account of a case that deserved more scrutiny and skepticism from the outset.

In the face of such an early media onslaught, DSK's stunned supporters in France could only cautiously plead for letting the American courts do their job and to question whether the perp walk was an unnecessary, prejudicial act of media humiliation in the United States. (By the end of the case, even many American legal experts questioned whether the perp walk had outlived its purpose or fairness.)

"The news we received from New York last night struck like a thunderbolt," French Socialist Party leader Martine Aubry would tell Reuters that first weekend. "I urge that we wait for the facts, respect the presumption of innocence and maintain the necessary decency." Added François Hollande, a Socialist Party candidate: "I'm flabbergasted. It's terrible news. There is a charge, but it's not proof of guilt. We have to react with emotion . . . but also with reserve."

While the official responses were reserved, DSK supporters almost instantly began to whisper about conspiracy theories of the wildest proportions. Sarkozy and French intelligence set up the whole episode, one went. The hotel maid was alternately described as a French intelligence operative from Africa who stole his phone and lured him into the incident or a hotel hooker who only reported the crime when she didn't get a big enough cash tip. Alternatively, DSK couldn't have done it because he was with his daughter. The theories went on and on. Some would eventually make it into the media, compliments of sympathetic writers. Most would not stick in the public's imagination for very long.

On Monday, a clearly exhausted and humiliated Strauss-Kahn appeared in court for his first hearing, looking every bit his sixty-two years of age and hardly resembling the invigorated, naked man Diallo reported attacking her in the hotel room two days earlier. He was wearing the same shirt and overcoat since his arrest two days before, and seemed lost in the cold, austere surroundings of a Manhattan criminal courtroom.

"Docket 2011NY034774, Dominique Strauss-Kahn step up," the courtroom bailiff bellowed in a classic New York accent. There were no dignitary titles, no diplomatic niceties, not even a "mister" for courtesy.

"Stand right here and face the judge, please."

Strauss-Kahn stood slightly hunched over in front of the judge. And the show began. Vance's team came armed to make the case that he was a flight risk, unworthy of bail, and the prosecutors' arguments appeared to be aimed as much for the media-consuming public as the judge.

"The People are requesting that the Court remand the defendant without bail," McConnell declared. It took but just a few seconds for the prosecutors to try to raise the uncorroborated allegation in France, even though they knew it was eight years old.

"We are obtaining additional information on a daily basis regarding his conduct and background," McConnell told the court. "Some of this information includes reports he has in fact engaged in conduct similar to the conduct alleged in this complaint on at least one other occasion, and we are attempting to verify all of this which will certainly take time."

The courtroom was riveted. What? Another sexual assault by DSK?

McConnell went on for a few seconds about Strauss-Kahn being a "noble, politically known" international figure with access to "substantial financial resources." He said that "it is our view if he went to France, we would have no legal mechanism that guarantees his return to the country to face these charges."

McConnell even declared, wrongly, that the Frenchman did not have ties to the United States. Strauss-Kahn is an "incurable flight risk," "virtually having nothing, no ties, not only to New York but to the United States," the prosecutor argued.

In fact, Strauss-Kahn and his wife have owned since 2007 a $4 million home in Washington, D.C.'s, posh Georgetown neighborhood, and he worked regularly at IMF headquarters in the nation's capital. His daughter also lived in New York and was willing to make her home his location for house arrest. And there was no mention of the defense's offer to surrender his passport and U.N. travel identifications, either.

Judge Melissa Jackson interjected, stopping McConnell's litany. The fleeting mention of another possible attack clearly caught her attention.

"Before you continue, may I inquire when was the prior occasion? Is that investigation something that's in the United States or some place else?"

"I believe that was abroad," McConnell answered, failing to mention that the purported attack was eight years old and not reported to police at the time.

The judge had her first red flag. An event in a foreign country would hardly sway her bail decision. "Thank you. You may continue," she said.

McConnell boasted about the strength of the case. "The proof against the defendant is compelling," he said, offering a preview of what the housekeeper would tell the grand jury just a few days later.

"The defendant restrained a hotel employee inside of the room.

He sexually assaulted her and attempted to forcibly rape her. When he was unsuccessful, he forced her to perform oral sex on him," McConnell explained, adding there was forensic evidence, "very powerful details," and a lineup identification from the victim.

McConnell had given a compelling, albeit one-sided argument, and sought to close a deal for no bail.

"The defendant has the personal, political, and financial resources to in fact flee and evade law enforcement," he argued. "He is a person of means. By all accounts, it appears he has resources to avoid capture and prosecution would he be released. He has an extensive network of contacts throughout the world and likely would assist him."

The DSK legal team was doing what it could to avoid rolling its eyes. A man on the cusp of being president of France wasn't going to flee. He would want to clear his name. And what was this network, some sort of IMF Underground Railroad? Still, they kept calm and waited for their turn to dispel what they saw as hyperbole from the prosecution.

But what came next from McConnell really miffed Brafman and Taylor.

"Certainly his ability to leave the country was demonstrated by the manner in which he left the hotel after the incident. . . . I have watched the video of the defendant exiting the hotel, through the lobby, minutes after the incident, and it appears to be a man who was in a hurry," the prosecutor said, leaving the clear impression he was rushing to the airport to flee.

True, DSK was late for lunch with his daughter. But he wasn't in a hurry to head out of town. He spent ninety minutes calmly at a Manhattan restaurant and even felt comfortable, after that, to call the hotel, the scene of the alleged crime, to ask them to look for his lost cell phone when he got to the airport.

And as for that flight to France, the one from which DSK was plucked by police, he had been scheduled aboard that for several days. Prosecutors already had the bookings and itinerary to prove it wasn't a last-minute flight to flee the country.

Brafman finally got his chance to correct the record and make a plea for bail. He pushed back on all the specifics, and tried to make the commonsense argument.

"The defendant, more than anything else, has a very important incentive to clear his name and the only way he can clear his name is not becoming a fugitive," Brafman argued. He added a first hint about a possible defense, that the event in the room may have been consensual.

"The forensic evidence, we believe, are not consistent with a forcible encounter. We believe this is a very, very defensible case," the defense lawyer declared.

Though a long shot, Brafman added more food for thought, suggesting DSK was being punished just because he was rich and powerful.

"There are people in this building who get bail, reasonable bail, who commit far more serious offenses and all the people in the courtroom understand that," Brafman said, himself playing to the public and media as much as to the judge. "I don't think the fact that he is an important man, it should provide one set of rules and an average citizen get a second set of rules."

Brafman made a suggestion of $1 million cash for bail.

The judge heard the populist plea. "Mr. Brafman, you are absolutely right. The same rules apply to your client as anybody else who appears before this court," she said, reminding the defense lawyer she was a "fair judge" and not there to decide innocence or guilt.

But she also signaled where she was heading. "When I hear your client was at JFK Airport about to board a flight, it raises some concern with this court," she opined. She clearly was hinting at how she planned to rule, though she thanked both sides for making "persuasive" arguments.

The judge asked the prosecution if it had any more to offer. It seemed like McConnell had already closed the deal. But Alonso, Vance's number two, who had sat quietly through the proceedings to that point, suddenly rose to speak, awkwardly interjecting a bit of Hollywood to the whole equation.

"On the whole issue of being a fugitive for the rest of his life, he would be living openly just like Roman Polanski. The State of California wanted him back for sex crimes for ten years," Alonso offered.

It was too much, and the judge let him know it. "I will note Roman Polanski has nothing to with this," she chided. "I am trying to be objective, and I am not going to judge this individual on the basis of what happened with Roman Polanski."

The prosecution had been slapped down. Brafman tried to attack the Polanski allusion further, but the judge cut him off and made a short, decisive decree.

"I am going to remand the defendant for grand jury," she declared. Strauss-Kahn would spend the next five days at Rikers Island. No bail. End of argument.

The first forty-eight hours of the investigation had come and gone, and the occasionally breathless nature of the players would foreshadow what lay ahead. There would be more stretching of the facts by prosecutors, more reckless rushes to judgment by the media, more conspiracy theories by DSK's defenders, and more oversights by investigators. This case would not bring out the best in twenty-first-century American jurisprudence or journalism.

For the next few days, the saga would move behind closed doors as the District Attorney's Office pressed to prep Diallo and her hotel colleagues for a grand jury appearance and race to get an indictment by Friday of the first week. McConnell and Prunty, working with the sex crimes detectives, spent Monday debriefing Diallo and going over her story and the evidence. Friel, the unit chief, was staying involved and planned to handle Diallo with McConnell when they brought her to the grand jury on Wednesday.

Friel, however, was raising her concerns to her superiors about whether they were rushing too fast. She knew there was another bail hearing scheduled for Thursday, and she wondered whether the grand jury appearances should be slowed down. She also worried that Prunty, a fabulous investigator and prosecutor, didn't have much experience debriefing sexual assault victims and could be intense in her interrogations. She and others felt there were legitimate questions about whether Prunty could create the right dynamic in the room to get all the truth they needed from this immigrant housekeeper, who spoke broken English and harbored a complicated life story of her own. Friel knew with her own tight schedule on Monday and Tuesday at the Cop Rape Trial that she'd barely get any time with the alleged victim before they headed into the grand jury on Wednesday. It made her uneasy.

Friel and McConnell showed up early Wednesday morning at One Hogan Place ready to question Diallo, hoping to get as much time as possible with the accuser before bringing her to the grand jury. But Diallo was no where to be found. Friel and McConnell called around frantically, trying to track down the detectives who were charged with protecting and transporting Diallo. Hours passed before Friel learned the detectives had taken Diallo to a different building where she was being debriefed by Prunty, with neither sex crime expert present. It was another misstep, which would have been comical except that it left Friel less than forty minutes to debrief Diallo before the grand jury.

At the NYPD crime lab, technicians were at work testing sections of carpet that had been cut from the floor of the hotel suite where Diallo said the attack occurred and where she remembered spitting out Strauss-Kahn's semen. Spots on Diallo's housekeeping uniform—which would prove the best evidence of a sexual encounter—were also being tested. The initial results showed signs of DNA and technicians were doing the necessary tests to see if it matched Strauss-Kahn.

At the Sofitel in New York, executives had brought in a high-powered private attorney from Washington to interview virtually every employee who had contact with Diallo and Strauss-Kahn over that fateful weekend. The hotel and its French owners—certain to be swept into the firestorm on two continents—wanted to understand everything that happened, and that meant leaving no stone unturned. The security personnel, the housekeeping supervisors, the room service attendant, and even the VIP concierges who had showed Strauss-Kahn to his room when he checked in Friday night were interviewed. A detailed timeline was created through the interviews with the hotel witnesses, one the Sofitel would later learn matched quite closely with Diallo's own account and physical evidence such as DNA and security records. The Sofitel's general counsel in Dallas, Texas, Alan Rabinowitz, decided early on to keep the hotel neutral and fair to all sides. He offered full cooperation to Vance's office, believing the company had an ethical obligation to cooperate with law enforcement as well as an obligation to help an employee, who had alleged she was sexually assaulted, get the full police investigation she deserved. But Rabinowitz insisted that no documents or materials be turned over unless prosecutors issued a subpoena. The Sofitel would make the same deal to cooperate with Strauss-Kahn's lawyers as well, requiring them to serve subpoenas for the same evidence prosecutors had requested. Such a strategy would allow the hotel, if needed, to argue back in France to DSK's supporters that it had no choice but to cooperate and thus treated everyone equally.

By midweek the Sofitel employees—their hotel lawyer accompanying them—met with the prosecutors and some headed to the grand jury to give their account of what had happened. Each worker who had encountered Diallo in the immediate aftermath of the incident was adamant that he or she believed the housekeeper had been attacked. Some described her as being in a traumatized state, trembling and spitting on the floor and at one point even feeling like she had to vomit, requiring her to excuse herself to a bathroom. The hotel employees were what prosecutors call "outcry witnesses," the first people a sexual assault victim reaches out to when reporting an attack. And their role in the case was critical in those first few days for four reasons.

First, the hotel employees were credible, hardworking witnesses who came to the aid of a distressed colleague and their accounts matched both Diallo's and the crime scene evidence. They were key corroborators, and in the early going they gave prosecutors an additional sense of confidence about the victim herself. They described Nafi Diallo as hardworking, shy, honest, and not one to flirt with men. One telling anecdote came shortly before the employees testified. The Sofitel lawyer was briefing Friel about what each employee told the hotel investigation when the question arose about whether there was any possibility that Diallo could have invited a sexual encounter, maybe to earn a tip.

"I asked that question of everyone I could find at the hotel, and everyone says Nafi is not that type of person, she doesn't give off even the slightest hint that she is flirtatious. She seems to only care about working and getting home to her daughter," the lawyer answered. "In fact, one of the security guards said none of the men even look at her that way. If anything she looks down and away from men when they talk to her."

"That's significant to me," Friel answered. "I trust men's instincts on this."

Such instincts and intuitions—combined with the prosecutors' own sympathy for Diallo after she, in tears, told them a story about an earlier rape in Guinea—and the time crunch may have substituted in the early days for a more forceful investigation of the victim, her associates, her motives, and her finances. In fact, it would be weeks before prosecutors would learn that she had given false statements to get into the country, made up the story about the earlier rape, and allowed a man in prison on drug charges to move money through her accounts. In the end, Vance's office found out about the most serious problems with the alleged victim's credibility because Diallo's new lawyer volunteered them. It was exactly the scenario that both Fairstein and Friel had fretted about if the victim wasn't properly debriefed at the outset.

Second, the hotel employees established that Diallo was reluctant at first to report to police the alleged attack. To prosecutors, that meant Diallo wasn't champing at the bit to call the cops on DSK, whether to seek revenge or to cash in with a lawsuit. The first four employees who had contact with Diallo all reported she raised her concerns with them that she might be fired if she reported the crime, simply because she had accidentally walked in on a VIP guest. They recounted how it took some coaxing and reassuring on their part before Diallo was willing to talk to police. The effort to calm and reassure her also helped explain the one-hour gap between 12:30 p.m., the time when the first hotel employee learned of the alleged attack, and 1:30 p.m. when police were called.

Third, the Sofitel's physical evidence was convincing—it created a clear timetable for when the alleged assault could have occurred and what each of the key players did before and after. When disputes and conspiracy theories arose, prosecutors and Diallo's own lawyers could turn to the Sofitel's evidence because the time stamps and video footage couldn't lie.

Finally, the hotel employees' good intentions and quick actions would unwittingly hand DSK's lawyers some fodder to raise questions and doubts in the weeks that ensued. Diallo's first housekeeping supervisor, who found her upset in a hallway, had taken the maid back into the same Suite 2806 where the alleged assault occurred. And for about twenty minutes, a handful of Sofitel employees entered that room trying to gain information and to calm their colleague. At one point, they also allowed Diallo to leave their sight and head into one of the suite's bathrooms when she felt sick. While well meaning, the hotel workers' actions violated the best practices of crime scene preservation. And they would give DSK's lawyers an opportunity to suggest the crime scene could have been corrupted, contaminated, or tampered with before police got control of it. Prosecutors, however, found no evidence that anything significant was affected at the scene.

Another problem occurred when some of the Sofitel security personnel had briefly showed Diallo a picture of Strauss-Kahn. The act, while innocent, required police to disclose the identification to Strauss-Kahn's lawyers, giving them an opportunity to argue if necessary that the later lineup identification could have been unduly influenced or tainted. As it turned out, DSK would not contest he was in the room so the lineup became less important.

Additionally, two hotel officials who had been instrumental in persuading Diallo to report her alleged attack to police would disappear for a few minutes after the 911 call was made. They went to a hotel loading dock to blow off some steam. For reasons they themselves could not explain later, the two men engaged in a brief but odd celebration, jumping into the air together and bumping chests. The celebration, lasting just thirteen seconds, was caught on a security camera. And a sharp-eyed lawyer for Strauss-Kahn would later spot the moment, helping DSK's supporters to weave a theory that the hotel officials were celebrating the fact that they had set up Strauss-Kahn to be arrested. The theory even made it into print, thanks to a ravenous press willing to publish just about anything. The two employees adamantly deny they were doing anything but expressing relief that Diallo had finally agreed to call the police and that detectives were on the way. They also speculated they might have been talking about sports for part of the conversation. But the seeds of one of the many conspiracy theories had been planted.

Away from the rush of the investigation, Strauss-Kahn was perhaps the only player with time that first week to reflect quietly on the drama. Wearing an orange prison jumpsuit, he was placed in a solitary confinement cell in the VIP section of Rikers Island, spending his time mostly reading or watching television. He and the guards got along fine and he had few complaints, beyond the obvious loss of his freedom. Perhaps his only concern was that he did not have a pair of glasses, which made watching TV difficult.

He had but one visitor the whole time. His longtime lawyer Bill Taylor made a single visit at midweek to help prepare for a planned Thursday court appearance, the second bail hearing. Strauss-Kahn smiled at seeing a familiar face.

"How are you, Dominique?" Taylor inquired.

"I'm doing fine," the Frenchman answered in a stoic voice, refusing to display any of the wear or humiliation of being imprisoned. Taylor described the bail package that was being prepared in an effort to free him, and the two discussed legal strategy briefly. Strauss-Kahn also was worried about the IMF and the state of the debt talks. An IMF official arranged with prison officials for DSK to make a call from his prison cell to his colleagues back in Washington so he could resign in person and apologize for the hardship his arrest had caused. They had been through so much together, including the 2008 investigation of his affair with a subordinate, and Strauss-Kahn wanted one last chance to bid farewell. When Taylor arrived, Strauss-Kahn handed him a signed letter of resignation to formally deliver to the IMF.

In perhaps the only lament during the visit, Strauss-Kahn mentioned to Taylor the troubles he was having seeing the television without eyeglasses. Taylor tried to get the prison to give Strauss-Kahn a pair of glasses, but to no avail. So he hatched a plan. He knew Strauss-Kahn would need a suit for his Thursday court appearance, so he sneaked a pair of contact lenses in with the suit. It worked. For some reason, the same prison officials who refused to give him glasses agreed to take the contacts.

The prosecutors and the defense would each score victories at the end of an exhaustive first week of the case. Though Friel had less than forty minutes to debrief Diallo before putting her before the grand jurors, the housekeeper performed convincingly in her testimony that Wednesday and Vance's office secured the indictment it had been seeking within the five-day limit. They walked the indictment right into the courtroom on Thursday morning, creating the headline they wanted for a hearing that was supposed to be about releasing Strauss-Kahn on bail.

Strauss-Kahn was officially charged with four felonies and three misdemeanors. The two sides battled anew that Thursday over the question of bail. Strauss-Kahn was mostly a spectator, this time looking much more crisp in his dark suit than during his first appearance. His wife, Anne Sinclair, had flown in from France and sat in the front row with his daughter Camille. He would eventually blow them a kiss as the legal bickering proceeded in front of a new judge.

When Sinclair, a prominent French journalist and millionaire heiress to an art collector's fortune, first got word in Paris of her husband's arrest and jailing, she was numb with pain. She was determined to stand by her man. After two decades of marriage, she was well aware of the rumors, the whispers, and his own admission to IMF investigators in 2008 of carousing and infidelity. But she would not believe a man destined for political greatness was capable of a violent sexual assault. Before leaving France for New York, Sinclair reportedly penned a brief statement of support for her husband to leave behind for the ravenous media back home. "I don't believe for a single second the accusations of sexual assault by my husband," she would write. "I am certain his innocence will be proven."

Sinclair was in the courtroom as Taylor laid out a detailed bail package that included $1 million bail and a house arrest at a specially rented apartment that would be secured by the same security firm that had handled Wall Street tycoon Bernie Madoff's house arrest.

McConnell, the young district attorney, again argued against any release. "The defendant has shown a propensity to impulsive criminal conduct . . . and a bracelet with a battery are not sufficient to assure he returns," he argued, as he repeated a favorite line from Monday's court arguments.

"He has the stature and resources not only to be a fugitive on the run but to live in ease and comfort."

Judge Michael Obus wanted more than just $1 million cash in bail to free Strauss-Kahn but he was careful to stress to the Frenchman that his request for an additional $5 million bond should not be viewed as a shakedown from the U.S. court system.

"Money alone is not going to be sufficient to give us the assurance. It is primarily these other conditions that will simply make it impossible for you to leave," Obus explained as he approved releasing Strauss-Kahn from Rikers under the restrictive terms.

The DSK legal team could breathe its first sigh of relief. Away from the courtroom, District Attorney Cyrus Vance made a cameo appearance outside his office, seemingly to address the political criticisms of his office back in France about the perp walk, the imprisonment, and the quick indictment. He didn't like even the faintest hint in the public's mind that there had been a rush to judgment. He also wouldn't take any questions.

"Fairness and impartiality in our American criminal justice system has been the bedrock of our democracy for more than 200 years. It has been rigorously upheld in New York courts, and by our office,"

Vance said, sounding both a bit defensive and scholarly. As the case wore on, both staffers inside his office and others outside it would witness Vance's sensitivities to the political winds. To some it was troubling; to others it was reassuring to see he understood the job of Manhattan district attorney involved more than being a straitlaced lawman like the fictional TV prosecutor Jack McCoy from *Law & Order.*

The shuffling inside Vance's office, however, wasn't finished. The trial division chief Karen Agnifilo already had been forced to recuse herself from the case because her husband had joined DSK's defense team. And John Irwin, Agnifilo's deputy, would deliver some unexpected news to Friel.

"We're going in a different direction and you're off the case," Irwin told the stunned sex crimes chief. "We're going to bring in Joan Illuzzi from homicide."

"That's ridiculous," Friel said. "I'm not taking this. I want to hear it from Dan."

Alonso, who had known Friel for years, obliged with a swift declaration that all but ended Friel's tenure in the Manhattan District Attorney's Office. "Cy just doesn't trust you on this one, Lisa," he said.

The prosecution would enter the second phase of the case without one of its most battle-tested sex crimes prosecutors. In Friel's place were two of the office's best homicide and violent crimes prosecutors, exactly the sort of "dream team" that Vance and Alonso wanted to handle the case. Joan Illuzzi-Orbon was proud of her record of having never lost a case at trial and was respected across the city, recently winning a conviction in the murder of celebrity real estate agent Linda Stein. Vance had just named her head of a new hate crimes unit in his office. Prunty enjoyed a similar reputation, and could dismantle even the most grizzled murderer on cross-examination. Back in 2008, she had won accolades for winning the conviction of a man who raped and tortured a Columbia University student, and earlier in her career she also had spent a brief stint in the sex crimes unit.

But neither had sought the assignment. They were drafted. And neither was quite ready for the dark secrets that were about to emerge from Diallo, a complicated victim who could lie about her past with such ease and cunning that she could bring others to tears and whose true life story was more intricate than she had let on initially. And adding to the complications, Team Vance was also about to experience a force of nature in the person of Diallo's new attorney, Kenneth Thompson, an impassioned, relentless defender who would be the first to uncover Diallo's past lies and then spend weeks fighting with the prosecutors over his client's honor.

Back at Rikers, Strauss-Kahn was readying to be released and to get his first taste of freedom in nearly a week. He still faced the tough task of confronting a wife and daughter whom he had humiliated with his conduct. He also had to more fully absorb the complete decimation of his once promising political career. About the only thing that rang true that first week for Strauss-Kahn was a single statement his lawyer made during the first court appearance.

"Life before this arrest is not going to be the same as life after this arrest," Brafman pronounced.

At times of reflection, Strauss-Kahn's mind would wander back to that fateful moment at 12:06 p.m. on May 14 when he first heard a woman's voice calling out near his bedroom.

"Hello? Housekeeping."

THREE

Her Story

BY ALL ACCOUNTS, Nafissatou Diallo treasured her 9 a.m. to 4:30 p.m. job as a housekeeper at the New York Sofitel. She could see her fifteen-year-old daughter off to high school and be back in time for dinner. And Saturday shifts offered an additional bonus—an hour later starting time that gave Nafi (as friends and family called her) extra time to share breakfast, gab, or just watch TV with her daughter. And May 14, 2011, was one of those late-starting, leisurely Saturdays. Diallo spent the early morning lazing around the apartment with her daughter, then donned her cream-colored maid's uniform, and left for the subway and the routine ride from her small apartment in the Bronx to the Sofitel on West 44th in midtown Manhattan. "Don't forget your homework," Diallo reminded as she left her daughter behind.

Little did she know at that moment that she would not see her daughter again for eighteen hours, sucked into a vortex of sex, politics, law, and international intrigue that would demolish the tranquil lifestyle she now enjoyed.

Mother and daughter had grown especially close since they were reunited a few years back, spending much of their free time together going to movies, cooking, strolling through a park, or watching favorite television shows like *Law & Order.* At age thirty-two, Diallo was finally satisfied with the life she had built since she fled her native Guinea after her husband died. She now had a steady, union-protected job paying $25 an hour with health insurance and benefits, and her daughter was a solid student aspiring to attend college one day. And most importantly for Diallo, her daughter had escaped the horror of female genital mutilation, a far too common ritual imposed on young women in Africa by their families that robs them of any future sexual gratification. The procedure, which carries cultural significances in Africa, is typically carried out by a female circumciser and involves the partial or complete removal of the external female genitalia. Diallo had suffered through it at an early age.

"I had bad things happen when I was young, when I was a little girl," she would tell me during an interview. "I got cut on private parts." A doctor's examination in connection with her immigration efforts confirmed she had the procedure.

She looks down to the floor frequently when talking to men, in this instance with a touch of shame or resignation about what had happened to her in Guinea. "I don't want them to do that to my daughter."

She says *that* was her primary motivation for fleeing the West African nation of Guinea in 2003, leaving her then seven-year-old daughter behind with relatives until she could earn enough to bring the young girl to join her four years later.

There were plenty of other reasons to long for America. Diallo grew up in a Guinean household led by her aging father, an imam who taught the Koran in the local village. But Nafi was never fully educated and instead mostly tended her parents' home and watched children. For a while, she worked at a sandwich shop run by a brother. One night, she says, she and another young woman were working past a government curfew for young adults at the shop when two soldiers walked in.

"The place I used to work. We closed late. We had a cafeteria. We sold sandwiches, coffee, things like that," she explains. "I was there for all night and all morning." The soldiers arrested the two young women in the wee hours of the morning and took them to a nearby prison camp, where in a small room they raped her repeatedly.

"They take me there. I was raped there. They let me go home in the morning," she relates in a monotone, matter-of-fact voice that sounds a bit awkward for the recounting of such a traumatic incident. "In the morning, they asked us to clean up," she continues. "Then they took us home." Diallo has trouble with dates and at first can't quite place the year that attack occurred. She later recalls it being in 2001, meaning she would have been around twenty-two years old.

The loss of a child to premature death and her husband's death a couple years after the rape only added to the hardship, leaving her with a young daughter and little economic future. So in 2003 she set out for America's brighter shores. Diallo entered the United States, using the visa and travel papers of another woman. Her original plan was to live with a relative who had emigrated earlier and to babysit that relative's children, but she soon aspired for more. She learned her way around New York City's bustling, West African immigrant community in the Bronx and Harlem, picking up odd jobs. First, she braided hair, then worked in a bodega, and finally she landed a job in a restaurant. "That was the choices because I don't speak English and don't have papers to work here," she explains of her circumstances when she arrived.

Diallo is not particularly glamorous, with flat hair and acne-pocked skin. But at 5'10" and with a shapely figure, she'd attracted the attention of some men at the restaurant and started to learn English. They liked to talk with her and tip her, though she didn't seem particularly interested in them, according to Blake Diallo, a Senegalese immigrant who managed the Café 2115 in Harlem where Nafi Diallo often picked up food or spent her free time. Blake Diallo, no relation to Nafi, became one of her few trusted male friends, and an unofficial spokesman-defender for her after her encounter with DSK catapulted her into an unwanted limelight.

"She don't like men. She don't trust them," Blake Diallo would tell my *Newsweek* colleague Chris Dickey in one particularly insightful story about the West African immigrant community that absorbed Nafi Diallo upon her arrival to America. "She don't hang out with nobody. What she knows is work, pick up her daughter from school, pick up food, go home, and watch Nigerian movies."

Diallo would have another "significant" male friend, Amara Tarawally, a fellow Guinean who would go around the community claiming he was Nafi Diallo's fiancé. Diallo insists they weren't betrothed but admits he showered her with gifts, like knockoff designer handbags. "Not very good ones," she would lament. He won her trust, though, and eventually access to her checking account before he landed in jail in Arizona as a result of a drug sting.

Both male friends, Blake Diallo and Amara Tarawally, would prove instrumental in the drama that changed Nafi's life forever.

Because she had entered the United States illegally, Diallo knew she needed working papers to get full-time employment and enough income to afford reuniting with her daughter. So in 2004, she applied for asylum in the United States as a woman fleeing political and sexual persecution from Guinea. Because she had been a victim of genital mutilation and had, as a teenager, been raped once by the two soldiers for violating curfew, she may have been entitled to asylum solely on the strength of her personal story. But an immigration adviser she consulted in Brooklyn—a shadowy figure she refuses to name—insisted she needed a more compelling tale.

Diallo could neither read nor write in any language, and her English was marginally proficient and broken. When she talks, she drifts back and forth between her native Fulani and English. So the immigration adviser gave her a cassette tape with a sure-fire story to win asylum from U.S. immigration officials. He instructed her to memorize every word, every detail.

The story was compelling but embellished beyond any relation to Diallo's real life. She was told to claim her husband and she had been political opponents of Guinea's ruthless regime, and their house was burned by soldiers in retaliation. They both had been beaten and her husband was tortured and ultimately withered away in prison as a political dissident. And Diallo herself was gang-raped by a band of ruthless soldiers, who ripped her then two-year-old daughter from her arms and threw the child to the ground before beating and raping her repeatedly.

Diallo would memorize the story perfectly and could tell it convincingly with emotion, tears, and even an animated reenactment. Her performance was so good that she would eventually even fool the most veteran of Manhattan prosecutors.

Diallo filed an application that recounted the political persecution—without the specifics of the bogus rape story—and it worked. She won asylum in 2007. And she filed away the embellished rape story in her memory, right alongside the real rape incident that had occurred earlier in her life. The two would become blended into one highly believable tale, the emotion, shame, and horror of the real attack merging with the sensational details of the contrived.

Now a legal green card resident of the United States with working papers in 2007, Nafi Diallo could finally begin to build the life and opportunity she always dreamed of. She reached out to the nonprofit International Rescue Committee, which helps immigrants find work, and soon was sent for temporary work in the laundry room of the Sofitel. Walking through its gold-plated front door, Diallo entered a strangely upscale world. It was alluring and exotic, an attractive home away from home for the rich and famous of France. Diallo was grateful for the laundry work, but it was temporary and she yearned for better pay. And after two or three months, the hotel unexpectedly laid off the temporary help in the laundry room.

Diallo had won the respect of her Sofitel supervisors during the short stint, and she went back to the jobs agency and managed to persuade them to find her a spot in a Sofitel housekeeping training program. Now, she was on her way to becoming a full-fledged maid at one of New York's luxury hotels, a job that would finally provide the full-time work, union benefits, and money to justify bringing her daughter from Guinea to live with her permanently in the United States. The two were reunited in 2007 after a four-year separation.

The Sofitel became a source of stability for Diallo. "I never miss my work. I always go," she would tell me. She quickly learned the routines of a housekeeper with precision. Each maid had a quota of fourteen rooms a day to clean, though suites could count for as many as three. Each room on average takes about forty minutes for a thorough cleaning. At the bottom of the housekeeping seniority list at the Sofitel, Diallo didn't have her own floor, instead picking up leftover rooms that needed to be cleaned on various floors. "We have a lot of people in housekeeping, but they don't hire a lot," she explains proudly. "Only one, after me." The key to her cleaning strategy was to minimize moving between floors, knocking off as many rooms as possible before moving to new locations. If rooms still had DO NOT DISTURB signs on a door, a maid often would use the time to go to a linen or storage closet and refill her supplies. Every minute counted if Diallo was to finish on time to leave at 4:30 p.m. sharp to see her daughter at home after school.

Diallo always left her cleaning gear in the room just cleaned, waiting to "clear" the next room and make sure it was empty before hauling in the vacuum and cart. And when cleaning a room, the door was always left ajar. To some, this seems like the minutia of a mundane job. But for the Sofitel, it was hotel policy. And for Diallo, the routine, the job security, and the camaraderie she found at the Sofitel were a source of pride.

"I like the job, and I like the people. I made friends there," Diallo says. But she quickly adds she almost never engaged with the guests. "When I go to work, I always mind my business," she says.

Raised to be Muslim by her parents, Diallo sometimes wore a traditional scarf to cover her hair at work; other times she did not. She also knew that many Muslim men in the West African immigrant community disapproved of women working as housekeepers, believing it brought them too close to strange men and the beds and bathrooms they used on travel. There were always whispers in the community that women who took such jobs were she-devils who might "whore around" with patrons for money. Nafi Diallo mostly shrugged off such talk. (Though DSK's private investigators would look to mine those rumors relentlessly when the legal war began.)

About a month before the incident that catapulted her to the global stage, Diallo caught a big break at work. One of her housekeeping colleagues with more seniority (and her own floor) left on maternity leave. Diallo volunteered to fill in, and she was now the proud custodian of the cleaning chart for the twenty-eighth floor of the Sofitel. It would turn out, however, to be an unlucky twist of fate.

After leaving her daughter on Saturday morning, May 14, 2011, Diallo arrived at the Sofitel at about 9:30 a.m., giving her a half hour to catch a quick breakfast in the hotel workers' cafeteria and get into uniform. About a year earlier, the Sofitel had changed the traditional maid's wardrobe from a blouse and pants that housekeepers found comfortable to a more traditional dress with a skirt at half calf. The maids chafed at the change, finding the new outfit less comfortable for work conditions and more prone to show their buttocks when they bent over to clean.

As she did most days, Diallo compensated for the short dress by wearing two pairs of pantyhose, a lighter colored pair over her panties covered by a darker, heavier set of nylons over the top. It hardly was the garb of a woman expecting to engage in a consensual sexual encounter.

Diallo's cleaning assignments for that Saturday included several rooms on the eleventh floor and then her now regular regimen on the twenty-eighth. Starting around 10 a.m., she did a quick inventory of all the occupied rooms on the twenty-eighth, then went down the elevator to the eleventh. Nearly all the rooms had DO NOT DISTURB signs on them, not unusual for a spring weekend when guests were tempted to stay out late and then sleep in. Diallo quickly checked a couple of unoccupied rooms that hadn't been rented, ensuring they were clean and fully supplied, then headed back to the twenty-eighth floor.

At about 10:30 a.m., she approached Room 2820, around the corner from the suite where Strauss-Kahn was staying. There was no DO NOT DISTURB sign on the door to so she knocked and then keyed the door.

This is how she recounted what happened next.

"Hello? Housekeeping," she announces. No one answers, and there's no sign of the guest. But the luggage is visible so she closes the door, with a plan to return in half an hour. She checks on a couple of other rooms, doing some cleaning, and then returns to Room 2820 at about 11 a.m. She knocks on the door and puts the key in, but a man with a French accent answers. He's a winemaker finishing a business trip before returning to Paris.

"I'm so sorry," she says.

"No problem. I'm going to be leaving soon," the man assures.

Diallo decides to wait in the hallway near the elevators. All the other rooms on the twenty-eighth are marked with DO NOT DISTURB signs. She's patient. She would have liked to check her cell phone for messages, but she mistakenly left it at home. So she just passes the time quietly.

About twenty minutes later, she returns to Room 2820. It's now empty, so she keys the door, props it open, and rolls in her cart to start cleaning. She vacuums and scrubs, and she changes the linens and towels. It's a larger room and takes close to forty minutes. She closes the door with her cart still inside (per hotel policy) and walks down the hallway toward the floor's largest and most expensive VIP suite. It's about 12:05 p.m. and she sees her colleague Syed Haque, a room service attendant, emerging from Suite 2806 carrying a breakfast tray.

"It's empty and ready to be cleaned," Haque assures her. By that time, the door to Suite 2806 had slammed shut again.

Diallo reaches for her security key in the hip pocket of her dress and slides it into the door latch, moments from a fateful encounter that would change her life.

She leaves the door ajar. "Hello? Housekeeping," she beckons, starting her routine all over again. There's no answer, and no sign of luggage as she eases into the large living room of the suite.

"Hello? It's housekeeping," she announces anew.

Again, no reply. She peers toward the door to the bedroom on her left. It's ajar and she can see part of an unmade bed.

As she approaches the bedroom, she tries another shout. "Hello? Housekeeping," she calls out for a third and final time.

Suddenly, a naked man with white hair approaches from a nearby bathroom. She looks down in shame. She has only a glimpse of this man, a stranger she's never seen before.

"Oh, my God, I'm so sorry," she says, her voice faint with embarrassment. She can't look him in the eye, and she doesn't even glance at his body to see if his penis is erect. She tries to flee the room.

The man moves right next to her and grabs her breasts, then slides his naked body around her so that she can't approach the open door of the suite. "You don't have to be sorry," he says in English. He slips through the living room and shuts the door to the suite.

Diallo had experienced this aura of impending doom before, when as a child the Guinean circumcisers robbed her of sexual pleasures and again as a young woman when the two soldiers took her to the encampment to be raped.

She's momentarily paralyzed, worried oddly about what will happen afterward. She'll almost certainly be fired for walking in on a VIP suite patron, she fears. As the white-haired man walks swiftly back across the living room and approaches her anew, he starts to push her toward the bedroom. He's a few inches shorter than Diallo, but he's forceful, almost like a "crazed man," Diallo would later tell authorities.

"Sir, stop this!" she pleads. "I don't want to lose my job." Her voice is faint with shame and her eyes wide with fear.

"You don't have to lose your job," he answers back invitingly.

For some reason, Strauss-Kahn interprets the look in her eyes as an invitation for sexual conquest, perhaps his last before a long interlude of summer work at the IMF and the start of a grueling campaign for the French presidency with his wife by his side. He knows, however, he must be quick, or he'll be late for lunch with his daughter Camille and her new boyfriend. The pursuit intensifies. "You're beautiful," he says. It's not what Diallo wants to hear. Diallo is a sturdy woman, but Strauss-Kahn somehow manages to pull her hard onto the bed. She's pinned on the edge, almost sliding to the floor, when Strauss-Kahn tries to insert his penis into her mouth. She keeps her lips pursed and thrashes her head from side to side, thwarting his first penetration.

Diallo shoves him hard, and he stumbles back a short way. For a fleeting second she worries if she's hurt him. (Another reason to be fired, she fears.) There's just enough space now for her to rise from the bed. She's looking for a distraction so she tries to scare him with a lie.

"Look, there is my supervisor right there," she says, pointing toward the bedroom door.

"There's nobody there," he says dismissively. "And no one can hear us."

The sixty-two-year-old Frenchman is right back upon her, seemingly enjoying the roughness. They begin a new round of shoving; Diallo is uncertain how hard to push for fear she might be accused of assaulting a hotel patron. He is more aggressive, pushing her down a long hallway that leads from the bedroom to a second bathroom. The hallway is narrow and both are panting. Strauss-Kahn pins her near a wall, a few feet from the bathroom. He pulls up her uniform dress, and partially pulls down the outer pair of pantyhose she is wearing. He's frustrated to find another pair of nylons in the way. This time he slides his hand beneath the second pantyhose and her panties, leaving behind a key piece of evidence, small cutaneous cells of skin from his hands. He grabs her vaginal area so hard that it sends a shock of pain through her body. Diallo lets out a tiny cry as the struggle continues.

She moves his hand away from her groin and tries to pull up her pantyhose, but he manages to press her to her knees, her legs folded awkwardly to the side on the floor and her head pinned near the wall. Her torso is twisted uncomfortably, and she feels a twinge of pain in her shoulder. It's hard to breathe in such an awkward position.

Strauss-Kahn grabs Diallo's neatly hennaed, straightened black hair, one hand on each side of her head, and pushes his penis into her mouth as she gasps for air. He's thrusting and grunting his way toward satisfaction.

"Suck my dick," he implores in the foulest of tones.

A few seconds later, Diallo tastes a warm, sour fluid come into her mouth. Strauss-Kahn gasps in satisfaction and releases her hair.

The maid quickly lifts herself from the floor and spits his semen onto the carpet and the walls as she bounds down the narrow hallway. She has tears in her eyes as she heads straight for the door, trying to straighten her hair and fix her panties in the process. She wipes her mouth as she walks out the door.

"I run. I run out of there," she would recount later. "I don't turn back. I run to the hallway."

She walks rapidly through the corridor and around a short hallway near Room 2820, the one she had cleaned just before entering Strauss-Kahn's room. She can hide there, able to see the elevators. She doesn't know what to do. The time is now 12:13 p.m. A mere seven minutes in Suite 2806 was about to prove consequential for both actors in this drama, wrecking his political future and the quiet, tranquil life she had made as an immigrant. She spits from time to time, still trying to eliminate the taste in her mouth. Her stomach is tied in knots.

"I was standing there spitting. I was so alone. I was so scared. I don't know what to do or who to tell," she would recount later. She's unaware at the time, but on her uniform top are three droplets of Strauss-Kahn's semen mixed with her saliva. It would prove the signature evidence that a sexual encounter had occurred.

Back in the suite, Strauss-Kahn had received a call at 12:13 p.m. on his IMF BlackBerry from his daughter that he did not answer as the encounter was coming to an end. Two minutes later, he calmly calls Camille back on his cell phone to say he might be a few minutes late for lunch. He quickly brushes his teeth, slips into a suit, grabs his top coat and bags, and heads for the elevator. It's now about 12:25 p.m.

As he approaches the elevator, Diallo is peering around the corner, still hiding by Room 2820. Their eyes meet for but a second. He says nothing before boarding the elevator.

"I just see the face I see attack me," Diallo recounts. "And I don't even want to look at him." One thing is certain, though. This man with the white hair and the French accent is a complete stranger to her. "I never know who he was. I never know," she insists.

Downstairs, Strauss-Kahn rushes through the lobby and checks out at 12:28 p.m., clearly in a rush to get to the restaurant to meet his daughter. The security video shows a female concierge grabbing his bags as he goes to the desk to return the keys. The desk clerk vividly remembers something odd about this otherwise prim and proper man. There's a touch of toothpaste foam around the lips, the faint evidence of a hasty exit from the room.

Back on the twenty-eighth floor, one of the most consequential moments of the entire case is about to transpire. The natural question is why Nafi Diallo at that very moment, her attacker now departed in the elevator, doesn't run to a room like 2820 (which she knew was empty after cleaning it) and call 911, or at least hotel security.

Her explanation isn't quite satisfying to prosecutors later on. "I don't know what to do," she explains to me a few weeks later, sounding a bit ashamed or frustrated at the course she chose in that split second. "I was so afraid to lose my job. I was so afraid of him, too. I don't know what he have. Sometimes people kill here. I don't know if he have a gun, or anything."

So Nafi Diallo does what she does best. She returns to housekeeping. At approximately 12:26 p.m., she keys the door to Room 2820, the one she had cleaned just before encountering Strauss-Kahn, and momentarily grabs her cleaning gear. She carts it over to Suite 2806, opens the door with her security key, and props open the door. She knows Strauss-Kahn has left for good. So this time she doesn't yell out, "Hello? Housekeeping."

Just entering the room so soon after the alleged attack leaves her suddenly ill and disoriented. She doesn't know where to start so she stumbles out into the hallway to the nearby linen closet. Maybe she should start by gathering some fresh towels and linens for the room, she thinks for a second.

Just then, she hears the ding of the service elevator bell. The doors open and off steps a familiar face, the housekeeping floor supervisor named Jessica Hollingsworth.

Their eyes meet, and Jessica can immediately tell that Diallo is not herself. She's trembling. She even spits uncharacteristically on the carpet. Something is seriously amiss.

"Nafi, what's wrong?" Jessica asks.

There's a pause. No one is ready for what transpires next.

FOUR

Outcries and Evidence

"Nafi, tell me what happened? What's wrong?" Jessica Hollingsworth implores.

"Oh, Jessica, thank God. I was going to call. But I don't want to tell you out here," Diallo says, gesturing to the hallway.

Hollingsworth can sense something bad has happened. Diallo looks distraught, disoriented. "Let's go inside," she says as she takes Diallo through the open door of Suite 2806 and has her sit in the living room.

It's about 12:30 p.m., or about seventeen minutes after the incident inside Suite 2806 ended. Diallo at that moment still isn't sure what to say, whether she wants to admit what really happened. She's worried still that she might be fired for walking in on a VIP client. She reaches instead for a hypothetical.

"If somebody try to rape you in this job, what do you do?" Diallo asks, almost embarrassed to ask.

Hollingsworth doesn't for a second believe this is a hypothetical question. She presses Diallo to tell what happened. Diallo finally relents and explains how a naked man with white hair came out of the bathroom, grabbed her, and then assaulted her.

At 12:36 p.m., Hollingsworth uses the housekeepers' radio system to call the chief of housekeeping, Renata Markozani, and summon her to Suite 2806. Though it is technically a crime scene, several Sofitel employees would wander through the room over the next twenty minutes. It would later be flagged as an issue by Dominique Strauss-Kahn's lawyers. But at the moment, the Sofitel workers are less worried about preserving evidence and crime scene integrity, and more worried about ensuring the well-being of their colleague while ascertaining what really happened.

Markozani arrives about two minutes after Hollingsworth paged her on the radio, and the two housekeeping supervisors again question Diallo about what occurred.

Diallo describes the incident, at times reenacting some of the pushing and shoving. At other times, she is quivering with her eyes welling with tears. During the retelling, she becomes so nauseated at one point that she feels like vomiting. One of her supervisors takes her to a small half bathroom in the suite where Diallo spits in the sink as she tries to settle her stomach. While there, Diallo notices a garbage can with a bloody bandage or tissue in it.

Again, she begins to worry.

Did I hurt him when I pushed him hard to get him away from me? she wonders, fearing anew for her job. She doesn't understand how the American legal system works. If it's like Guinea, the female accuser is always at a disadvantage and might even be killed if she comes forward to report an assault, she would later tell an investigator in explaining her fears. And she can't afford to lose her job for striking a client. (It turns out, the blood on the tissue was unrelated to the attacks. Strauss-Kahn suffered from a skin condition that weekend that caused the tips of his fingers to occasionally bleed.)

"I don't know what to do," Diallo says after describing the incident. She's fishing around to see if she is about to get in trouble for having walked in on a VIP guest.

"If this was me, I would call the police," one of the supervisors tells her. For much of the next hour, several colleagues would try repeatedly to convince Diallo that the right thing to do is to report the assault to police. Diallo's reply is deferential, almost submissive. "Whatever you think," she says.

Markozani has heard enough. She calls the security office and asks one of the officers to come up to Suite 2806 for the report of a possible sexual assault. At 12:41 p.m., officer Derrick May heads into the elevator for the twenty-eighth floor to take the report. Before he leaves, May decides to call Sofitel chief engineer Brian Yearwood and asks him to join him. Though not a security officer, Yearwood is that weekend's acting hotel manager, and thus the top Sofitel official on scene.

At 12:45 p.m., Yearwood keys the door to Suite 2806, and he and May question Diallo there. Again, the housekeeper recounts what happened. She is calming down a bit and no longer spitting, the handiwork of her housekeeping colleagues' compassion and attentiveness. When it becomes clear the alleged attack has occurred in the room where everyone is currently sitting, May decides it would be best to leave the room and preserve the crime scene, and to continue the interview downstairs in the Sofitel security office. May, Markozani, and Diallo leave the suite and head onto the elevators at around 12:51 p.m. arriving a minute later at the first-floor security office.

As soon as the others leave, however, Yearwood keys the door to Suite 2806 one more time. The exact reason for his last visit inside the suite remains unknown, a mystery that Strauss-Kahn's lawyers want to solve if they get a chance to question the outcry witnesses in connection with a civil trial. Over the next hour, Yearwood drifts around the hotel, bouncing between various locations, making calls, and encountering various people. There's nothing unusual about his behavior since he is the acting hotel manager at the moment and dealing with more than just Diallo's complaint.

In the hallway outside the security office, Diallo sits quietly on a bench for about thirteen minutes. She is trying to process everything that has happened to her. She is still dressed in the cream-colored housekeeping uniform she was wearing when the incident occurred. She's seemingly unaware of the small spots of semen and saliva staining the top of her dress. These would become crucial pieces of prosecution evidence proving a sexual encounter had occurred. Security officials are buzzing around her, and eventually May and fellow security officer Adrian Branch stop by at around 1:05 p.m. to ask a question or two. While standing, Diallo becomes more agitated as she talks about the specifics of what happened in the suite with the white-haired man, whose name at this point she still does not know.

At one point, Markozani asks Diallo again how she ended up moving from the suite's living room to the narrow hallway by the bathroom. Diallo is caught on the security videotape reenacting the shoving match she says occurred with Strauss-Kahn. She plays the role of DSK, while Markozani is pushed back down the hall near the security office. Diallo will give that reenactment several more times over the course of the next few days.

Behind the scenes, the first notifications to senior management of the Sofitel are beginning to occur. Those working that Saturday recognize that there are going to be large repercussions from an alleged sexual assault incident between a VIP client and a housekeeper, and so everyone wants to do things "by the book."

Shortly after 1 p.m., a Sofitel security official phones the hotel's chief of security, John Sheehan, who is out enjoying the spring weekend in New York City's suburbs. Sheehan, a former military officer, recognizes he is going to need to head to the hotel himself, so he fires off a couple of text messages to rearrange personal plans and then heads for midtown Manhattan. Soon, a decision is made to call the police, whether or not Diallo is reluctant to do so.

On his way in, Sheehan makes a call at 1:28 p.m. to Florian Schutz, a German-born, French-trained hotel executive who had worked his way up the Sofitel chain of command from the restaurant-beverages division to become the New York hotel's manager. Schutz decides to return to the hotel as well. At 1:31 p.m., Sheehan phones Yearwood, the engineering chief who is the acting hotel manager that Saturday, to get an update and give the go-ahead to call police.

At that same minute, Sofitel security officer Adrian Branch picks up the phone in the security office and calls 911. From that moment forward, Diallo's and Strauss-Kahn's lives would forever change. A case tailor-made for the NBC drama *Law & Order: SVU* is about to be forged. (In fact, five months later, the show about NYPD's Special Victims unit opened its 2011 fall season with a fictionalized account of the case.)

The 911 operator answers.

"Hello, I would like to report a domestic, uh, I'm sorry, a sexual assault," Branch begins.

The dispatcher inquires about the location and the status of the victim. "This is actually a hotel and it's one of the attendants who was assaulted by one of the guests," he explains. Uniformed officers and Special Victims detectives who specialize in sexual assaults are dispatched to the scene.

Yearwood and May had been fretting for some time about whether Diallo would report the crime to police. They were taken aback a bit by her reluctance to summon police and had to assure her she would not be fired for what had happened. With the 911 call now finally made, the two men, who often pal around inside the hotel, take a brief break, walking out to one of the hotel's loading docks. They are oblivious to the fact that they are being recorded by security cameras. They simply, by their own account, went to blow off some steam after feeling relieved that police were finally getting involved.

Months later, however, the footage of their awkward thirteen-second celebration—a classic guys' handshake and chest bump—would be broadcast across the globe and used by Strauss-Kahn's defenders to suggest the two hotel workers may have been part of some conspiracy to set up the French politician to be apprehended by police.

The footage leaves much to be explained, and lots to be interpreted. DSK's supporters see some sort of celebration of the fact that police are now involved and their client is about to be arrested. Diallo's lawyers watch the same footage and think the two men might be mockingly reenacting some of the sexual assault scene, like the housekeeper had done for the two men. The hotel workers, and their bosses who have seen the tape multiple times, however, think both sides' interpretations are preposterous.

Sofitel executives and the hotel's outside counsel pressed the two men aggressively about what really happened. Their answer, more than six months later, was a bit vague, their recollections perhaps faded by the passage of time. They weren't exactly sure what they were talking about or celebrating. Perhaps it was about sports, one of their favorite pastimes. All they remember was feeling a sense of relief that police had finally been summoned.

Nearing the hotel, Sheehan continues calling up the command chain of the Sofitel. At 1:33 p.m. he calls Jorge Tito, the hotel's general manager, and describes what is happening. At 1:38 p.m., he makes another call to Yearwood to pass along some instructions.

And then at 1:40 p.m., nearly an hour and a half after Diallo alleges the incident with Strauss-Kahn had ended, Sheehan finally makes his first call to France and Sofitel's parent company, Accor. He is trying to reach the duty manager in Paris to report what has happened at the

New York property. He has two discussions with Accor officials over the next twenty minutes.

Soon police would arrive at the scene, at 2:05 p.m. to be exact, and the Sofitel officials would transition from being first responders for a sex assault victim to the all-important outcry witnesses who can help make or break a sexual assault prosecution.

Around 2:30 p.m., Diallo is sitting in a small security office with NYPD officers and hotel officials when one of the security officials shows her a picture of Strauss-Kahn from the Internet. She quickly identifies him as her attacker. The brief episode, however, violates police protocol and prosecutors would eventually have to disclose to Strauss-Kahn that she was shown a photo of their client long before she made a positive identification from a police lineup. It was an innocent mistake, but one that weeks later would be flagged as a potential concern inside Vance's office.

Over the next hour, police and security officials begin to map out a strategy. Diallo must be taken to the hospital for a rape kit, and the alleged crime scene must be secured. Eventually, detectives will want to take Diallo back to the twenty-eighth floor, tracing her every step to and from Suite 2806. And if DSK calls the Sofitel, there are clear instructions to the hotel switchboard to route the call to security. To everyone's surprise, a seemingly calm Strauss-Kahn makes a call to the hotel around 3:30 p.m. looking for his lost cell phone, allowing police and Sofitel security officials to stage a ruse to ascertain his whereabouts and secure his arrest at John F. Kennedy International Airport before he can leave on a flight to Paris.

Around 3:30 p.m., detectives take Nafi Diallo from the hotel and drive her to St. Luke's-Roosevelt Hospital, the place where many of New York City's sexual assault victims are taken for the all-important Sexual Assault Forensic Exam (SAFE). It is clear Diallo's shift won't end at her normal 5:30 p.m. So she calls her daughter to explain what has happened. While at the hospital, she also reaches out briefly by phone to her friend Blake Diallo, the coffee shop manager in Harlem.

"Somebody tried to do something very bad to me," the housekeeper confides to her friend, sounding in distress. "Somebody tried to rape me."

Blake Diallo tries to calm her down, and asks where she is. "I am at St. Luke Hospital with the police and the doctors," she explains. "They are checking for evidence."

The call is short. The doctors and nurses need the time to check Nafi Diallo's body and clothing for evidence. Even with the most trained of technicians, the task can be stressful and demeaning. Diallo had removed her uniform dress and her two pairs of pantyhose, and her underwear. Everything is bagged, marked, and sealed as evidence.

The maid's uniform, like the infamous blue dress White House intern Monica Lewinsky wore the day she had oral sex with President Bill Clinton, the event which led to his impeachment case, would yield irrefutable forensic proof that a sexual encounter took place. Lab technicians found three stains on the upper portion of Diallo's uniform dress containing semen, two which were mixed with amylase and saliva as would be expected from an oral sex encounter. The significance of this discovery is almost understated in the typically dry narrative of the prosecutors' records. "A single DNA profile matching the defendant's was obtained from these three stains," the records state. In other words, the police lab confirmed Strauss-Kahn's semen was on the housekeeper's dress.

But there was additional DNA evidence that proved Strauss-Kahn had inserted his hand into Diallo's stockings. Strauss-Kahn's DNA from epithelial cells—the type found on the outside of hands—was found on both the interior and exterior waistband of Diallo's two pairs of pantyhose as well as on the waistband of her underwear. This all but proved that Strauss-Kahn's hand had tried to get inside

Diallo's panties, as she had described. Moreover, the lab technicians also found DSK's skin cells on the exterior crotch of the light-colored pantyhose. The forensic evidence confirming a sexual encounter was piling up for police, and it would only continue to get more solid.

Strauss-Kahn's undergarments likewise yielded proof that he had engaged in a sexual encounter shortly before he got dressed and left the hotel room for lunch with his daughter. Both his boxer shorts and a penile swab taken by police a full day after his arrest contained the presence of semen that matched his DNA.

Over the course of two hours at St. Luke's, Diallo's entire body is examined from head to toe. There are no scratches or visible bruises. But Diallo complains of pain in her left shoulder, "which is mild, constant and non-radiating," the hospital notes state. She is diagnosed that evening by the emergency room doctor to have suffered a muscle strain and contusion. There was no need for X-rays or pain medicine, though.

The shoulder injury was originally viewed by prosecutors as consistent with Diallo's description of being pushed to the floor and pinned to the wall by her alleged attacker, but it would later become a source of contention. When the pain persisted, Diallo went in late June to have an MRI done on the shoulder and was diagnosed by an orthopedic surgeon to be suffering from a SLAP Type 2 ligament tear. For some reason, prosecutors would come to doubt the injury was related to the alleged attack, theorizing it could have been caused by something like repetitive motion from cleaning rooms or the like.

The doctors also observed "redness" in Diallo's vaginal area about five hours after the attack, right in the area where the housekeeper claimed DSK grabbed her forcefully between the legs before she fell to the ground. The medical staff took a picture of her vagina, and highlighted the inflamed area with a circle and two arrows. Diallo told me and my *Newsweek* colleagues weeks later that she had suffered pain urinating for some time after the injury. "Too much pain for too many days when I have to go the bathroom," she said in a July interview. Again, prosecutors would later come to doubt that the redness on the vagina was related to the attack. And they claimed she never told them until weeks later that the pain in her vaginal area persisted after the attack.

Diallo declined to have a test for sexually transmitted diseases, the records state. She was told she could get a prescription for doxycycline to prevent any infection, and that "STD risks were discussed."

The hospital records provide one of the best written accounts in the first twenty-four hours of what Diallo told the various outcry witnesses. The doctors' and sexual assault examiner's notations closely match the recollections of the Sofitel employees, and the consistency of accounts between all the people who encountered Nafi Diallo that first day impressed the detectives and prosecutors enough to proceed quickly toward securing an indictment of Strauss-Kahn.

Diallo was "tearful" as she retold the incident "in narrative fashion, paused while she was describing act of" oral sex, the notes from St. Luke's related. The patient "reports that as soon as she was inside, a male, naked with white hair, locked the door and pushed her onto the bed, that he stood in front of her and put his penis in her mouth," the notes added. "Pt [patient] reports that she told him to stop and tried to get away from him and that he pulled her towards the direction of the bathroom, and put his hand under her clothes and inside her stockings, grabbing outside of vaginal area."

After the man grabbed her vagina, "she fell onto the carpeted floor and he penetrated her mouth with his penis ('deep'), holding her by the hair and forcing her head onto his penis for a longer time," the hospital report added. "She felt something wet and sour come into her mouth and she spit it out on the carpet."

There was, however, one inconsistency in the hospital records that would later catch the attention of DSK's defense lawyers. "Pt [patient] reports he got dressed + left the room and that he said nothing to her during the incident." In her interview with police, her testimony to the grand jury, and her account to *Newsweek*, Diallo recalled Strauss-Kahn making several statements during the attack, and she insisted she fled the room as soon as the attack ended. So how could she have known Strauss-Kahn got dressed?

Cyrus Vance's prosecutors hadn't noticed the discrepancy, but after Strauss-Kahn's lawyers pointed it out, they went back to the sexual assault examiner at the hospital, who opined that the report might simply have tried to "conflate different portions of the complainant's narrative in the same sentences," court records show. Diallo could obviously tell Strauss-Kahn had gotten dressed and left the room because she saw him at the elevator, just before he checked out.

The hospital exam, however, mostly corroborated what police believed had occurred in Suite 2806. But they now needed Diallo to return to the scene and walk them through everything she had done. Diallo was reluctant to return to the hotel room, but she was told it was essential for police. Around dinnertime, Diallo left the hospital and returned to the $3,000-a-night luxury hotel room where her tranquil life's routine as a housekeeper had been shattered.

Back on scene on the twenty-eighth floor of the Sofitel, Diallo that Saturday night patiently walked detectives through her steps that day. She pointed out where she entered Suite 2806, where Strauss-Kahn first grabbed her near the doorway of the bedroom, the location on the bed where he first tried to attack her, and then the hallway where he pushed her down. She was tearful, especially when she showed authorities the location where she had fallen to the floor in the narrow hallway, near the bathroom, and where he inserted his penis into her mouth and ejaculated. She also showed detectives how she fled the room, pointing out the locations inside and outside the suite where she remembered spitting out his semen. It included the hallway area near Room 2820 where she fled and hid until after Strauss-Kahn left. At each location, police lab technicians placed evidence markers and began the tedious process of swabbing for DNA evidence.

In a few locations, they cut sections of the carpet or wallpaper to be taken to the crime lab for further analysis. In all, five areas with distinct stains from human fluids were found. One of them from the narrow hallway, approximately six to eight feet from where Diallo claimed she was attacked, tested positive for Strauss-Kahn's semen and her saliva. It was the location where Diallo remembered spitting the first time as she fled down the hallway in an effort to leave the suite. Many of the other stains in the room also tested positive for semen, but they were from other men and were ruled to have occurred in earlier instances. (After all, the glorious confines of Suite 2806 were likely a hotbed for romance inside the Sofitel for many years.)

The crime scene walk-through drags on for hours, and Diallo begins to appear emotionally drained and tired. Shortly after 10 p.m., the detectives decide to take the housekeeper back to their Harlem squad room to finish the paperwork and review any remaining questions. She doesn't know it, but behind the closed door of the squad's interrogation room, Strauss-Kahn is sitting patiently. He's contacted his lawyer and been instructed not to talk to the police.

Diallo tries to take her mind off the nightmarish day she's been through so she glances at the television in the office where she is seated, looking for a brief mental reprieve. Soon, the eleven o'clock news opens and the arrest of a man known as DSK is blared on the headlines. She sees the photo of the man from the suite and she turns away. Detectives realize their mistake and change the channel. Sitting in the squad room, Diallo begins to cry as the detectives occasionally ask follow-up questions.

"I want it to be over," she says. "I just want to go home."

Shortly before 3 a.m. on Sunday morning, after police formally booked Strauss-Kahn on multiple felony charges, detectives drive

Diallo back to her apartment in the Bronx and she is reunited with her teenage daughter. It's one of the longest periods they have been apart since her daughter moved to the United States four years earlier. She explains to her daughter briefly what has happened and then tries to sleep. But her mind is racing with all that has transpired, and she tosses and turns, only able to nod off for short periods of time.

When the sun rises, Diallo is back up. When she can't sleep, she usually turns on the TV. She does, and on comes the morning news. One of the lead stories is the arrest of Strauss-Kahn. The night before she only glanced at his photo on the TV screen. But this time she watches more intently. The man arrested for sexual assault is one of the world's most powerful politicians, a likely candidate for the French presidency, and the head of an international agency at the center of the global financial crisis.

"I watched Channel 7 and they say this is guy—I don't know—and he is going to be the next president of France. And I think, 'Oh my God, they are going to kill me,'" Diallo would later confide to me and my *Newsweek* colleagues, describing the moment she first realized the man she had accused was the leader of the International Monetary Fund and a potential presidential candidate in France.

Soon, the apartment phone rings. It is a reporter for a French media outlet looking for the housekeeper who made the criminal complaint. She hangs up. Then there are knocks on the door. Diallo can't stand it any longer. She and her daughter pack their bags to flee for the anonymity of a niece's home. She grabs her cell phones and some clothes. It's the last time she would set foot in her apartment for weeks. Soon, she'll be placed in protective police custody, first at a hotel in Brooklyn and later in a hotel in upscale Westchester County, near the Connecticut border, when her lawyers raised concerns about the lack of security at the Brooklyn location.

Over the course of that Sunday, Diallo's friends begin to ring her cell phone. Blake Diallo calls back. After their first conversation while at the hospital, he had become angry and rifled through the Internet Yellow Pages looking for a lawyer to represent the housekeeper, ultimately choosing a civil attorney named Jeffrey Shapiro. He sets up a Monday appointment for her to get a legal consultation.

A second ring of the phone brings another familiar voice, Amara Tarawally, another of her male friends from the neighborhood. Tarawally's uncle owns the bodega where Diallo once worked and the two became friends. Diallo also became friendly with Tarawally's wife, and the housekeeper believed he had a business selling designer handbags and T-shirts both in New York and Arizona. She comes to trust him enough to lend her checking account information to him via her debit card. She is surprised to learn from prosecutors in June that he and his friends ultimately used her account to move tens of thousands of dollars through it over the prior year. She eventually becomes angry by what prosecutors tell her and cuts off her relationship with Tarawally. But not before two consequential phone calls in the early days of the DSK case.

In recent months before the Sofitel incident, Tarawally has been held in an Arizona immigration detention center, after being convicted in a drug sting. He has arranged for calling cards so he could phone Diallo, the woman he calls his "fiancée" and stay in touch. This Sunday is just a normal call to check up. Soon he learns his friend is in distress, the victim of an attempted rape.

In her native West African Fulani dialect, Diallo tells Tarawally she had been attacked at the hotel where she worked. "A man attacked me, a man tried to rape me," Diallo recalls telling Tarawally that day.

Tarawally is concerned for Diallo's well-being. At the detention cell in Arizona, he watches television and sees the news reports about this powerful Frenchman nicknamed DSK who has been arrested for attacking a chambermaid at a luxury hotel in New York City. He quickly puts two and two together, and he plans the next day to call her and make sure she can handle herself against such a formidable defendant. That follow-up call would later tarnish Diallo's credibility and the outcome of the criminal case.

For now, though, Diallo has to return to the reality of being treated as a crime victim. Detectives plan to pick her up from her niece's house and bring the housekeeper and her daughter to a safe house for protection. But first she has one more important task before Strauss-Kahn can be brought to court: she must officially identify him in a police lineup.

Diallo is driven back to the Harlem Special Victims squad room around mid-afternoon. Standing behind a one-way window, five older-looking men stream into a room, each holding a number. Diallo's heart is racing, and she is sweating from nerves. She can only glance up for a second.

"I don't even look at clothes. I look at the face," she recalls.

"Do you see the man who attacked you, Nafi?" a prosecutor asks.

"No. 3," she answers.

"Are you sure?" the prosecutor prods.

She nods and then tries to leave the room as quickly as possible.

She won't have to come face-to-face again with Strauss-Kahn. But she is just beginning to witness the rigors of the judicial system. There are numerous interviews, a grand jury appearance, and countless meetings with her lawyer and prosecutors in the days ahead. After that, there are weeks of loneliness at the safe house.

On Monday, May 16, as Strauss-Kahn is paraded into a courtroom for the first time and is ordered held without bail, Diallo meets with her friend Blake Diallo and the new lawyer he has picked for her, Jeffrey Shapiro. Prosecutors have told Nafi Diallo that she has done nothing wrong and doesn't need an attorney. But Blake Diallo wants to make sure the housekeeper, his friend, has a lawyer watching her back while going up against a global figure with limitless resources.

While the meeting is occurring, Diallo's cell phone rings. It's

Tarawally again from the Arizona detention center. He's seen all the news reports and wants to make sure his friend understands what and who she is up against. Because Tarawally is in prison, his call is being recorded. The exact transcript of this call would become a matter of great dispute between the prosecutor, Diallo, her lawyers, and even the two interpreters asked by the prosecutors to translate the Fulani dialect used on the phone. (Fulanis are a mostly Muslim people scattered across several countries in West Africa who speak various dialects of the Fulani language. Diallo's particular dialect is common in her homeland of Guinea.)

A full six weeks later, the public would first learn about this call from a leak made by a "well-placed law enforcement source" to *The New York Times.* The story claimed that during the call Diallo said "words to the effect of, 'Don't worry, this guy has a lot of money. I know what I'm doing.'" The newspaper also reported the call occurred the day after the attack. In fact, the call occurred two days after the attack. And when Diallo, her lawyer, and a Fulani interpreter finally got to listen to the tape, they discovered Diallo never raised the issue of money. It was Tarawally who had done so, and Diallo responds by saying it was an issue for her lawyer, not her, to deal with.

The call was generally consistent with what Diallo told prosecutors originally, that she wasn't interested in money and no one could "buy" her. And it was consistent with what she told me and my *Newsweek* colleagues in a later interview. "I never said that," she said, strongly disputing the idea that she ever raised the issue of Strauss-Kahn's money. It would, however, not matter in the end. The image of her as a money-grubber was blasted into the public by the anonymous leaker to the *Times* and prosecutors would do little to correct the impression.

Monday, May 16, was important for another reason. It was the first time that Diallo told detectives and prosecutors a contrived but graphic tale of how she was gang-raped in Guinea. She would repeat the story in even greater detail a few weeks later in an interview session on May 30 in which even the most grizzled prosecutors got moist eyes. Prosecutors would later marvel at how masterful Diallo was in weaving the false story.

"She offered precise and powerful details about the number and nature of her attackers and the presence of her 2-year-old daughter at the assault scene, who she said was pulled from her arms and thrown to the ground," Vance's team would later tell the court. "During both interviews, she identified certain visible scars on her person, which she claimed were sustained during the attack.

"On both occasions, the complainant recounted the rape with great emotion and conviction: she cried, spoke hesitantly, and appeared understandably distraught, and during that first interview, even laid her head facedown on her arms on a table in front of her."

Diallo would admit readily in those first interviews that she entered the United States illegally, using another woman's visa. But for some reason, she insisted on sticking to the rest of the bogus story her immigration adviser purportedly had given her, including the false story of the rape.

It would turn out that May 16 would become one of the most crucial days in the case, the day Diallo's credibility suffered irrevocable harm in the prosecutors' eyes. The call from Tarawally and Diallo's performance in the interview room would eventually prove too much for prosecutors to tolerate.

Over the rest of May, though, Diallo enjoyed a good relationship with the prosecutors, who remained oblivious to the pitfalls that lay ahead. The forensic evidence was substantial, better than most sexual assault cases. And the outcry witnesses, those compassionate Sofitel workers who comforted Diallo in the early minutes after she emerged from her encounter with Strauss-Kahn in Suite 2806, had provided solid, consistent testimony that bolstered Diallo's own account.

On the other side of the case, Strauss-Kahn's lawyers were gathering their own evidence and shared little optimism that the criminal charges would be dropped anytime soon even though they believed the accuser suffered serious credibility issues. To defense attorneys Benjamin Brafman and William Taylor, the prosecutors seemed enamored in their early court appearances with their evidence and their star witness, the immigrant chambermaid.

Near the end of the first week, right after Strauss-Kahn was finally released from Rikers Island on bail, the DSK investigators stumbled onto a piece of evidence that sent shock waves of alarm through the defense team. While researching Diallo's past and talking to her neighbors and friends in the West African immigrant community, they discovered that she and her daughter were living in an apartment building in the Bronx where many units are subsidized by Harlem United, a nonprofit organization that provides housing and care to patients with HIV and their families.

The defense lawyers had just learned about the forensic lab results confirming a sexual encounter had occurred between their client and Diallo. So they alerted Strauss-Kahn to the possibility he might have been exposed to the HIV virus or other sexually transmitted diseases. There was little Strauss-Kahn could do at that moment. He was in house arrest, under the strictest of detention conditions. Even after those restrictions were eased in the early summer, DSK did not do much about the HIV scare. He knew reporters would be staking out his every move if he left the house and went to a doctor. So he just waited. Finally, when he returned to France in the fall, he got tested for HIV. The test results came back negative, and the Frenchman was relieved to have dodged yet another bullet.

As the first month wound to an end, Diallo made one last decision that was certain to change the course of the case. Some of her friends and family in the West African immigrant community had worried that her first lawyer, Jeffrey Shapiro, was skilled in civil matters but had little experience in criminal law. With the complexities of the case obvious, they had reached out to a former federal prosecutor named Kenneth Thompson, who was a hero of sorts in the community for his role in successfully prosecuting NYPD police officers who had sodomized a Haitian immigrant in a police station back in the 1990s in one of New York's more racially charged episodes.

Over the Memorial Day weekend, Diallo formally switched lawyers. In his first sit-down with the housekeeper, Thompson made a bold promise. "Nafi, I will fight for you and won't stop fighting for you no matter how tough this case gets," he vowed.

Little did she or the prosecutors know at the time just how fervent Thompson would be in fulfilling that mission.

FIVE

The Beginning of the End

SITTING IN A HOTEL ROOM in the ritzy tourist trap of Lake George, New York, attorney Kenneth Thompson frantically tried to reach prosecutors in the Dominique Strauss-Kahn case. He was just hours away from rubbing elbows with federal and state judges attending the prestigious Second Circuit Judicial Conference at the Sagamore Resort—the first time he had ever been invited—and he suspected he'd be peppered with questions about his new high-profile client, Nafissatou Diallo, the hotel maid who had accused Dominique Strauss-Kahn of sexual assault the previous month.

"Joan, I need to reach you. I need to know what's going on," Thompson said in a phone message asking the lead prosecutor in the case, Joan Illuzzi-Orbon, to call him back the afternoon of June 9.

Thompson had a pit in his stomach. In the days before he left for the three-plus-hour drive to the conference, Diallo had informed him that she had made false statements to prosecutors about her past—specifically in connection with her efforts to win asylum. The lies included her tale of an earlier gang rape in Guinea at the hands of soldiers. Diallo had embellished the tale—given to her years earlier by a man who helped her win asylum to the United States as a victim of persecution in Guinea—by crying in those earlier sessions. Diallo actually had been raped in an different episode, but for some reason she stuck instead with the bogus story her immigration adviser gave her. And she told it convincingly enough to even bring prosecutors to tears.

Diallo faced a tall task to restore her credibility with prosecutors. Shortly after Thompson took over, Diallo confided to him that she had made earlier false statements to prosecutors about her past a how she got into the United States.

As best Thompson knew, though, Diallo's problems simply involved misstatements about her background and she was still sticking by her story of what happened in the hotel suite with Strauss-Kahn, a story she had told over and over again with a consistency that had impressed the detectives and prosecutors. But as a former federal prosecutor, Thompson knew the case was at a make-or-break moment. Any story concocted about an earlier rape could undercut the trust essential between an accuser and the prosecution team, and perhaps, end the whole case.

Before jumping in the car on Wednesday, June 8, 2011, with his wife for the Lake George trip, Thompson informed the prosecution about the problems and instructed Diallo to come clean about any and all falsehoods she had told during her debriefings. And he assured prosecutors she was ready to come clean about any prior misstatements.

As he traveled upstate along the New York Thruway, he didn't question the wisdom of leaving Diallo behind under such difficult circumstances. After all, he had only been representing her for two weeks and she had handled nearly all of her prior debriefings with detectives and prosecutors without her lawyer present.

Still, there were reasons to be worried. Diallo's English was uneven, and she couldn't read or write, so she would be left to the mercy of a Fulani interpreter and a group of prosecutors suddenly leery of her tale. The language gap only made the chance for miscommunication worse with a woman still in a fragile mental state nearly a month after the alleged attack.

But the prospect of meeting judges would be good for his career, so Thompson left behind, for a fleeting but consequential moment, the "mess in Manhattan."

Within forty-eight hours, Thompson would see it as his biggest mistake in the case.

Back in a windowless room at the prosecutor's office, the dynamic between Diallo and the assistant district attorneys had changed. They began questioning her on June 8 and the session spilled over to June 9. There no longer was the sympathy afforded a rape victim. Ann Prunty and Joan Illuzzi—two veteran violent crimes prosecutors seemingly cut from an episode of *Law & Order*—felt personally offended at having been lied to so convincingly, especially about the Guinean gang rape. For countless hours, they repeatedly pressed for answers. There was a personal nature to the inquisition, and a stunning degree of distrust.

"Tell us the truth, Nafi," Prunty would say over and over again, her voice raised.

"Please step yelling at me," Diallo would counter in broken English. Her fifteen-year-old daughter, sitting nearby, could hear the raised voices.

For weeks the prosecutors had coddled and protected Diallo, arranged for detectives to put her in a safe house, and drive her anywhere she needed: shopping, dinner with friends, her daughter's school. They gave her living money and helped pay her rent.

For a woman of few means, the treatment was unusual. Now, the sensation of watching the prosecutors turn against her, doubting her every word, left Diallo feeling victimized anew.

By the afternoon of June 9, prosecutors had ascertained a bevy of lies—all of them related to Diallo's past and her entrance into the

United States. She had lied about her husband's death. He hadn't died at the hands of Guinean soldiers who had beaten, imprisoned, and tortured him, the victim of a repressive regime that tried to silence its critics through murder. Rather, he died from Africa's other great scourge: AIDS. Diallo posed as another woman to illegally enter the United States and began working without proper papers.

In fact, most of the story she gave immigration officials to win asylum in 2004 was mostly fictional, the workmanship of a shadowy figure in Brooklyn who gave her a sure-to-win account to memorize and provide to U.S. immigration authorities to support her asylum claim.

Under penalty of perjury during her asylum interview years earlier and in her interviews with detectives and prosecutors after the alleged attack in May, Diallo had claimed that she and her husband had been persecuted by the dictatorial regime running Guinea in the late 1990s and early 2000s, and that their home had been destroyed by authorities. She and her husband were beaten by the authorities because of their opposition to the regime, and her husband ultimately was imprisoned and tortured by the regime until he died from maltreatment, she had claimed quite convincingly. None of it was true.

In two earlier private sessions with prosecutors, Diallo also claimed that during her persecution in Guinea she was raped by Guinean soldiers, breaking into tears as she recounted the brutal attack in such vivid details that even the two female prosecutors, veterans of many sordid, violent cases, welled up with tears of sympathy. Again, the tale was a figment of the immigration adviser's script from years earlier, designed to improve Diallo's chances of winning asylum as a victim of political persecution.

Diallo's pattern of lying continued after she got into the United States, too.

She had cheated on her taxes, claiming another friend's child as her own to get another deduction on top of her fifteen-year-old biological daughter. She lied about her income—which topped out over $40,000 with a maid's salary and tips—to attain low-income housing in the Bronx. The list went on, according to prosecutors.

Diallo had to justify why she had provided so much misinformation. She explained that she had stuck to her embellished immigration story because she didn't want to take any chances being deported. She, in fact, had been raped by Guinean soldiers, but earlier in her life and under different circumstances. Cheating on her taxes and the housing application was a simple effort to get a better life for her and her daughter, who scraped by in expensive New York City on a housekeeper's salary. There was nothing easy about the interrogations—for Diallo or the prosecutors—as these facts were laid out.

Illuzzi returned Thompson's call on June 9. "Ken, it's worse than you think. She is changing her story," the prosecutor reported. "No one with half a brain would ever put her on the stand."

"Is she changing her story about what happened in the hotel room?" Thompson pressed.

"I don't know. I haven't got to that part yet," Illuzzi answered.

"When are you going to get to that?"

"I don't know. Probably the end of the day."

"Joan, you need to do it now," Thompson pleaded. "I need to know if we're dealing with another Tawana Brawley."

Brawley was an iconic figure in New York sex crime annals. The young black woman had alleged she was raped by six white men back in 1987, an allegation that inflamed an entire city during an era of racial tensions. A young Reverend Al Sharpton had taken up Brawley's cause, as had many others. A special prosecutor and a special grand jury were convened, but Brawley declined to participate, hiding behind an entourage of advisers and lawyers. The reasons soon became clear. She had made up the entire story, the grand jury would conclude in a sensational report months after the initial accusations garnered headlines.

Thompson was young back then, but the memory was still fresh. And his fear that Diallo—an African immigrant accusing one of the world's most powerful men of sexual assault—might go the same route was palpable.

Perhaps, just as importantly, he needed to know how to play the room at the judicial conference a few hours later when the black robes and their clerks came up and asked him to dish on the celebrity case.

Illuzzi agreed to continue the interrogation. Thompson left another message trying to find out what happened. She called back hours later, just as Thompson was about to leave for an evening reception at the conference.

"Ken, we've got a problem. She's changed her story," Illuzzi said, opening the conversation on a dreadful note.

"What? What's changed?" Thompson asked, his heart racing.

"She is now saying Strauss-Kahn told her to 'suck my dick' and get down on her knees. It's all new," Illuzzi related.

"What? Joan. Get familiar with the case, will you!" an exasperated Thompson shot back. "She told that from the very beginning. Do you even know her story?"

The error of Thompson's decision to leave for Lake George was now self-evident. Illuzzi, a homicide prosecutor, had supervised the case for a couple of weeks but up to that point had not really spent much time attending the interviews with Diallo about what actually occurred in Sofitel Hotel Suite 2806 on May 14.

Thompson had left his client behind with a prosecutor unfamiliar with the specifics, and she now was declaring parts of the core allegations untrue. A train wreck was clearly in the making.

"Joan, you need to stop questioning her. You need to wait for me to come back. It has to stop right now," Thompson demanded.

"Ken, we want to continue," Illuzzi protested, clearly miffed at

Thompson's eruption. His tone felt personal, a trait that would grind at Illuzzi and the other prosecutors in the following weeks.

"No, you must wait until I get back. I'll come back as soon as I can," Thompson insisted. He paused. "Joan, don't abandon the case. You can't do it. It would be wrong," Thompson implored.

During the call, Diallo was left sitting in the prosecutor office's where the inquisition had stopped momentarily. She didn't know what to expect next. After all, without Thompson, or the detectives who shuttled her from place to place, she was lost, an alien in a legal world that both mesmerized and scared her.

"Get out of here. Just get out of here," Prunty shouted as she opened the door to the office where Diallo had been sitting quietly. Prosecutors were frustrated that Thompson had cut off the interview.

Diallo cried, then left. Her daughter was appalled by the way she saw prosecutors treat her mom that day. She could hear them yelling at her in the nearby interview room and was indignant with the way her mother was kicked out, she would later tell me.

It was the beginning of the end for Diallo's criminal case against DSK.

A fateful decision by Thompson to leave his client behind to pursue an unrelated career advancement opportunity had opened the door for prosecutors to turn on their star witness. And the prosecution team and Diallo's lawyer would, in the ensuing days, wander down a path of escalating insults, and a very public feud.

Strauss-Kahn could simply sit aside and watch, marveling. His lawyers hadn't even fired their first shot and already the foundation of the case was cracking. Soon it would implode.

Defense lawyers Brafman and Taylor became more convinced

the case was coming apart when Thompson reached out to them, unexpectedly, in mid-June to explore the possibility of reaching a monetary settlement on the civil side of the case. Thompson was becoming concerned the charges would be dropped, unable to extinguish from his mind Illuzzi's statement that she couldn't put Diallo on the witness stand. He knew no sex assault prosecution could succeed if the victim couldn't be put on the stand. So he wanted to at least explore the second best option for getting justice for his client, a civil settlement.

Diallo hadn't yet sued, but both sides knew a suit against DSK was likely at some point. So both signed nondisclosure agreements for the talks, and they met on June 15 to explore the parameters of a settlement process. Thompson and his partner, Douglas Wigdor, suggested some names of high-profile legal mediators, former judges mostly, who could oversee the talks. Brafman and Taylor asked what sort of figure Diallo might be seeking, but Thompson was nowhere ready to talk money. A few days later, DSK's lawyers countered with a different name for a mediator, a former prosecutor whom Diallo's lawyers were also comfortable with. Still, DSK's lawyers continued to press for a dollar figure to be put on the table. Thompson wasn't willing to suggest one yet, preferring instead to focus on the mediation process. Thompson did not, and legally could not, suggest that Diallo would drop the criminal charges in exchange for a civil settlement. Instead, the two sides carefully talked about approaching the prosecutors together if a civil deal was struck.

It's unclear whether DSK had a real intention of settling with Diallo at that moment, but the discussions allowed Taylor and Brafman to spot the first signs of weaknesses in the prosecution's case. Eventually, the magnitude of the problems would become clearer and the DSK legal team would use targeted news leaks and its communications with the District Attorney's Office to fan the flames of dissension between the victim and prosecution team. The goal was to imply Diallo had even more secrets and lies, and that the case was unwinnable in court.

Thompson juggled the two fronts, telling neither the district attorney nor DSK's lawyers of his conversations with the other.

What occurred out of the public's view in the second half of June, however, would be misreported at the time. News media would claim, according to anonymous law enforcement officials, that Thompson stubbornly kept his client from being further interviewed by the prosecution for eighteen straight days after the infamous interrogation was cut off on June 9. These reports were wrong.

In fact, Thompson returned from Lake George and met with the prosecutors the very next day, June 10, to map out a plan for continuing the interviews, and he brought his client to the District Attorney's Office several times the following two weeks. But unexpected circumstances intervened to keep the prosecution and Diallo from doing more interviews: translators didn't show up, Diallo had doctor appointments and an MRI for the shoulder pain that had persisted since the alleged attack, and prosecutors had other meetings or vacation plans.

The back-and-forth began on Friday, June 10, when Thompson and Wigdor met with the prosecutors to get a full report on what had gone wrong the day before during Diallo's latest interrogations. The housekeeper's two lawyers were pressing to see Vance, too, hoping to get a sense of his commitment to the case. But Vance didn't show, and at one point Diallo's lawyers could see the district attorney sneak out the back door of his office, avoiding the meeting with Thompson and Wigdor. They found it odd, creating a perception that would grow over time that Vance wanted to stay out of the fray. The meeting ended with an agreement for Diallo to be interviewed anew after the weekend.

Thompson and Diallo showed up at Vance's office the following Monday morning, June 13, ready to resume the interview. Though spooked by the unexpected turns and tenor of the June 9 session, Thompson remained convinced Diallo could redeem herself with prosecutors. All she had to do was explain her misstatements and recount the alleged attack by DSK to show she had remained consistent about it. He also was banking on the fact that prosecutors would credit Diallo for coming forward to correct her story, rather than waiting for prosecutors to be blindsided.

Likewise, Thompson also was glad when Illuzzi admitted to him that she had talked to the detectives and had been "mistaken" about Diallo changing her story on June 9 about what DSK said and did to her during the attack. Thompson saw it as a sign that there was still enough goodwill to try to get things back on track.

Thompson started the morning of Monday, June 13, by going into one of the prosecution rooms to question Diallo himself, alone, for a short period. Prosecutors remained outside, waiting for the chance to resume their questioning. As in the past, the prosecution's Fulani interpreter was there to help, but the interpreter cut off the session for another meeting before prosecutors could get started. It was the first of several false starts.

Thompson and Diallo prepared to return the next day, Tuesday, June 14, at 11:30 a.m. for another session. Thompson even had canceled other meetings so he could spend the whole day with prosecutors. But he got word shortly before leaving for the District Attorney's Office that the interpreter was unavailable. Another session was off.

Both sides had conflicts the rest of that week, and they agreed to try again on Monday, June 20. Thompson and Diallo arrived at the District Attorney's Office at 11:30 that day, but the interpreter didn't show for two hours and the session was again canceled. Thompson had begun to hear whispers inside the prosecutor's office speculating that he might be playing a game of "keep-away" with his client. He would eventually shoot an email to Daniel Alonso, Vance's supervisor of the criminal division, to try to set the record straight. Thompson and Alonso had worked together as young federal prosecutors in the U.S. Attorney's Office in Brooklyn a decade earlier, and they were cordial and respectful of each other.

"While I understand that your schedule is important," Thompson emailed Alonso, "you may be unaware of the efforts by the victim and me to meet repeatedly, even when the victim has been in pain, only to have our efforts thwarted by the lateness and/or unavailability of the interpreter."

A new wrinkle surfaced that same week that only further nurtured the growing distrust on both sides.

The New York Times reported on the morning of June 20 that a member of Strauss-Kahn's high-powered legal team, Marc Agnifilo, was married to Vance's chief of the trial division. By title and practice, Karen Friedman Agnifilo oversaw all the prosecuting attorneys in the Manhattan D.A.'s Office, including those handling the Strauss-Kahn case. The *Times* reported she recognized she had a conflict of interest and had recused herself from the DSK case early on. Thompson and Wigdor were flabbergasted that they hadn't been told.

Thompson was furious and demanded a meeting directly with Vance and Alonso to clear the air. Vance obliged, and on Wednesday, June 22, a powwow took place. In the annals of the case, the meeting would become just a footnote, referenced only briefly in a handful of emails and letters. But in the crucial relationship between an alleged victim and the prosecutors seeking justice for her, the meeting would prove to be a pivotal moment, a lost opportunity to put the relationship back on track.

Distrust had been building for two weeks on both sides. Prosecutors like Illuzzi and Prunty had taken it personally that Diallo had lied to them so convincingly, and they were equally upset when Thompson cut off their interrogations June 9 just as they were digging into the extent of her deceptions. They also felt Thompson was becoming increasingly accusatory in his tone with them. Managers in the office, like Alonso and top deputy John Irwin, also had suspicions that Thompson might be using excuses like Diallo's purported shoulder injury to cancel or delay further interrogations of the housekeeper. They wanted to get the reinterview finished and move on.

On the other side, Thompson and his partner, Douglas Wigdor, felt their client was not treated with the respect due a sexual assault victim, and that prosecutors had failed to take into account that she came forward voluntarily to disclose her lies, all of which involved matters outside the alleged attack—finances, shady friends, and a false asylum application. Thompson had only been on the case a few days when he discovered the issues and he went right to prosecutors to disclose them. He felt that he and his client deserved some credit and a more respectful process for sorting out the facts.

Finally, Thompson did not believe the current team of prosecutors led by Illuzzi, a veteran of homicide cases, and Prunty, who handled sexual assaults and other violent crimes but wasn't a rape victim expert, knew how to handle the immigrant housekeeper. After all, Diallo was still dealing with trauma and injury, the intricacies of a legal system she had never before experienced, and the challenges of getting Americans to understand the subtleties of her culture and the horror of her past experiences in Guinea. She had been coached to lie to get into the country, and that dissembling needed to be understood separately from the facts and evidence of what occurred in the room with Strauss-Kahn, Thompson believed. And Diallo needed to be managed differently during the debriefings, he concluded.

He wasn't alone in sharing those concerns. Both Linda Fairstein, the former sex crimes prosecutor and novelist who advised Vance from the outside, and Lisa Friel, the sex crimes unit supervisor removed from the case early on, had concerns about whether the right team was in place to handle such a complicated sex case.

Thompson soon made clear he didn't like Illuzzi's and Prunty's interactions with Diallo. They seemed to Thompson only to want to go to trial, against DSK's all-star team, if they had a perfect victim. But sexual assault victims are seldom perfect, ranging from prostitutes and petty street crime players to wealthy debutantes hiding secret sex lives. Most have secrets and skeletons in their closets, which veteran sex crimes prosecutors frequently learn to navigate around while securing convictions.

In Diallo's case, the housekeeper had followed the path of many West African immigrants who are coached to lie on their asylum and immigration paperwork in hopes of securing a better life in America. Thompson wondered whether Illuzzi could separate her personal anger about being lied to from the facts about the attack. She seemed to be looking to catch Diallo in a lie about the actual incident involving DSK, one that would give the prosecution a reason to jettison the case and remove the risk to her perfect trial conviction rate, Thompson perceived. Whether a fair assessment or not, the perception drove his suspicions and his desire to keep Diallo from being victimized anew by the prosecutor's office.

Illuzzi and the rest of the prosecutors saw it differently. They believed a victim they had treated early on with respect and compassion continued to be evasive and inaccurate, and that her lawyer was poisoning the relationship with his own demands and vitriolic criticisms. If anyone was jeopardizing the case, it was the victim and her lawyer, the prosecutors believed.

It was against that complex backdrop that the two sides met in Vance's office on June 22. The prosecution was represented by Vance, Alonso, and top deputy John Irwin. Thompson and Wigdor were there to advocate for Diallo.

The meeting offered the perfect opportunity for both sides to reboot the relationship after a rocky couple of weeks, and to craft a strategy for how best to resume the questioning of Diallo and resolve the legitimate questions that prosecutors had about her credibility.

Vance, still new to his job, could cast himself in a pontifical role for the meeting, brokering the peace and setting a course forward for resolving the tensions. Thompson could flash his past experience as a prosecutor and make helpful suggestions for how the debriefings could resume in a way to keep his client calm, collected, and accurate.

The problem was, neither side took the high road.

Thompson and Wigdor, believing their client was being mistreated and still waiting to see how the settlement talks would go with DSK, aired a list of grievances and questions that struck an accusatory tone in the prosecutors' mind. Wigdor played the main aggressor. Why wasn't Strauss-Kahn questioned for more than four hours while in the custody of the police that first day? Are you willing to remove Prunty from the case for the way she yelled at Diallo? How come we didn't know about the potential conflict and recusal involving the Agnifilos? And is there any paperwork to back up the recusal?

Alonso and Irwin fired back, stressing they were suspicious about Thompson's willingness to get Diallo back in for questioning. When Thompson raised Diallo's shoulder injury and her need for an MRI, Irwin apparently dismissed it by saying he had had a similar injury and all that was needed was "to go to physical therapy and pull on some rubber bands." Irwin also made clear he wanted to get the reinterview done before he left for a vacation in Barbados. Alonso defended his prosecutors' work and integrity, and stressed how important it was to get Diallo back in the room to wrap things up.

Though polite, Vance seemed to Thompson and Wigdor to be disengaged. The two lawyers were still smarting from the fact that they had seen Vance try to dodge the earlier meeting, and they wondered whether that was an omen that Manhattan's chief prosecutor was looking to escape the tensions and controversy of the case.

Vance did weigh in forcefully one time during the meeting, suggesting to Irwin it was inappropriate to question or dismiss Diallo's shoulder injury. "John, you're not a doctor," Vance chided. And he tried to find some common ground with the victim by noting he had once traveled to Guinea. "I'm probably the only district attorney in the country to ever set foot in Guinea," Vance urged Thompson and Wigdor to tell their client. But Vance couldn't answer any of the key questions, about the recusal, the failure to question DSK, and so on. Prosecutors, for instance, had the email showing Karen Agnifilo had recused herself at 10:45 p.m. the first night of the case, as soon as she learned her husband was involved. They could have shared it with Thompson and Wigdor to lessen their concerns. But they didn't. And as a result, the distrust continued to fester.

Vance promised to get back to Thompson about the unanswered questions, but never did. His chance to fill a pontifical role in easing the tensions went essentially unfulfilled. Neither side felt satisfied, but they sought anew to arrange the elusive follow-up interview that prosecutors wanted with Nafi Diallo. A new tone of seeming pettiness, however, dominated the next round of conversations, which were mostly conducted via email.

Alonso sent a polite prod on Monday, June 27, to inquire whether Diallo was planning to come in to be interviewed as planned. "I'm told there is an issue as to whether you and your client are coming in today," Alonso emailed. "I don't wish to minimize any health issues but want to reiterate the difficulty we are in every day she doesn't come in."

Thompson immediately escalated.

"It appears that the District Attorney's office does not actually care about the health of the victim," Thompson fired back in an email that rehashed the litany of complaints that he and Wigdor had brought to Vance's attention in the meeting a week earlier.

Thompson took a personal shot at Irwin for his comment in the Vance meeting, saying the prosecutor had showed a "callous disregard for the victim's well being" when he suggested the "victim should somehow disregard her pain and meet again with your office the next day because he wanted to go on vacation to Barbados."

And Prunty's treatment of Diallo at the June 9 interrogation also was brought up anew. "As you know, one of your prosecutors screamed at and threw the victim out of the office," Thompson continued. He added for emphasis later in his missive: "I repeat that Ms. Diallo is a rape victim," seemingly pleading for some mercy.

Alonso, who had tried to keep relations cool and calm with Thompson, took the bait this time. "Your email contains inaccuracies and its tone is unhelpful," he wrote back, reminding Thompson that Vance himself had told the group a week earlier that "it is important for us to move forward and speak with the victim."

Thompson, ever the fighter, persisted.

"What inaccuracies does my email contain? Please describe those inaccuracies," he demanded. "I'm concerned about the way the victim has been treated by your office and the insistence that she meet with the prosecutors handling the case on Thursday of last week and today when she has been determined by a doctor to have suffered a serious injury."

Thompson added a few more grievances, alluding to the conflict of interest question. And then he ended on a hopeful note. "We will be there tomorrow at 10 a.m., and I will see you then."

Prosecutors had finally gotten their meeting. But the terse email exchanges that preceded it would start a new phase of the case in which leaks, letters, and literary bravado seemed to overtake the law.

SIX

The War of the Proses

LOOKING BACK WITH THE BENEFIT of hindsight, Tuesday, June 28, was destined to be a disaster for the case known as the *People of the State of New York v. Dominique Strauss-Kahn.* A slow-building tension was about to reach a crescendo among the once harmonious players on the prosecution side of the drama.

Nafissatou Diallo, once the star witness in the case, now felt humiliated by the way prosecutors had yelled at her back on June 9 and threw her out of the office after her last interview, one where she thought she was doing the right thing by correcting her previous misstatements. And the pain in her shoulder seemed to be worsening, providing an additional distraction in recent days with an MRI, a visit to an orthopedist, and physical therapy.

Her attorney, Kenneth Thompson, was upset at the unprofessionalism he perceived inside the prosecutors' office. He believed Cyrus Vance's team had mistreated a sexual assault victim, seemed unaware of the specifics of the evidence, and had made missteps ranging from failing to question DSK the first day to informally handling the recusal of a prosecutor who had a conflict of interest. Even relatively minor comments like John Irwin's statement about Diallo's shoulder injury seemed inflammatory in this tinder-box environment.

And Vance's team felt increasingly antagonized by Thompson's aggressive style, his accusations, and what they perceived was his effort to slow down the follow-up interview with the housekeeper that prosecutors had been seeking since June 9.

But perhaps more than anything else, the prosecutors suffered a deep, sudden distrust of the alleged victim, as well as a sense of personal angst at having fallen so easily for Diallo's false account of the gang rape in Guinea and the stories she had used to win asylum in the United States. Veteran prosecutors of some of New York's toughest cases pride themselves at having strong "BS detectors" able to spot falsehoods while interrogating defendants and accusers alike. But in this case, the prosecutors were mesmerized by Diallo's dramatic retelling of her life story, with all of its embellishments and falsehoods. And it further grated them that it took Thompson, the victim's lawyer and a former prosecutor himself, to discover the credibility problems rather than their own investigation. Such sullied pride can—and in this case did—intensify the emotions of these legal professionals headed into the most important interview of the case.

If the sour moods of the key players weren't enough, there was an added complication. The Fulani translator who had worked with Diallo and the prosecutors through the entire first phase of the case and earned their trust had left for a summer trip to Africa. It soon became evident the substitute translator would become a source of contention, especially when the nuances of Diallo's specific Fulani dialect were at issue.

Thompson and Diallo arrived at the District Attorney's Office and the high stakes of the interview became instantly clear. Daniel Alonso, Vance's number two, was going to sit in on the questioning. He joined Joan Illuzzi, the lead prosecutor, and Artie McConnell, the sex crimes unit prosecutor. Missing from the picture this time, though, was Ann Prunty, the hard-nosed assistant district attorney who had handled many of the prior debriefings but had raised her voice and expelled Diallo from the last session on June 9. Vance and Alonso had decided to pull her from this interview, hoping to neutralize Diallo's and Thompson's complaints of mistreatment.

McConnell, as he had done so many times before, asked Diallo to walk through all of her steps on the fateful day of May 14. And, as she had done so many times before, Diallo recounted everything she had said previously. She even fell to her knees, reenacting the sexual assault scene vividly. Thompson, who had left her alone to handle the prior interviews, was present this time. And both he and Diallo interjected to correct or contest the Fulani translator's interpretations several times.

To prosecutors, most of the story appeared and sounded the same. But they heard, for the first time, what appeared to them to be a major change of story in what Diallo claimed she had done after the alleged assault. Since the beginning, Diallo had told detectives, prosecutors, and the grand jury that after Strauss-Kahn had ejaculated she immediately fled Suite 2806 and then hid in a hallway across the way, near Room 2820, until her floor supervisor Jessica Hollingsworth found her.

But this time, prosecutors believed Diallo had told them she had gone inside another room, 2820, and then returned to Strauss-Kahn's suite before she met Hollingsworth. They stayed calm, though, and kept asking questions.

"Nafi, did you spit in Room 2820 when you went in?" McConnell asked.

"No, I clean the room," Diallo answered.

McConnell and Illuzzi asked her to describe how she cleaned the room, and she did so in great detail. She then described how she went back to Strauss-Kahn's suite to start to clean it after he left down the elevators. She opened the door and then went to the linen closet to pick up supplies, and it was then that she encountered Hollingsworth and reported the attack, Diallo would tell the prosecutors.

Prosecutors believed Diallo had once again admitted to a change in her story. But this one seemed more consequential. All the previous falsehoods involved her past life and her efforts to get into the country. This one involved her actions on the day of the attack and her behavior immediately afterward, essentially altering the timeline of the case. It would allow Strauss-Kahn's lawyers to directly impeach her credibility about the event itself.

The problem was, something apparently got lost in translation. Diallo did not mean to tell the prosecutors that she had cleaned Room 2820 *after* the alleged assault. She had cleaned it *before* the attack. The only thing she had done after the alleged attack was key the door to 2820 so she could get her cleaning supplies that she had left behind.

Prosecutors were blind to this fact because they had never asked to get *all* of the security key card records for Diallo's whereabouts inside the Sofitel that day. They had mostly just focused on Suite 2806, the scene of the crime. When the interview ended, McConnell called the Sofitel and asked for the records to Room 2820. The hotel pulled them and put them in an envelope to be picked up. But no one would show up for three days to pick up the records. It would turn out to be a blunder on the part of the prosecution team.

If prosecutors had retrieved the records immediately, they would have noticed that the account that they believed Diallo had just given them on June 28 couldn't have been true. Diallo had keyed the door to Room 2820 at 10:30 a.m., 11 a.m., and shortly before 11:30 a.m. on May 14, the last time spending forty minutes cleaning that room before she headed at 12:06 p.m. to Strauss-Kahn's suite where the infamous encounter occurred. Diallo only keyed the Room 2820 again at 12:26 p.m. for less than a minute, ostensibly to pick up her cleaning gear after the alleged assault.

Such a supposed change in story deserved more investigation.

But that didn't happen. Instead prosecutors would run straight to court and undercut their star witness's credibility for the first time, only to learn a few days later when they belatedly got the key card records from the Sofitel that they would have to revise their suppositions again.

In fairness, Diallo's second change in her story on June 28 was important. During all the hours of prior interviews, she apparently had never told prosecutors that after Strauss-Kahn left the twenty-eighth floor, she went back to his Suite 2806, keyed the door at 12:26 p.m. (after getting her gear out of Room 2820 a few seconds earlier) with the intention of cleaning the room, and propped the door open.

Such a change was important because it is odd for a sexual assault victim to willingly, and so soon after, return to the scene of an attack. She later offered a plausible explanation for her conduct—that at the time she feared she might be fired for walking in on a VIP client, and she wasn't sure she was going to report the alleged attack to supervisors or the police. That reasoning seemed supported by the outcry witnesses as well, who described Diallo as expressing concern about losing her job and seeming reluctant to call police.

As it turned out, Diallo didn't really clean Suite 2806 when she returned at 12:26 p.m. By her own account, she simply moved her cleaning gear into the suite from Room 2820 but couldn't figure out where to start. So instead she headed to the linen closet in the hallway outside, where her supervisor found her.

Once again, though, the fact that prosecutors were surprised by these facts six weeks after the case had started underscored the incomplete work detectives and prosecutors had done at the beginning of the case. They mostly had accepted Diallo's account at face value. But if they had scrutinized the evidence they had in their possession more closely, they might have spotted an incongruity almost immediately.

Hollingsworth had told authorities she took Diallo back to Suite

2806 around 12:30 p.m. to calm her down and figure out what had happened. But there was no security card record showing Hollingsworth ever keyed the door at that time. The only key card entry around that time was 12:26 p.m. And it showed that it was Diallo who opened the door. If Hollingsworth took Diallo to the room later, and there was no record of entry, the door must have been open already.

Real gumshoe work should have uncovered the discrepancy much earlier and led prosecutors to question Diallo and Hollingsworth to figure out what really happened. Refreshing witnesses' recollections with contemporaneous evidence is a common practice. But it didn't happen here. Prosecutors would simply go to court and accuse Diallo of a change in story. And then, when they belatedly got called from the Sofitel and were pressed to look at the timeline of the security cards more closely, they recognized problems. In fact, they didn't even get the security card records until Friday, July 1, after they had gone to court and declared Diallo had changed her story.

Eventually, a month later on July 27, prosecutors would go back and interview Diallo again, this time getting the correct sequence, timeline, and account. But rather than explain to the court the evolution of the story in a way favorable to Diallo that might salvage the prosecution, Vance's team simply accused Diallo of giving a "third," different account of what she had done in the immediate aftermath of the alleged incident.

In all likelihood, the "third" account was the accurate account, and the one Diallo intended to tell all along on June 28. I know this because when I interviewed Diallo right in the middle of the drama in July I walked her through the key card records and she gave a precise account that made sense and matched the records. She admitted going back to Suite 2806 after the alleged attack, and she explained her short stop at 12:26 p.m. in Room 2820 was simply to pick up the cleaning gear she had left behind when she had cleaned the room earlier that morning. There was no hesitation, no ambiguity.

The more precise the question, and the more familiar the questioner was with the evidence, the more complete Diallo was in her answers.

Prosecutors, however, would never admit that it was possible that they might have misunderstood Diallo on the time sequence or that they had failed to get the hotel records that would resolve the questions before they interrogated her. They were never pressed to explain whether their investigative missteps contributed to the evolution of Diallo's account. Part of the reason may be that Diallo had already told lies about her past, especially the earlier gang rape. And that made it easy for the media to assume she was lying about everything, especially when most reporters had little familiarity with the detailed facts and evidence in the case.

Prosecutors also surprised Diallo during the June 28 interrogations with evidence that large sums of money, nearly double the $40,000 a year she made as a housekeeper, had run through her checking account. Men in four different states had made large deposits and then quick withdrawals. Diallo didn't know what to do. She didn't seem to know about the money and she looked to Thompson for guidance. He didn't know either. Soon, they would discover that Diallo's friend Amara Tarawally had gained access to Diallo's checking account through her ATM card and had moved the money in connection with his activities. Diallo immediately cut off her friendship. Still, prosecutors had yet another reason to suddenly doubt the housekeeper.

The new concerns aside, prosecutors at least managed to keep the tenor of the June 28 interview mostly peaceful. There was no screaming or shouting, no crying and no finger-pointing. The only disputes seemed to center around a handful of translations from the substitute translator. In fact, prosecutors did such a good job of suppressing their fears about Diallo's latest credibility issues and perceived new falsehoods that Thompson had no inkling that a major salvo against his client was approaching.

After the interview, Vance's team decided what they needed to do. Under a Supreme Court standard known as the Brady rule, they felt they had an obligation to disclose Diallo's falsehoods in the case to the defense and the court as exculpatory evidence. For those members on the prosecution team that had already decided Diallo would make a terrible witness at trial, the notification seemed to formally set the course toward a dismissal of the charges. Not everyone, however, shared that sentiment. Some—inside Vance's office and at the Sofitel—would plead for more time and more investigation. And for weeks afterward, members of Vance's team would hold mock court sessions inside their office, sitting around a conference table trying to see if there was a way to successfully overcome Diallo's credibility problems to secure a conviction.

The next day, Wednesday, June 29, Vance's prosecutors summoned Strauss-Kahn's lawyers to their office for a meeting. They laid out the falsehoods they had discovered in Diallo's earlier account and their plans to send the court a Brady notification. The prosecutors also disclosed they were willing to ease Strauss-Kahn's restrictive house arrest conditions.

DSK's lawyers were struck with glee. A case that looked so ominous just a few short weeks ago—enough so that they even discussed a civil settlement with Diallo's lawyers—now seemed on the verge of collapse. They plotted to give a few more nudges in that direction with a handful of targeted media leaks and a special private presentation to Vance's staff designed to remind the prosecutors of the flaws in the case.

On Thursday, June 30, Vance's team formally sent the Brady notification letter to defense lawyers Brafman and Taylor and filed it with the court. The letter, signed by Illuzzi and McConnell, in bland factual terms identified all of the falsehoods—real and perceived—in Diallo's earlier account to authorities. And it ended with a line, whether by design or accident, that set the stage for a new media narrative about an accuser who apparently couldn't tell a straight story. "Finally, during the course of this investigation," the prosecutors declared, "the complainant was untruthful with assistant district attorneys about a variety of additional topics concerning her history, background, present circumstances and personal relationships."

The last actions for prosecutors before heading into the three-day Fourth of July holiday weekend were to inform Thompson and then head to court to loosen Strauss-Kahn's bail conditions on that Friday. Late Thursday afternoon, Alonso and Illuzzi called Thompson and explained they were sending a Brady letter to the court and the defense. Thompson had expected that would happen since the moment he first brought Diallo's inaccuracies to the prosecutor on June 7. It might have felt a little early, but Thompson as a former prosecutor understood the obligation under the Brady requirement.

What Thompson didn't expect was the second subject of the conversation with prosecutors. Alonso told him prosecutors had obtained a recording of a phone call from a federal detention center in Arizona where an inmate named Amara Tarawally, a friend of the housekeeper convicted on drug charges, had called Diallo in mid-May, shortly after the alleged attack. The tape, Alonso told Thompson, captured Diallo saying "words to the effect of, 'Don't worry, this guy has a lot of money. I know what I'm doing.'"

Thompson was numb. The body blows just kept coming. And he knew he would have to ask Diallo about this new twist. But Alonso assured Thompson he had some time because prosecutors weren't mentioning the tape in the Brady letter that was about to become public. Certainly, though, it would be fodder for Diallo's next interview session.

The next morning's newspaper headlines inflicted more pain, suddenly putting the accuser on trial in the court of public opinion. *The New York Times* led with a story reporting the purported contents of the prison tape—that Diallo had been captured on the recording talking to her friend Tarawally about Strauss-Kahn's wealth.

"The phone call raised yet another problem: it seemed as if she hoped to profit from whatever occurred in Suite 2806," the *Times* reported, citing a "well-placed law enforcement official." The information about the content of the tape was attributed to one source, not the two usually required for anonymous stories in the news industry. There was a second source mentioned in the story, but about other matters, not the specifics of the tape recording.

The newspaper's report would turn out to have several errors in it. It said prosecutors had a full transcript of the call. In fact, prosecutors didn't have a full transcript yet. They had a "digest" that gave the translator's general sense of the conversation. It also reported that the conversation about money occurred on May 15, just twenty-eight hours after the alleged attack. In fact, there were two calls merged into one in the digest. In the first call on May 15, Diallo simply had told Tarawally that she had been attacked at the hotel. In the second call, on May 16, Tarawally raised the issue of Strauss-Kahn's wealth, not Diallo.

Some in the office, including Alonso, were furious about the leak. They knew that they did not yet have a full transcript. They knew they had decided not to disclose the call in the Brady letter. And they knew the leak would only further set off Thompson and further poison the relationship even before prosecutors had a full story about what had happened on the prison phone. They also knew by the attribution in the newspaper that the leak had come from within their own ranks, perhaps by someone hoping to speed the end of the case. "It was not helpful. It was not authorized. And it was not accurate. No prosecutor in their right mind should have done it," a senior manager in the office would tell me later. Vance's office, to this day, has steadfastly refused to say whether it ever investigated the leak or held someone accountable.

At that moment on July 1, however, the public would have no inkling the leak was erroneous. The story essentially transformed Diallo overnight in the public's mind from a poor immigrant hotel housekeeper who was sexually assaulted by a powerful foreign leader to someone scheming to shake down the wealthy Frenchman she had accused. To make matters worse, the leak coincided with the Brady filing in court and created a double-barreled assault on Diallo's credibility in the court of public opinion.

Thompson expected the court filing, but the leak blindsided him. Diallo insisted to her lawyer that she had never said what was attributed to her in the *Times* article. In fact, she claimed, Tarawally had raised the issue of money—not on May 15 but in a later call—and that she had responded in a way that indicated she wasn't interested in money and would leave those issues to her lawyer. Weeks later, a translator working for the prosecutor would agree with her—the *Times* story was wrong on both the date (the conversation about money occurred on May 16) and the substance. ("The translator told us she could not find that statement on the tape," Thompson would later tell me.) But neither the newspaper nor Vance's office would do much to correct the record in the ensuing days.

A leak that Thompson knew could only have come from Vance's office had severely damaged Diallo's credibility. And he quickly fired off an email to prosecutors. "I want to make sure that your office has taken steps to investigate" the leak because it had a "devastating effect . . . on the victim's current state of mind and her personal and professional reputations." Thompson wrote that the leak was a "very serious breach of the ethical obligations of those two law enforcement sources and we will do all that we can to make sure they are held accountable."

Thompson, who often wears his passion on his sleeve, also took to the courthouse steps the afternoon of July 1 to excoriate the prosecutors about the leak and the way they had suddenly turned on

Diallo. His verbal barrage, caught on national television, accused Vance's office of trying to sabotage and abandon his client.

"This stuff that they leaked to *The New York Times* was designed to discredit this woman," Thompson bellowed from the courthouse steps, laying out his complaints, ranging from the police failure to question DSK when they first had him in custody to the way Vance handled the recusal of the prosecutor with the conflict of interest.

Three weeks of frustration and distrust boiled over. And Thompson even went X-rated for a few seconds, almost forgetting the cameras were running as he described a picture taken of Diallo's bruised vagina at the hospital the day of the incident.

Strauss-Kahn "grabbed her vagina with so much force that he hurt her. He grabbed her vagina with such force that he bruised her vagina," Thompson declared, trying to remind reporters of the brutality of the alleged attack. "When she went to the hospital, they took pictures of the bruises on her vagina, and the district attorney has those pictures."

Some prosecutors watched the footage, and would later mockingly refer to the press conference as Thompson's "vagina moment."

The surreal scene amounted to an impassioned monologue. Thompson didn't care. He had promised Diallo he would fight however he needed to win her justice. And he wanted the media to know his client was being victimized anew, this time by the prosecutors themselves.

"We believe that the district attorney is laying the foundation to dismiss this case. Anyone can see that," Thompson predicted, at times sounding like a revival-tent preacher demanding that prosecutors repent and do the right thing.

"The district attorney of New York County has an obligation to stand by this rape victim. He has an obligation to stand up for all women who have been raped or sexually assaulted," Thompson added.

"Now, it is a fact that the victim here made some mistakes, but that doesn't mean she's not a rape victim."

His comments would echo on national TV for hours.

Late that Friday afternoon, as most were preparing for the long Fourth of July holiday weekend, Thompson's cell phone started buzzing. It was a text message from Illuzzi, the lead prosecutor in the case.

"Ken please call me at your earliest convenience. I have a concern about Nafi," she texted. By the time Illuzzi's text message had arrived, Thompson had cooled a bit. He figured Illuzzi was going to carp about some new problem the prosecutors had with Diallo's credibility. He returned the call anyway.

"Ken, the detectives are with Nafi back at the hotel. She's looking for sleeping pills. They're worried she is going to hurt herself," Illuzzi relayed. Thompson wanted to snap back that it was the prosecutors' fault. But he thought better of it. Instead, he called Diallo to check on her well-being.

"I got no sleep. I got no sleep," an exhausted, tearful Diallo lamented.

Diallo's daughter was also pleading with her mother. "Please Mom, don't hurt yourself. I know one day the truth will come out," the teenager would say to me later, relating what she told her mom that day.

("I was so happy when she says that," Diallo told me a few weeks later, finding solace in the fact that her daughter still believed and stood by her mother.)

Thompson explained to Diallo that the detectives were worried she might commit suicide. Diallo assured him that she would not, and that she simply wanted to sleep away the nightmare of the past seventy-two hours. Thompson told her to call him anytime over the holiday weekend if she felt troubled.

Months later, Thompson would recount to me in vivid detail the never before revealed suicide scare. "She was emotionally destroyed and so confused about how this could have happened," he told me.

Thompson figured a good night's sleep and the festive patriotic spirit that typically floods New York City over the Fourth of July would provide a welcome reprieve from the intensity of a quickly crumbling case. The next morning, he woke up to another devastating headline, this time in the *New York Post.*

DSK MAID A HOOKER, the tabloid's front page blared that Saturday morning.

"Dominique Strauss-Kahn's accuser wasn't just a girl working at a hotel—she was a working girl," the story began. "The Sofitel housekeeper who claims the former IMF boss sexually assaulted her in his room was doing double duty as a prostitute, collecting cash on the side from male guests, *The Post* has learned."

This time the character assassination had come from DSK's side. The story, attributed to a "source close to the defense investigation," had little corroboration and was so thinly backed up that Thompson would sue the *Post* for defamation and libel on behalf of Diallo soon after. The lawsuit is pending.

Thompson realized his client was now caught in a vicious cycle. Not only had the prosecutors turned, so had the media. The same news organizations that had blared DSK's perp walk photo under headlines like "Le Perv" had flip-flopped overnight. The news media's performance had proven a vicious seesaw.

The *New York Post* had a second story over the holiday weekend suggesting Diallo was also "turning tricks while at a hotel" in Brooklyn under police custody. The story infuriated Thompson in part because a senior prosecutor in Vance's office was quoted anonymously in the story as saying "I can't say with 100 percent certainty that it's not true."

Thompson and his partner, Douglas Wigdor, decided that weekend that desperate straits called for desperate measures. With leaks and letters to the court, prosecutors and the defense team had lobbed their first volleys in what was increasingly becoming a battle of words in the public domain. Thompson and Wigdor decided it was time to return fire in the war of the proses.

Thompson was already on record at the July courthouse press conference preparing the public for Vance to dismiss the charges. Now he had to do what he could to pressure the district attorney into sticking by the victim. If he couldn't succeed at that, at the very least, Thompson would do what it took to rehabilitate Diallo's public image so she could seek justice in a civil trial.

The first strikes were launched on July 5 after New York City returned from the long holiday weekend. Early in the day, Thompson and Wigdor sued the *Post* for the prostitution stories over the weekend, saying they were false, defamatory, and libelous. Then later in the afternoon, Thompson sent an email directly to Vance entitled "urgent need to meet." Vance didn't respond; instead his deputy engaged. "Happy to discuss. What's the topic?" Dan Alonso replied, trying to keep the temperature cool.

"We will tell you when we get there," Thompson emailed back.

A few minutes later, Thompson renewed his request to meet directly with Vance. "Dan, again we ask to meet with District Attorney Vance regarding the case," he pressed.

Alonso wouldn't yield on Vance. "If you want to meet, we have to talk in advance," the deputy wrote back. "Please give us that courtesy."

Alonso was cognizant by this time that both Thompson and Diallo felt victimized by the developments of the previous week, and that there even had been some concern over the weekend about Diallo's well-being. So he inserted a P.S. designed to show that Vance's office still cared about Diallo, even if the prosecutors believed she had lied in a way that might make the case impossible to bring.

"P.S. If the urgency involves safety, I urge you to tell us immediately," Alonso wrote.

Thompson chafed at the cat-and-mouse game going on in email. "It is simply improper for District Attorney Vance to refuse to meet with us about a pressing matter in the case," he fired back.

The next day, Wednesday, July 6, 2011, that pressing matter spilled into the public. Thompson and Wigdor sent a letter to Vance asking him and his team to step aside from the case.

Entitled "Request for Immediate Recusal," Thompson's letter declared Vance's office unfit to take the case to trial. "We do not make this request lightly but believe in the interest of justice the people of the State of New York have a right to a fair and impartial prosecution of such an important case," the letter stated. "Your office unfortunately has demonstrated that it is incapable of meeting these standards and must therefore immediately recuse itself from the case."

The letter put into the public domain the complaints that had built up inside Diallo's camp over the past month. But one passage particularly rang in Alonso's ears. Thompson noted that the language that Alonso had used on June 30 to inform Diallo's team about the contents of the prison tape was eerily similar to the language that leaked to the *Times*. Alonso felt like Thompson was accusing him of personally being the leaker when, in fact, he had been as angry about the leak as anyone. Whatever goodwill Alonso and Thompson enjoyed as former colleagues of the Brooklyn U.S. Attorney's Office years back was fading. Alonso had repeatedly tried to keep the temperature low with Diallo's team and acted as the unofficial complaints department. But the implication in the letter that he might be the leaker steamed him for weeks. He never got an apology, either.

Thompson's barrage of letters, emails, and court filings was just beginning. He was intent on pressuring Vance's office into sticking by the victim, or at least in rehabilitating Nafi Diallo's reputation so she could seek justice through a lawsuit. Part of that strategy involved a dramatic decision to let Diallo tell her story in public, a decision that

I would ultimately benefit from. *Newsweek* would get that exclusive print interview just a few short weeks later.

The rest of the strategy involved creating pressure wherever it could be created or sustained. Thompson would reach out to the hotel workers' union to rally behind Diallo and to even raise questions about the hotel's decision to change housekeepers' uniforms to dresses about a year before the attack. The Sofitel agreed to let maids go back to their uniform pants to avoid any negative publicity in the aftermath of the DSK headlines. Thompson also reached out to victims' advocates and civil rights advocates, including exploring the idea of involving the Reverend Al Sharpton in Diallo's cause. But Sharpton's connection two decades earlier to Tawana Brawley and her false sex assault accusations made that idea a nonstarter.

Victims' advocates had been a critical part of the election alliance that swept Vance into office and the district attorney was concerned about the perception that he was abandoning a sexual assault victim or setting a new standard of proof for victims with troubled pasts. Since the revelations on June 30 that Vance might reverse course and drop the case, there were increasing murmurs in the public about whether his team was guilty of a rush to judgment and too inexperienced to handle such a big case.

VANCE BUNGLES ANOTHER ONE, the *New York Post* had declared in one headline over the long holiday.

Vance decided he needed to push back, and redefine the public debate. Prosecutors shouldn't be afraid of being lampooned for doing the right thing when a case goes bad, he believed. He needed some allies to make the argument.

First he called the former sex crimes prosecutor and novelist Linda Fairstein over the holiday. He knew she made plenty of TV, radio, and print appearances. "Linda, if you truly believe we did the right thing, it would be helpful if you could say so," Vance asked politely.

Fairstein dutifully hit the airwaves, starting with a prior engagement she had set up on radio. "The first week, there was no reason to disbelieve her. . . . It seemed like everything made sense," she told the Don Imus radio show, still one of the most powerful in influencing debate in New York City. "He'd have been damned for not believing this woman in the first place: a minority woman in a powerless job."

Fairstein claimed on the July 5 Imus show that the problems were uncovered because the district attorney continued to aggressively investigate and gather evidence about the victim. "You get all these things, hoping, of course, that they're going to support your witness' story," she said. "And in this case, almost every piece of supportive evidence turned out to be unhelpful, to contradict her; in fact, in many instances, to catch her in very brazen lies."

While Fairstein worked to slap down the rush-to-judgment claims, Vance also reached out to the biggest gun he could find. He wanted his legendary predecessor and mentor, Robert Morgenthau, to come to his defense. The two met July 7, and Morgenthau, as he had done so many times before, came to the aid of his protégé once again. At the suggestion of one of Vance's staffers, he issued a statement suggesting Vance handled the turnaround in the case the same way he would have if he were still in charge.

"For decades we instructed line prosecutors at the Manhattan D.A.'s Office to seek justice over everything else, to investigate, to find the truth, and to proceed without fear or favor," the statement said. "The most important attribute I looked for in hiring junior prosecutors was a strong ethical sense. The recent actions from the District Attorney's Office show me that these attributes are alive and well," Morgenthau's statement declared.

The news media bit on Vance's shrewd PR ploy and soon reporters and pundits were talking about Vance's courage in doing the right thing. EX-MANHATTAN DISTRICT ATTORNEY PRAISES HANDLING OF STRAUSS-KAHN CASE, *The Wall Street Journal* declared. It was exactly the headline Vance's team wanted. And they could get it because few reporters had dug enough behind the scenes to uncover the way prosecutors had overlooked early evidence or lost control of the relationship with their victim.

Thompson's offensive, meanwhile, continued. In public, he tried to restore Diallo's credibility. In private, he continued to hammer away at the prosecutors for sloppy investigative work, the backup translator, and the way they continued to handle the case. In fact, he was accusing the prosecutors essentially of tricking Diallo into misstatements.

"Had you or other members of the prosecution team bothered to get the electronic records to room 2820 before your last meeting with Nafi on June 28, 2011, you would have known that it would have been physically impossible for her to have cleaned 2820 after she was sexually assaulted by Dominique Strauss-Kahn," Thompson wrote in an email on July 21, 2011, to Illuzzi that dripped with antagonism and disdain.

"You can continue to send me emails with false statements but please keep in mind that your emails may be discoverable and end up in the hands of Strauss-Kahn's defense attorneys, which given your actions, may be your intent," he wrote in another insulting email.

Thompson also demanded that Vance's office let him and his client hear the infamous prison call tape. He decided that if prosecutors wanted to keep talking to Diallo, they needed to let her hear the recording and clear her name.

Illuzzi insisted the terms be reversed, first an interview followed by the tape. "Like any other victim, she must be interviewed without being given the means to tailor her narrative," Illuzzi wrote back. Such a concept was fair, *if* authorities hadn't already leaked the purported contents of the tape first.

Illuzzi and Thompson tangled by email several more times. "You and she claimed she was going to come clean and give us the entire truthful story," Illuzzi wrote in one barb. "... However, you now recognize (after looking at objective records) that she was, in fact, not truthful."

Thompson fired back, "I completely reject your false claims that Nafi was 'untruthful' about her actions."

The exchanges took on the air of an intramural spat among high school friends, underscoring that for much of June and July 2011 the real struggle was not between prosecutors and DSK, but rather between Diallo, her lawyer, and the prosecutors. In fact, Strauss-Kahn's lawyers enjoyed an increasingly cordial relationship with Vance's office, even securing an opportunity in July to drop by for a private meeting with prosecutors to make their arguments for why the charges should be dropped entirely. The defense lawyers routinely began sharing information they thought prosecutors might want to know about, all of it aimed at undercutting the victim, her attorney, or the evidence.

Without the benefit of knowing what was going on behind the scenes, Thompson's tactics seemed to be counterproductive. In fact, after the case was over, a citizen lawyer with no connection to the case filed an ethics complaint against Thompson, accusing him of disserving his client. The New York City bar rejected the claim but the complaint nonetheless highlighted a prevailing sentiment among many reporters and lawyers who couldn't see the undercurrents of the case at the time.

Months later, I asked Thompson why in public and private he had persisted in antagonizing the prosecution when there was still a chance, however slight, that they might continue with the criminal case. Thompson's answer was insightful.

On June 9 when Prunty yelled at the victim and Illuzzi declared she wouldn't put Diallo on the stand, Thompson had come to conclude that Vance's team was looking for reasons to jettison the case and avoid an embarrassing loss. He saw sloppy investigative work and a politically sensitive prosecution team who was worried about Vance's uncertain public image.

On June 28, Thompson believed, prosecutors had actually tried to use the confusion over the Fulani translations to lure Diallo into making false statements so they could run to the court with one set of problems, then leak another issue to lay the groundwork for dismissal. "This translator kept getting a lot of what Nafi said wrong. They should have shut it down right then and there. But it was clear to me they were looking to dismiss the case," Thompson explained months later after he had had time to reflect.

So, long before the public could see the case was heading for dismissal, Thompson recognized the unfavorable circumstances. And he and his partner, Douglas Wigdor, crafted a Hail Mary strategy, a relentless effort to generate public pressure to try to sway Vance. They knew it was a long shot. But if it failed in its primary goal, it would still help lay the groundwork for Diallo to seek justice though a second path: a civil lawsuit.

Prosecutors were heading toward one final, cataclysmic interview with Diallo on July 27, 2011. The interview would provide three final footnotes for the case.

First, Thompson offered Illuzzi an apology for all the vitriol of the past month or two. "If I said anything to offend you, that wasn't my intention," he offered. That conciliatory sentiment, however, didn't last very long.

Second, Diallo—with the benefit of the security card records—gave a correct, complete version of what she did after she fled the alleged assault in Suite 2806. Prosecutors, unwilling to acknowledge publicly their mistake, simply told the court it was a "third" account from Diallo about the same event. In fact, there was substantial evidence that prosecutors could have, and should have, gotten the correct story much earlier if they had simply done thorough gumshoe work at the start.

And finally, Diallo got to listen to the tapes of her conversation with Tarawally, and her recollections proved mostly correct. She did not talk about money at all the first day he called on May 15. And when he called the next day again, Tarawally raised Strauss-Kahn's wealth first, not Diallo, Thompson would disclose.

Thompson wanted to underscore the inaccuracy of the *Times*'s leak. So after the translator had finished offering the English translation as the tape was playing in Fulani, Thompson read the quote from the original "digest" that Alonso had told him about on June 30 and which appeared the next day in the *Times* article.

Did Diallo say words to the effect that Strauss-Kahn has lots of money and I know what to do because I have a lawyer? Thompson inquired.

"Those words aren't there," Thompson recalls the translator answering.

The prosecutors tried to interject, insisting that the general essence or sentiments of such a statement were on the tape.

"I'm sorry, but those words aren't on there," the translator responded, according to Thompson's recounting of the event.

The recording of the discussion about money was played before lunch. And at that moment, Thompson still believed it was a tape of the very first conversation between Diallo and Tarawally that had occurred twenty-eight hours after the alleged assault.

When prosecutors, Diallo, the translator, and Thompson reassembled after lunch, Thompson asked to hear what he thought was the second conversation, which occurred on May 16.

"Okay, I want to hear the second tape," Thompson requested.

"No, no, no. You already heard the second tape. The tape I have now is the first time they talk," Illuzzi explained.

Thompson was incredulous. He believed the prosecutors once again were trying to mislead, perhaps in an effort to pretend the *Times*'s leak was justifiable and accurate.

"Why would you play the second tape first?" Thompson inquired. "Why not play them chronologically like they happened?"

There was no satisfactory answer.

And so the final interview ended with little drama. Prosecutors proceeded to begin drafting a motion to dismiss while Thompson persisted in his war of words, hoping to sway the court of public opinion.

Diallo gave interviews to *Newsweek* and ABC in late July, then held a brief press conference so all the world could see her face and hear her story unfiltered by the prosecutors. Thompson brought a lawyer from France representing Tristane Banon, the journalist who claimed Strauss-Kahn assaulted her back in 2003, to meet with Vance's team and offer her cooperation. He also forwarded an anonymous letter he received from an Air France employee alleging Strauss-Kahn "may have engaged in sexually inappropriate conduct towards Air France employees at the Los Angeles International Airport."

None of it seemed to move the needle enough inside Vance's office or in the court of public opinion to alter the inevitable path toward dismissal.

On August 5, 2011, Illuzzi lit Thompson's fuse one last time, sending a request for his own law firm records detailing any confidential settlement discussions he held with Strauss-Kahn's lawyers back in June. Thompson saw it as an intrusion on the attorney-client privilege that he enjoyed with Diallo.

So he prepared his final three volleys in the war of the proses.

On August 8, he sent a letter to Vance's team excoriating the request for attorney-client-privileged documents. "It is patently evident that the only purpose of your letter is to further harass and retaliate against Ms. Diallo and her counsel," he wrote. The letter itemized five pages of complaints about the conduct of Vance's office. For the first time, Thompson was putting many of his behind-the-scenes grievances into the public domain by making the letter public.

That same day, Thompson filed a civil lawsuit against Strauss-Kahn, choosing Diallo's home borough of the Bronx as the venue instead of Vance's Manhattan, where the assault had occurred. He was seeking a home field advantage. And the document's rhetoric was aimed at the court of public opinion as much as the court of law. Strauss-Kahn committed a "violent and sadistic attack" that robbed Diallo "of her dignity as a woman," the suit declared.

And finally, on August 22 as prosecutors readied their motion to dismiss the criminal case, Thompson resurrected his request that Vance step aside, filing a lawsuit asking a judge to appoint a special prosecutor. The suit had little chance of succeeding in court, but it gave the Diallo team one more venue to air its grievances in public.

While most of the world was relishing its August vacation, prosecutors were gliding toward a dismissal of the criminal case. Meanwhile, the housekeeper had staked a claim for justice in a new venue, hoping to put her future in the hands of jurors in a civil trial.

The Interview

ONE OF THE BENEFITS of working for Tina Brown is her infectious belief that journalism's greatest days are still ahead and that the possibilities for compelling storytelling are limitless. Her fervor is especially welcome in this era when so many other editors see a profession destined for doom and gloom and settle for thin reporting, quick aggregation summaries, and speculative opinion as a substitute for the hard-core news we used to get in the heyday of *Time, Newsweek, 60 Minutes*, and Woodward and Bernstein's *Washington Post.* In Tina's world, no story is too hard to uncover, no interview subject is too hard to get, and no magazine cover too provocative to consider. (Remember the nude, pregnant Demi Moore cover at *Vanity Fair*? Or how about Michele Bachmann's crazy eyes at *Newsweek*?) So it shouldn't have been a surprise that I would be handed a tall order on my first week on the job at *Newsweek.*

I had met Tina back in fall 2010, thanks to my good friend Howie Kurtz, the longtime *Washington Post* media writer. He surprised the journalism world earlier that year by jumping to Tina's *The Daily Beast,* an upstart news Web site that put a touch of British tabloid flair on America's news and had a healthy following, especially among liberal readers. Tina and I hit it off immediately during coffee at Washington's ritzy Hay-Adams Hotel, right across from the White House. At the time, I was working as the executive editor of the nonprofit Center for Public Integrity, home to some of the country's best investigative reporters. Tina was putting the finishing touches on a plan to merge her *Beast* with the failing *Newsweek* magazine, rescued just weeks earlier by millionaire businessman Sidney Harman.

I wasn't interested in leaving the Center, so Tina brought me aboard as a consultant to advise her on the merger. It soon became clear she craved access to more investigative reporting and editing, seeing it as a key ingredient to reviving a sleepy newsweekly with a long record of financial losses. First, we struck a deal to syndicate some of the Center's best investigative exposés to *Newsweek*. But the courtship continued. And in early May, just days before the DSK affair rocked the world, I decided to leave the Center and head to *Newsweek* to work as director of news and investigations in its Washington bureau.

On June 16, 2011, my third day at *Newsweek*, I went to New York to meet with Tina. I came prepared to wow her with a list of what I thought were irresistible investigative stories: a tear-jerker about the children of deployed soldiers going to school in unsafe classrooms on military bases, solid examples of political corruption in Congress, big-name interviews with big newsmakers. I thought I had an impressive list. Tina listened dutifully, occasionally looking down at her well-worn BlackBerry to check messages.

When I exhaled after rattling off my list, Tina chimed in with one I hadn't mentioned. "You *know* we'd have a bloody incredible scoop if we got DSK or the hotel maid to talk," she said, with the slightest hint of a smile. In my head I was immediately thinking, there's no way a rape suspect or his alleged victim is going to talk in the midst of a pending case, especially one with international ramifications. But I kept that to myself and gave a cautious answer back. "Let me see what I can do. No doubt, it would be a barn burner."

I had already dabbled in the DSK story in its early days. During the first week of breathless coverage in mid-May, Tina reached out to me while I was winding down my tenure at the Center. It was four days into the scandal and she sent one of her typically cryptic, but always tantalizing, BlackBerry messages late at night.

"A tabloid ed in UK used to yellowest material does raise some interesting counter thoughts to me," Tina wrote. "Wld a man who just raped a maid call a hotel about his cell or just want to get out of town asp without any contact with place?

"Maid from Guinea therefore French speaking. French hotel. The frame up charges are not wholly ridiculous," she added. "Wld love an investigative type to really look at this aspect before we just assume, and feed u what learns."

Eager to make a good first impression, even before I officially started, I made some calls to legal sources the next morning on my commute into Washington. I got a lead on some of the specific details that the housekeeper had purportedly told the prosecutors and her hotel colleagues—along with details about corroborating forensic evidence—and passed it along to Tina's team. That was Thursday morning on what was shaping up to be a busy end of the week for me. Things at the Center had me consumed for the next couple of days, and I didn't check back until Saturday morning. When I did, I got a disappointing word. No one at the *Beast* had gotten time to confirm the tips I had picked up.

I was headed that afternoon to a concert with my family but didn't want the source material to get any staler. I hate waking up and seeing another publication with a story I knew about. So I made a half dozen quick phone calls that Saturday morning and got enough sourcing for a fairly compelling story about what the maid had alleged and the evidence to support it.

I drafted about seven hundred words, and sent it up to the *Beast* hoping they might want to use it over the weekend. Tina and one of her top deputies, Tom Watson, responded immediately.

"This is great. Home Page, plse post. We also need to blast out as news alert," Tina ordered the *Beast* editing desk from her BlackBerry.

By late afternoon, the *Beast* was crowing it had an exclusive on the DSK case, blasting out email alerts and leading its site with my story.

> *The luxury hotel maid who alleges she was sexually assaulted by Dominique Strauss-Kahn was found by a supervisor in a hallway where she hid after escaping from the former International Monetary Fund director's room. Hotel workers described her as traumatized, having difficulty speaking and immediately concerned about pressing charges and losing her job, according to sources familiar with the investigation.*
>
> *The maid also repeatedly spit on the walls and floors in front of her hotel colleagues as she alleged that Strauss-Kahn locked her in his room and pushed and forced her into oral sex acts. That saliva is being tested for possible DNA and could become a crucial piece of evidence in the case, the sources said.*

The story was picked up around the globe, and the next day police came back with word that the DNA found at the alleged crime scene did, in fact, match Strauss-Kahn.

Now a month later, Tina was sending me on a new mission to get one or both of the key players in the drama to talk. Where to start?

I decided the best way was to get myself back in the case by writing a few stories on the state of the evidence. I started making calls, reintroducing myself to the key players. In the month that had ensued, the maid had changed lawyers, and I hardly knew Kenneth Thompson, so I did a deep dive on his background as part of my initial research. Then I made a call to his office. I struck out. A professional public relations firm called me back to say Thompson was too busy to return my calls but they'd let him know of my interest in talking to him.

Little did I know at the time that brewing in the background was an epic dispute between the victim and the prosecutors that would soon spill into the public. On the night of June 30, I got a call from one of my best sources in the investigation alerting me to the fact that prosecutors were considering dropping the case because they had uncovered serious concerns about the alleged victim's credibility. I alerted the New York desk at *The Daily Beast* and started burning up the phones like a madman. I soon got confirmation that prosecutors were filing a Brady notice in court laying out concerns about Diallo's credibility and started writing. *The New York Times* beat me to the punch, going live with a piece suggesting the maid had lied to prosecutors and may have wanted to cash in on the DSK incident. I filed what I had to the *Beast.*

> *In a shocking turnaround, New York prosecutors in the sexual assault case against Dominique Strauss-Kahn plan to tell the judge Friday they have serious concerns about the credibility of the hotel maid who made the allegations against the former International Monetary Fund chief, two sources tell The Daily Beast.*

The next few days were chaotic. I was already juggling another big story in Washington. A law enforcement scandal I had helped uncover with CBS earlier in the year—detailing how federal agents had knowingly let semiautomatic weapons flow through the hands of straw buyers to Mexican drug cartels in a bungled operation known as "Fast and Furious"—was coming to a head. And I was hearing from sources that a key figure, the embattled director of the Bureau of Alcohol, Tobacco, Firearms and Explosives, was thinking of going to Congress to blow the whistle. I knew I had to work both stories simultaneously.

The turnabout was almost surreal. The prosecutors had filed a document in court officially accusing the hotel maid of a series of lies. Most dealt with her past in Africa and how she got into the United States claiming asylum, including a fabricated account about a prior gang rape at the hands of Guinean soldiers. The news media, which had all but convicted Strauss-Kahn during the first month of coverage, suddenly turned on the victim with a vengeance, publishing headlines and speculation that suggested she must be a liar and may even have been involved in some effort to shake down DSK.

Thompson, the maid's lawyer, was exasperated at the breathless abandonment of his client by prosecutors and the media, and took to the courthouse steps after the Brady filing to excoriate the prosecutors. His televised personal attack against Vance's team caught even veteran court watchers by surprise for its ferocity. Quite frankly, I didn't know what to make of it, except that all the TV pundits were declaring the case was on life support.

That's when I got the call. I almost didn't take it.

I was on another line trying to confirm the ATF story with a congressional staffer when a person close to the DSK evidence reached out, unsolicited. "You know that story you wrote back in May about the evidence?" the source asked. "Well, not a whole hell of a lot has changed. The evidence still supports an unwanted sexual attack occurred in that room. But some are getting cold feet. They going to walk away from all that evidence."

The source was even more concerned because prosecutors had failed to check key evidence at the hotel before making a sensational allegation to the court that the maid had changed her story about what she did immediately after fleeing Strauss-Kahn's room after the alleged attack. For weeks, prosecutors believed the maid had hid in a hallway around the corner from Strauss-Kahn's luxury suite until he checked out. But during a contentious June 28 interview, prosecutors believed Nafi Diallo had changed her story and told them she went and cleaned another room.

Of all the allegations attacking Diallo's credibility, this was among the most serious because it involved her account of what happened during and right after the attack. If she was changing her story about key events in the alleged crime, what else might she be lying about?

The source, however, insisted the prosecutors had it wrong and had failed, since the day of the alleged attack, to review all of Diallo's hotel security key card records. If they had, the source opined, they would have known the maid could *not* have gone to clean Room 2820 *after* the alleged attack in Strauss-Kahn's suite. The records showed she cleaned Room 2820 *before* the attack and only stopped back to Room 2820 after the attack for less than a minute, probably to pick up her cleaning cart, the source insisted.

I called my sources in the district attorney's office, and inquired about the key card records for 2820. "Where are these key card records because folks here claim they don't have them?" one prosecutorial source asked me.

I shot back, "I'm told your office requested them before the court filing but then failed to pick them up from the hotel, and that they're still sitting in an envelope waiting to be picked up from the Sofitel security office." Vance's office then asked for the records to be faxed over, prodded in part by the Sofitel's own attorney and my inquiry.

A few hours later, I got a callback with the material I needed.

The hotel cards showed the maid entered 2820 three times before the alleged incident in 2806, and then for only a minute after the incident in Strauss-Kahn's room. She couldn't have cleaned the room after the alleged attack. She did it beforehand. Now prosecutors had two problems: they had assailed their victim's credibility, perhaps unfairly, because they had not checked the hotel records earlier. And they had not searched Room 2820 or treated it as part of the crime scene.

By late on the evening of July 2, I had confirmation about the hotel security card records and had a strong story that prosecutors still believed the physical evidence supported that an unwanted sexual encounter had occurred. But authorities were wrestling with the question of whether they could proceed to trial given other issues with the maid's credibility. The next day we moved a story on the *Beast,* complete with a rough timeline of key events we had dug up from our reporting.

Little did I know then the impact that story would have. The famed Harvard appellate lawyer Alan Dershowitz would later tell me the story was one of the most influential in changing his mind about the case. And the story finally got the attention of Thompson, who called and had his first substantive contact with me. I made the pitch that Tina wanted—that we'd like to do an interview with the maid and get her side of the story.

"I've gotten hundreds of requests from media all over the world. What makes you think I should do it with *Newsweek*?" Thompson asked. "And why would we do an interview at all right now?"

"Well, right now the maid is a nameless, faceless accuser whose credibility is being attacked, even by the prosecutors," I answered. "There's no substitute for looking someone in the eye, giving her a name, and asking her whether she's telling the truth about what happened in that room."

"And why *Newsweek*?" I rattled off all the stories we had done and the exclusive facts we had obtained about the evidence, the hotel outcry witnesses, and the possible mistake in the court filing about Room 2820. "We've done the gumshoe work. While others speculated, we dug up facts," I responded.

"But what do you know about rape, much less the experience of an African immigrant?" Thompson persisted.

"Well, I don't claim to know what your client has been through, but back in 2009 when I was executive editor of *The Washington Times* I shepherded a project on how troops were using rape as a tool of war in the Republic of Congo and it was so compellingly done by our photographer and reporter that it finished as a Pulitzer finalist," I answered.

That seemed to catch his attention. "Send me that project, John, along with everything else you've written on this case and let's see what happens," Thompson said. I emailed everything he had asked for, and I was suddenly hopeful that I had made a connection. Thompson promised to keep in touch and gave me contact information so I could bypass his public relations team.

At the time, I didn't know it, but the Sofitel's outside counsel was making his own pitch for why Thompson might consider having his client go public. Lanny Davis, the Sofitel's private attorney, had become a fan of my reporting and I suspect he may have put in his own word vouching for me as this process rolled along.

Rape victims, for decades, have received anonymity in the press, meaning they never had to put their names to their allegations in the court of public opinion. Even when the accused are acquitted, the alleged victim's name remains out of the news media. Diallo was willing to throw all of that away, and it soon became clear to me that her legal team had already concluded that Vance's office was going to dismiss the charges, even though prosecutors were insisting they were continuing to investigate.

Thus, the act of going public was an act of desperation, a carefully calculated tactic that Thompson hoped would engender sympathy for a woman he truly believed was victimized. He wanted to create public pressure—from the hotel workers' union, the West African immigrant community, the rape victim activists, and other influentials in the New York City community who had sat silent for weeks—to get Vance and his team to reconsider.

Thompson had spent enough time with Diallo to know she was a sympathetic character. He knew that if the public saw Diallo's rather ordinary looks and intensely shy, asexual personality, they'd reject DSK's wild notion that she was a sexual provocateur and a willing participant in seven quick minutes of spur-of-the-moment, consensual sex. The *New York Post*'s theory that she was a part-time hotel hooker looking for tips also would be challenged. And, Thompson hoped, she'd convince the world she wasn't sophisticated enough to be part of any plot by Sarkozy's French intelligence agency to sting Strauss-Kahn and eliminate a political rival for the French presidency.

But the strategy carried enormous risks. She could say things in the interview that were contradictory or omitted from her previous testimony, thus opening new doors for her credibility to be challenged in public and eventually in cross-examination by defense lawyers. Prosecutors almost certainly would be alienated, and some pundits, especially those aligned with Strauss-Kahn, would suggest she was more interested in publicity than in letting the judicial process take its course.

Thompson understood the risks. He wanted justice, and he and his client felt let down by the court of law, especially after *The New York Times* and *New York Post* leaks. His only venue, he believed, was a long-shot appeal to the court of public opinion. Even if it didn't change the prosecutors' minds, it would set the stage to create sympathy for a civil jury since Thompson now planned to sue Strauss-Kahn on behalf of Diallo no matter the outcome of the criminal case.

As I negotiated the terms of an interview, I still wondered whether Diallo herself understood the risks of going public. I'd soon get my answer.

After I sent all the articles Thompson requested, we began talking regularly about what an interview might look like. I insisted that the maid would have to be on the record and yield the normal anonymity afforded rape victims, allowing her name to be used and her photo to be taken. Thompson seemed open to the idea. He asked whether we would be willing to work with a TV outlet and an embargo for publication. And I even began to suggest a date—the edition of July 18.

I kept Tina apprised of the developments, telling her I was increasingly confident we might get an interview. She seemed pleased.

Things were going along swimmingly when Thompson called me one morning. I could tell from the curtness in his voice that there might be a setback.

"Tina Brown runs *Newsweek,* right? And she's your boss?" he asked.

"Yes."

"And she knows you're trying to get this interview, right?" he asked.

"Yes. I've briefed her," I answered.

"Well, then why on earth would she send a request to me personally offering Henry Louis Gates to do *your* interview?" he inquired.

"What? I have no idea what you're talking about."

Thompson read me an e-mail directly from Tina in which she suggested that Gates, the provocative Harvard intellectual with a history of exploring racism in law enforcement, be the interviewer. The email was dated July 5, and I hadn't been cc'd. It was marked "Urgent message from Tina Brown, Editor in Chief of Newsweek."

Dear Kenneth

Given how much your client Nafissatou Diallow is being pillaried [sic] in the DSK affair I wanted to suggest that professor Henry Louis Gates, the distinguished African American scholar and head of African American Research at Harvard University, does an interview with your client for Newsweek that paints a portrait that is fair and unsensational by one of the most predominant and influential figures in the African-American firmament.

I have spoken to Professor Gates and he would very much like to do it. Can I talk to you about this?

Best
Tina

I was blindsided, and felt undercut. But more importantly, the e-mail didn't sit well with the maid's legal team. They were locked in a life-and-death struggle with prosecutors trying to keep the case from being dismissed, and the last thing they wanted was an inflammatory interviewer like Gates, whose run-in with a Cambridge, Massachusetts, cop in 2009 unexpectedly ensnared President Obama in a contentious debate over race and law enforcement.

I was embarrassed and caught off guard, and promised Thompson I'd get back to him. I tracked down Tina and inquired about her surprise email. She told me she thought it would be helpful to have "more than one iron in the fire." I explained Thompson's response, and she instructed me to withdraw her request.

I got back to Thompson on Friday, July 8, and he thanked me for the quick response. I felt like things were back on track. But more surprises were awaiting.

The following Monday, Thompson contemplated holding a press conference with his client at his church, the Christian Cultural Center in the Bronx. He wanted her story out for fear prosecutors might dismiss the charges soon. He asked me how I would cover it.

"Well, it's going to be a classic New York media circus and it will be impossible to get a read on your client or to have a thoughtful discussion about the facts in that environment. I'd probably not go and just send a reporter from our New York office," I explained, trying to be as candid as possible.

He paused for a second, then acknowledged there were some in his inner circle who worried that such an event would turn her into a media circus character.

A few hours later, he called back and said the whole idea was off the table and he was seriously thinking about the interview with *Newsweek*. One complication, Thompson offered, was that his client was staying at the DA's expense in a safe house, a hotel room in Westchester County, and he needed to find her an alternate location. "They're going to kick her out on the street once she goes public," he worried. "I've got to find her a new place. So there's no way we could do an interview in time for the 18th."

I took a deep breath. The July 18 edition was a planned double issue, meaning we were dark the week of July 25 and wouldn't publish again until the first Monday in August. "That's too late, John," Thompson cautioned when I told him. "We can't wait that long because the prosecutors might drop the charges already. We've got to go sooner."

I mentioned putting it on *The Daily Beast,* but Thompson didn't think a Web story would be as valuable as a magazine cover story. He'd have to look at other options if *Newsweek* was dark.

I asked for more time, and promised to get back to him quickly. I talked to Tina, explaining the progress that had been made and the complications. And for the first time, we discussed the idea of doing a special, unplanned issue for the 25th of July just for the maid's interview.

Once again, Tina's belief in journalism's possibility was on display. She'd create an entire edition on a week *Newsweek* was supposed to be dark if she could get the defining interview.

I got back to Thompson with Tina's idea. He loved it, and we began talking about logistics. He would work on finding his client a new safe house, and I'd work on getting photos lined up, drafting questions, and finding a suitable location for the interview to be held.

Tina was willing to use her home for the interview, so that Diallo wouldn't have to worry about slithering through the near daily media stakeouts outside Thompson's office. Separately, Thompson was talking to ABC's Robin Roberts about doing a companion interview for television. The magazine would go first with a detailed account, and TV would follow with a quicker, more visual story.

I also suggested that I wanted Tina to join me for the interview. Having a woman in the room, I hoped, would change the dynamic, helping build rapport and making it easier for Diallo to talk about the very personal details of an alleged sex assault.

The word we were waiting for arrived Thursday afternoon, July 14.

"I'm willing to give *Newsweek* the opportunity to do the exclusive print interview of the victim of the sexual assault by Dominique Strauss-Kahn," Thompson wrote Tina and me. "However, my willingness to do so requires that we reach an agreement on certain conditions, such as timing, coordination with a TV broadcast interview and other matters."

Thompson invited us to his office the next day to talk logistics. I took the train from Washington and headed to the *Newsweek* office in New York. I was used to taking a cab or walking to interviews, but Tina arranged for one of her chauffeured cars to pick us up and take us the ten blocks from *Newsweek* to Thompson's office.

When we got there, Thompson and his partner, Douglas Wigdor, and a media consultant joined the meeting. We sat in a long, sunlit conference room, the place where Diallo would meet us just a few days later.

At the outset, Thompson made clear the sole reason he picked *Newsweek*, making sure the Henry Louis Gates idea was not even remotely on the table. "The *only* reason we're doing this is because of

John. He's kept to the facts and we'll trust you'll continue to do that with this interview," Thompson said, looking directly at Tina.

I felt a bit embarrassed, and didn't want Tina to think I had set Thompson up to toot my horn. But she hardly noticed. She went right into explaining how *Newsweek* was creating a special July 25 edition just for the interview. But to do so we'd need access to his client by the following Wednesday so we would have time to write and close the article by a Friday deadline.

Thompson explained the embargo and the companion piece by ABC. And he again reiterated the one hang-up: the interview could not occur until he found Diallo a new safe house to live with her fifteen-year-old daughter.

"We could probably put her up for a few weeks if that would help," Tina volunteered.

I winced, and then interjected. "I don't think that's a good idea, Tina. We don't want any semblance that this is a checkbook journalism exercise or people will not trust the interview."

Thompson agreed. "Let us worry about the housing issue. We have options. I just need to be clear that no matter what timetable you have, we can't go forward until that issue is resolved."

The rest of the meeting went well. Tina had graciously offered her home as the site of the interview, and by joining us for the meeting, she also got a good sense of the maid's legal team. We tentatively settled on Wednesday, July 20, as the date for the interview.

Tina and I decided to summon our Paris Bureau chief, Chris Dickey, to join us in New York. He had done a fantastic job covering the case—including writing a fascinating look inside the Special Victims unit of the NYPD that had worked the investigation. And he was one of the best writers I'd ever met. I couldn't wait for his help to make the interview come to life in prose.

Waiting patiently isn't easy for Tina, especially when a big scoop is near at hand. By phone and by BlackBerry, she pinged me often to see if there was any word. She was worried about the housing search delaying the interview.

On Monday, July 18, Tina's latest prod arrived. "What news on maid meeting?" she inquired in her usual BlackBerry shorthand.

"Just talked to Ken. He doesn't have a safe house set up. Still working on that. Expect an update at day's end," I wrote back.

Again, Tina couldn't resist the temptation.

"Ask him if she would like to stay this week at the house of a senior editor in Brooklyn who is willing to have her stay?" she e-mailed back.

My ears turned red. This was the third time she had raised *Newsweek* providing Diallo housing, a move that would almost certainly discredit our interview. I called *Newsweek*'s executive editor, Edward Felsenthal, and asked him to have his own conversation with Tina. Edward called back an hour or so later and promised that Tina wouldn't make any further mentions of an offer to house Nafi Diallo.

But I wasn't convinced. I was concerned Tina might make another end-around and go to Thompson behind my back. I knew any interview we did would almost certainly be subpoenaed in the case, and even the slightest hint of a financial inducement would harm *Newsweek*'s credibility. Ironically, Thompson and the maid weren't seeking any such help. It was simply Tina's desire to remove any roadblocks to getting the scoop.

I decided on Tuesday, July 19, to make sure the idea couldn't be revived. I called Thompson and told him I was worried Tina might try one more time to raise the housing issue and I was going to send him a preemptive e-mail—with Tina copied—making clear that housing was his responsibility and we were focused solely on the interview logistics. He liked the idea. He sent me an e-mail saying the housing situation still wasn't resolved, opening the door for me to send an e-mail back.

"I still haven't been able to find the victim an alternative place to live. I will continue to try to do so today. But if I'm not successful we will have to push back the interview until next week," Thompson wrote. In fact, Thompson had almost resolved the housing issue. But his e-mail provided the perfect fodder for me to "manage up" on Tina and end the temptation inside *Newsweek.*

I alerted Tina and Edward to Thompson's e-mail and drafted a reply that I hoped would put the entire issue to rest.

Ken,

We're all geared up for the interview at 4:30p tomorrow. As you know, Newsweek made a decision to add an edition to the lineup that wasn't planned for this Monday and it is our best shot for a cover story.

We remain hopeful you can resolve any other issues in time to make the interview. As you know we won't be publishing until Sunday or Monday which means you'd have additional time for resolving other logistics.

Regards
John

The e-mail worked perfectly. Tina instantly sent an e-mail back, essentially switching sides on the whole issue of finding Diallo alternate housing. "Yeah, I don't like the quest for housing," she emailed. "But hope to God we can resolve it or no cover ideas."

I never heard another word about providing housing. And good thing. The day after the *Newsweek* interview was published, scurrilous rumors and questions emanated from France about whether we had paid or provided financial inducement to get Diallo to talk. We could honestly answer, "No."

The last e-mail on the housing issue was exchanged midday on Tuesday, July 19, a day before our internal deadline for getting the interview. About seven hours later, as Thompson hinted earlier in the day, he formally lined up alternate housing for his client and she was ready for the interview. He wanted to do it Thursday afternoon, July 21, with *Newsweek* and then schedule ABC News to come in that Sunday.

I was thrilled, but we had lost another day of writing. If we did the interview Thursday, we'd have less than twenty-four hours to turn around a cover story before the Friday night deadline to close the magazine.

"We're set for maid interview," I emailed Tina early that evening, laying out the logistics and details. No video, but we could do audio with a transcript. The interview was slated for Tina's home. I was sending up a list of fifty questions we should ask so she and Dickey could review them ahead of time.

Tina seemed pleased, though cognizant of the tight turnaround. "Yikes. Will be tight," she emailed back.

The next morning, some of the logistics changed. Thompson refused to let us record audio, fearful it might be subpoenaed later. But he would allow us to bring three additional people into the room for note-taking and photos. That was perfect. It allowed me to slip Dickey into the room as a note taker so he could get his own sense of the woman. The other change Thompson wanted was to move the interview to his office for security reasons.

We were finally a go. We spent Wednesday inside *Newsweek* mapping out the questions and the pace of the interview. Tina wanted to open the questioning herself, creating a woman-to-woman bond. I liked that idea. I'd jump in midway through the interview with harder questions designed to challenge Diallo's credibility and to compare her answers to the extensive physical and outcry evidence we knew about. And Dickey, masquerading as the note taker, would wrap up the questioning with anything we missed that we would need to make the story sing.

I took Thompson and Wigdor out to dinner that Wednesday night, trying to learn everything I could about Diallo's state of mind, her time in protective custody, and the odyssey with prosecutors. I needed dates, times, names, and places. It was a fantastic prep session. As journalists, we were armed and ready for the Big Interview.

The next day, the *Newsweek* team—Tina, Dickey, and one additional note taker, a portrait photographer, and myself—met around the corner from Thompson's office on Fifth Avenue, just off Broadway in midtown Manhattan. He had instructed us to enter his building through a side door usually reserved for maintenance, so we could avoid any media stakeout at the front doors. A secretary ushered us up the elevator and into the law firm's conference room. There, we waited a good forty-five minutes.

Then Thompson opened the glass doors to the conference room with a plainly dressed, and clearly shy, Nafi Diallo in tow. She was wearing a tan sweater, a modest blouse, and dress slacks. While tall and voluptuous, we were struck by her utter lack of glamour. She was no eccentric West African beauty as the press had intimated, and it was hard to see the irresistible temptation DSK was allegedly allured by. In fact, after his first look at her Dickey leaned over to me. "She isn't what I thought at all," he whispered in disbelief.

I nodded. I felt a bit sexist, and the last thing I wanted to do was insult a woman's looks. But I couldn't agree more that her appearance added a whole new dimension to the question of whether this could be a consensual sexual encounter as DSK's lawyers had begun to whisper.

Dickey found the most graceful way to address this delicate question, with a passage in the eventual story that angered Diallo's lawyers but needed to be written anyway if we were going to help the public understand.

"'Nafi' Diallo is not glamorous. Her light-brown skin is pitted with what look like faint acne scars, and her dark hair is hennaed, straightened, and worn flat to her head, but she has a womanly, statuesque figure," Dickey would write. (Thompson thought the reference was insulting to Diallo, but we explained to him her looks were a key part of the evidence.) But for now, it was time to set aside our impressions about her looks and get to the formalities of the interview.

"I'd like you to meet my client, Nafi Diallo," Thompson bellowed. Diallo looked down at the ground, seemingly embarrassed by all the fuss as she shook hands. She didn't seem to know where to sit. When we suggested the chair at the head of the table, she almost seemed taken aback. And as Tina prepared to ask the first question, Diallo fidgeted, clearly uncomfortable with being a media celebrity.

"Nafi, tell us in your own words how your story, your life began," Tina asked.

There was a momentary pause, and then in a voice that was meek and hard to hear, we got our first answer.

"My name is Nafissatou Diallo," the housekeeper said, speaking in fairly clear English salted with a clear Guinean accent. She spelled out her name, almost like it was another grand jury appearance or deposition. And then she added, "But they call me Nafi."

For the first time, the immigrant housekeeper who rocked the world two months earlier by leveling sexual assault charges against Strauss-Kahn had offered her name and her story in public.

She spoke so softly at the start that Thompson had to interject a few times. "Nafi, you have to speak louder so everyone can you hear you."

As I listened in those first few minutes, it was hard to imagine this soft-spoken housekeeper had wielded so much influence on the global stage, toppling one of the world's most powerful politicians with a humbling five-day trip to New York's notorious Rikers Island prison. Diallo's allegations had truly ended DSK's assumptive bid for the French presidency and his tenure as head of the powerful International Monetary Fund, which was grappling with the Greek debt crisis and a wobbly euro, both serious threats to the global economy.

The magnitude of her impact aside, Diallo in person seemed almost disconnected from that world of power and finance she had so seriously affected. She preferred to talk about taking her daughter to movies and watching TV, and couldn't even explain what DSK's role was at the IMF when asked.

"I never know who he was. I never know," she insisted when pressed whether she knew Strauss-Kahn's position when she entered his room.

Her explanation seemed plausible, and in the end even Strauss-Kahn's own lawyers would come to surmise it was unlikely this simple woman was part of a grand conspiracy to set up DSK for his downfall.

For three hours we peppered Diallo with questions, extracting every tawdry detail about the incident and the aftermath. No question was off-limits, and we repeatedly pressed her about inconsistencies, rumors, and accusations. When we were done, we had exhausted our fifty original questions and a whole lot more.

Diallo seemed tired but she still had to pose for the cover shot. There was a quick makeup and lighting session conducted by the photographer and then the cameras starting snapping. Thompson brought Diallo's fifteen-year-old daughter into the conference room. She had been sitting quietly in the law firm's back room waiting for her mother for these three long hours. But she was used to it. She had done the same many times before when prosecutors summoned her mother for their own question sessions.

I tried to strike up a conversation with the daughter. Unlike her mother, she had no hint of a Guinean accent. But she was guarded and obviously frustrated that her mother's seven minutes of infamy had disrupted what had otherwise been a normal teenager's life going to high school in the Bronx. I asked her about school and her plans for a career and how her mother and she coped living in a safe house away from families and friends. Her answers were short and to the point. And there were awkward moments of silence. At one point, the daughter related how angry she was when prosecutors had yelled at her mother within earshot of her during the June 9 session at Vance's office.

Soon the photo shoot ended and Thompson brought in some cold cut sandwiches so everyone could take a few minutes' break. Nafi Diallo was sitting alone by herself so I pulled up the chair next to her and tried to strike up some small talk. Soon, the *Newsweek* photographer started snapping pictures of us talking, what we call "candid shots" or "b-roll" in the journalism business. About a half dozen flashes in, Tina noticed and shouted out to me. "John, why don't you get out of there?"

I thought Tina wanted more solo photos of Diallo, a reasonable request. But within seconds of my getting up, Tina shot into my seat so she could be photographed alongside her prized interview subject. For weeks after, Thompson and Wigdor would tease me about the episode. "Last place you want to be is between a camera and Tina," they'd joke. "You got a face made for radio, too ugly for a magazine shot, my friend." I took the ribbing in good nature. It actually was kind of funny.

Once the camera stopped, Tina got up and bid Diallo and her lawyers a gracious farewell. She was late for another appointment. I sat back down, right between Diallo and her daughter. And we returned to small talk. I don't remember much of what was said as we finished up our sandwiches. It was mostly chitchat about the hot summer, school, and the interview session. Just one thing stuck out for me. Both Diallo and her daughter said they loved watching *Law & Order* together each week and that they had all but overdosed on the TV show's reruns during the eight weeks trapped in the police safe house. I remember thinking, they themselves had become a classic episode of the show. By September, that prediction would prove right. The *Law & Order: SVU* series opened its fall season with an episode based on the case. About the only major change in the fictionalized account was that the accused wasn't a Frenchman. He was an Italian.

Most of our interview is now history, an epic cover scoop for *Newsweek* that caught prosecutors, DSK's defense, and much of the world by surprise. But during nearly three intense hours of questioning, there were five indelible takeaways from that face-to-face session with Diallo that I think benefited the public beyond her graphic description of what allegedly occurred in Strauss-Kahn's $3,000-a-night suite on the afternoon of May 14, 2011.

First, we came to understand that Diallo did not want to report to police the sexual assault at first, fearful that she would be fired for walking into a room where the VIP guest was still present. It helped explain why it took a full hour for the Sofitel to report the incident to police. "I was so afraid. I didn't want to lose my job," Diallo told us, repeating that line several times over the course of the interview.

In fact, when Diallo emerged from Strauss-Kahn's suite and was first found in a nearby hallway in a clearly distressed state by housekeeping supervisor Jessica Hollingsworth, she didn't admit at first she had been attacked. Instead, she asked Hollingsworth somewhat sheepishly: What would you do if someone tries to take advantage of a maid? Hollingsworth reacted forcefully, insisting the police should be called and demanding to know what happened. Diallo eventually described the attack, stopping at one point to go into the bathroom because she felt like vomiting.

Security officers at the Sofitel similarly reported that Diallo was reluctant to call the police and that it took some time to calm her and convince her to call authorities. Likewise, all the hotel employees are adamant she had no way of knowing beforehand that the man she encountered naked in VIP Suite 2806 was Strauss-Kahn. There are no pictures of VIP guests hung in the maids' quarters or identities listed on the housekeeping floor reports. In fact, a full two months later, Diallo hardly mentioned Strauss-Kahn by name in the interview, still referring to him instead as the "white man with the white hair."

Diallo ultimately—she says grudgingly—consented to report the alleged attack because her colleagues said it was the right thing to do. "I don't know what is the law here," she recalled telling officers when she finally authorized a call to the police. "But I have to tell."

Less than twenty-four hours later, however, she would have buyer's remorse, when she turned on the TV and the morning news proclaimed the man she had accused, the Frenchman Dominique Strauss-Kahn, was one of the world's most powerful politicians and poised to become president of a country with the world's third largest arsenal of nuclear weapons. A panic set over Diallo and her daughter, especially when her family back in Africa began to get calls from the media. Eventually she saw her mother on TV being interviewed in Africa, crying. "I think, oh my God, they are going to kill me," Diallo said, recalling how she quickly packed up her bags with her daughter and fled her apartment to a niece's house.

DSK's lawyers could easily dismiss this part of her account as the planned theatrics of a woman who was so convincing in her lying that she brought veteran prosecutors to tears with a false story of being raped in Guinea. All that would be true, and will certainly be used as weapons if and when her case goes to civil trial. That's when DSK's lawyers are expected to offer an alternate theory, arguing that Diallo only reported the crime when she returned to Strauss-Kahn's suite to find he had not left any money behind to pay her for what he believed was a consensual encounter.

But in the course of three hours of questioning by *Newsweek*, there was a simplicity to Diallo's life story and a genuine feeling to her declaration of what ultimately motivates her. Diallo wanted out of Guinea after her husband died and she declared she would do anything, including lying, to get her daughter into the United States before her young girl became a victim of genital mutilation. Diallo herself suffered the procedure, designed to rob a woman of her sexual pleasure, at the age of seven.

"I got cut on my private parts," she said softly, with just a hint of shame in her voice. "I was afraid. I don't want them to do that to my daughter. I don't want her to be cut like me."

Getting her daughter to America and keeping her here has been a life's mission and Diallo's commitment to her job at the Sofitel was unmistakable in the interview. She described in excruciating detail her routine—cleaning rooms on multiple floors a day, how housekeepers check for DO NOT DISTURB signs, and how they try to minimize shuffling between floors to save time. Even the story of how she got to the twenty-eighth floor—where DSK's suite was that fateful day—involved career advancement, no matter how modest. As one of the junior members of the Sofitel maid staff with just three years of seniority, Diallo didn't qualify for her own housekeeping floor, instead moving up and down the hotel wherever rooms needed to be cleaned. When a colleague that spring left on maternity leave, Diallo volunteered to take the twenty-eighth. "I had my own floor," she said with excitement.

To an onlooker, these might seem like mundane, boring details. But to Diallo, they are her lifeblood and source of pride, so much so that her voice perks up when she explains that it was a bonus to clean Strauss-Kahn's room that afternoon because it counted as three rooms toward her quota of fourteen that must be cleaned each day.

"I never miss work. I always go," she said at one point, beaming with pride. "I love my job. I love to work." In fact, she sounded bitter about the fact that the case had kept her locked up in protective police custody for two months and away from her colleagues. "I miss them," she said.

You're left in the end with the unmistakable sense that the Sofitel job and the ability to stay with her daughter in the United States are all that really matter to this thirty-two-year-old West African immigrant. And if she believed reporting a sexual assault might jeopardize that life, causing her to lose her job for walking in on a VIP hotel client, then her reluctance to report the attack makes more sense. It also likely explains why she persisted initially in telling Vance's prosecutors the same bogus story about her life in Guinea—complete with a false tale about an earlier rape—that she gave during her immigration proceedings.

"Yes, I did make mistakes," she told us when pressed about lying during the asylum process. "But I make those mistakes because I was afraid to go back to my country."

The fear of losing her job and of being forced to return to Guinea is an essential part of Diallo's story.

The second takeaway from the interview was that there is little doubt that Diallo's American experience—and her vulnerabilities in the court of law—have been forged in the rich, exotic atmosphere of New York City's West African immigrant community, where hardworking immigrants (some who told similar false tales to win asylum), fast-talking con artists, and drug dealers socialize together inside bodegas and restaurants and on the doorsteps of row houses in the Bronx. Women who came from a Guinean culture of male dominance, female genital mutilation, and frequent rape and suppression remain subservient to the men of their American ethnic community.

So Diallo apparently thought nothing of letting one of her male friends, Amara Tarawally, use her check cards to move thousands of dollars through her checking account. In return, she got a handful of knockoff designer purses. "They weren't very good," she said of the gifts, seemingly oblivious to the more serious possibility that the transactions he ran through her account might be laundered proceeds from the drug dealing that ultimately landed him in an Arizona detention center awaiting deportation. "He was my friend that I trust—that I used to trust," she added.

Likewise, another male friend in her new life in the Bronx, shopkeeper Blake Diallo, was the one that got her a personal injury lawyer on the second day of the case, one he had plucked out of the Yellow Pages. Though only trying to be helpful, Blake Diallo's intervention only increased the opportunity for DSK's defense team to suggest her allegations were motivated by greed and a financial incentive to make a rich Frenchman pay.

Blake Diallo also couldn't help being sucked into the notoriety of the case, granting several interviews to U.S. and foreign press, one in which he is quoted—he says misquoted—as claiming Diallo told him she suffered bruises and cuts during the attack, evidence that did not show up in the housekeeper's hospital exam. Strauss-Kahn's lawyers combed every word that Blake Diallo uttered to reporters, finding plenty to impeach his accuser's testimony. Blake Diallo was clearly well-meaning, but it would not always help Nafi Diallo in this case of international intrigue where the defendant would use high-priced lawyers and private eyes to wage a relentless effort to destroy her reputation.

Even the shadowy figure in Brooklyn who helped get Nafi Diallo into the country with an asylum claim in 2003 contributed to her complications in this case. Diallo probably could have won asylum under the immigration rules at the time simply by proving she was a victim of genital mutilation. But instead, that man gave her a script of an embellished and more sympathetic tale: she was raped by soldiers as political punishment and her husband died at the hands of the regime, a victim of persecution. Diallo memorized the account and told it convincingly. And when prosecutors questioned her years later, she stuck to her bogus asylum account.

Diallo told us she was, in fact, raped in Guinea as a teenager, but not under the circumstances she had initially told immigration authorities or Vance's prosecutors. She said she and a friend had stayed out one night past curfew to work to make a few extra dollars at a sandwich shop when they were picked up by Guinean soldiers, taken to a detention camp, and raped repeatedly through the night in a small square room. The next morning, she told us, the soldiers released her, but only after "they asked us to clean up" the site of the attack, she related.

None of this, of course, proves one way or the other whether Diallo was telling the truth about what happened in Sofitel Suite 2806 on the day she encountered Strauss-Kahn. But our interview helped bring into sharp focus the life of a woman with a complex victimology and a cast of friends and a home community certain to provide DSK plenty of fodder to attack her credibility, rightly or wrongly.

The third takeaway from our *Newsweek* interview was that we experienced some of the same behaviors that led prosecutors to distrust parts of Diallo's story. Often a function of her imperfect grasp of English, Diallo got confused about facts, only to correct herself after a perplexed look or a follow-up question. Her concept of time was often vague at best. She couldn't recall her exact age when she left her daughter in Africa for the United States, the year she was raped in Guinea, or even the month or day she first arrived in New York.

Asked how or when her husband died in Africa, she demurred, looking to the ground. Finally prompted by her lawyer to answer, she quietly whispered, "he had an illness," an answer open to wide interpretation on a continent where AIDS and other diseases ravage the population. She declined to be more specific, but made clear he did not die at the hands of the government as she had been coached to say on her asylum application. Later her lawyers would tell us her husband died of AIDS.

Her entire account of how she came to the United States was also vague, likely reflecting her lawyers' concerns that she could be deported now that New York prosecutors have declared in an official court filing that she lied during her asylum process. Asked how she got to the United States, she'd only answer "through a friend" whom she admitted told her to rehearse a more dramatic but false tale of persecution in Guinea.

The evasive, halting recounting of her past instantly gave way to a dramatic retelling of what happened in the Sofitel room that Saturday afternoon with DSK. Diallo, in fact, shocked all of us at one point. She had been sitting in her chair quietly and with little animation for the first half hour of questioning, when she suddenly dropped to her knees as she described how Strauss-Kahn forced her to the ground for oral sex. She grabbed her shoulder to show where she suffered an injury and continuing pain, and even thrashed her head from side to side to demonstrate how she tried to keep his penis from penetrating her mouth.

Her voice was raised and her breathing became heavy as she recounted the sordid details, right down to the pain she felt in her vagina when Strauss-Kahn suddenly grabbed her between the legs and tried to lift her panties. That meek tone she started off the interview with suddenly, and momentarily, dripped with incredulity when asked why DSK might think the episode was consensual.

"If am I to agree with that," she said scornfully, "how I'm going to be hurt between my legs? How am I going to be hurt on my shoulder?"

And that led to the fourth big takeaway from our interview. Diallo's account that day of what happened in the room was remarkably consistent with both the forensic evidence recovered by police in the room and every other statement she gave previously. It matches what she told her hotel colleagues in the first minutes after she was found, and to what she told detectives.

Even her explanation for the discrepancies about cleaning Room 2820 seem plausible. She believes a guest translator mixed up what she was trying to say to prosecutors during the June 28 reinterview. She believes she told prosecutors she cleaned Room 2820 before going to Strauss-Kahn's room and then returned afterward to 2820 momentarily to get her cleaning gear. Prosecutors believe she told them through the translator that she cleaned 2820 after the attack, which would be a major change in her story. The hotel security records, though, seem to back Diallo's account to *Newsweek*.

The quiet housekeeper became indignant when prosecutors questioned her honesty, and even started yelling at her in later debriefings. She's adamant she never changed her story about the alleged attacks and its aftermath. "It's the same," she told me. "I tell them what this man did to me. It never change. I know what this man do to me."

Now the final takeaway from the interview was personally important to me. I wanted to know whether Diallo understood the consequences of coming forward and going on the record or whether she was simply a pawn following her lawyers' instructions. Tina, Chris, and I all pressed her on the issue, and she was unequivocal that she knew what she was doing and why she was doing it. In short, she felt the prosecutors had abandoned her, and going public was the only way she could see to press for justice.

"I want him to go to jail," she said emphatically. "I want him to know there are some places you can't use your money, you can't use your power." She continued for a few more minutes, seemingly seizing a soapbox for victims' rights before settling back into her shy demeanor.

"He hurt me. He hurt all of my people," she continued, clearly referring to her family and friends who were inundated with media and private detectives and had to endure scurrilous, defamatory stories. "Because of him they call me a prostitute. All my life nobody ever called me that name." I left that day with a better understanding of the woman, her complex life, and a deep belief she understood what she was doing by going public. Of course, none of that would settle the questions of law or fact that would follow.

EIGHT

The Sofitel's Legal Two-Step

THE SOFITEL, WITH ITS GLASS tower stretching thirty stories into the sky and its gold-plated entrance, has yearned to be the high-class French traveler's destination in New York City since it opened in 2000. Nestled in midtown Manhattan right next to the New York Yacht Club, the hotel's attention to Old World France atmospherics is unmistakable. A chef schooled in Bordeaux named Sylvain Harribey serves up fine French food and wine at the hotel's Gaby restaurant, the gift shop offers an eclectic collection of French perfumes, and the architecture captures the elegance of Paris's own modern limestone buildings.

Likewise, the furniture, amenities, artwork, and linens all smack of French aristocracy, right down to the separate showers and European soaking tubs certain to pamper the world traveler in one of the hotel's fifty suites that top out at $3,000 a night. In the mammoth lobby, the greeting *Bon Jour* is frequently heard. (The lobby staff is bilingual, able to carry on conversations in English or French at a moment's notice.) And young, elegant women that appear ripped from the covers of European fashion magazines staff the concierge desks.

If ever there was a hotel to cater to Strauss-Kahn's whims and sexual escapades in New York City, the Sofitel was it. And though it didn't need any further French frills to lure a man like Strauss-Kahn, about a year before the alleged incident in Suite 2806, the hotel issued a new dress code for its housekeepers. Gone were the comfortable trousers maids had worn for years. In were new French-style skirts. As one person close to the hotel management told me, the goal was to "sex up" the place a bit, giving it a bit more European flair.

Diallo and the other housekeepers chafed at the change. They feared that when they bent over, the mid-calf skirts might show their buttocks, and overall they were simply less comfortable when hauling vacuums and cleaning carts between floors in such attire. In fact, soon after Diallo's case emerged, the hotel allowed the housekeepers to go back to uniforms with pants if they wanted. (And eventually the union for housekeepers and New York City hotels agreed on a new plan to equip chambermaids with panic buttons in case they are attacked, a lasting positive effect from this otherwise dark episode.)

The moment Sofitel security called the police the afternoon of May 14 and helped detectives arrest DSK at John F. Kennedy International Airport, the hotel management braced for a firestorm certain to spread across two continents. By late evening that first Saturday, Sofitel executives in Paris and New York had all been alerted. If the hotel cooperated too closely with authorities, its executives knew it would be accused by DSK's backers of becoming part of a U.S. lynch mob aligned with Sarkozy and designed to derail Strauss-Kahn's rise to the French presidency. Cooperate too little, and the hotel faced the outrage of its workers, their union, and women's rights advocates who would interpret complacency as abandoning a victim and caving to a powerful world leader. Adding to the pressures, Sofitel's parent company, Accor, was based in Paris and its list of board members and investors was filled with both Strauss-Kahn defenders and antagonists.

The job of navigating these treacherous waters fell to seasoned hotel industry lawyer Alan Rabinowitz, the executive vice president and general counsel for Accor's North American division, based in Dallas. The French-based Accor owned and operated the Sofitel in New York through its North American arm. Though stationed fifteen hundred miles away from the madness unfolding in Manhattan, Rabinowitz was no stranger to high-profile controversies. After all, any hotel chain with a thousand properties and fifteen thousand employees is certain to have its share of controversies and legal issues.

Back in the 1990s after Accor acquired the Motel 6 discount chain, for instance, Rabinowitz crafted the company's legal and public relations strategy when several African American customers alleged that Motel 6 discriminated on the basis of race, prompting a class-action lawsuit. The suit became a cause célèbre for the civil rights movement as it wound its way through the courts, and the company faced an uphill battle in both the court of law and court of public opinion after one of its own employees, an African American manager, alleged he was encouraged in training to reserve inferior rooms—"ghetto rooms" he called them—for black customers. Other black customers coming forward, armed with tales of being turned away for rooms that went to white customers, only added fuel to the fire. Soon President Bill Clinton's Justice Department had launched a civil rights investigation.

Rabinowitz turned to a Washington lawyer he had been referred to by a former Republican U.S. Attorney in northern Virginia, who used to debate the lawyer on television during Bill Clinton's fundraising and impeachment scandals that engulfed his presidency. Lanny J. Davis, by that time, had left the White House as special counsel and returned to private practice to craft a new area of legal practice that merged legal advice, crisis management, and crisis communications into one package. On TV and in a high-profile book entitled *Truth to Tell*, Davis advocated that it was essential for clients to be ready to fight in the court of public opinion as well as the court of law. And he espoused an approach, anathema to lawyers a generation earlier, that involved going public with derogatory information about their clients before critics and enemies got the chance. In short, he advocated telling bad news on the client's own terms as a preemptive strike. "Tell the truth early, tell it all, and tell it yourself before anyone else tells it for you," he would advise clients.

Davis had turned the concept into a science during his years as a special counsel in the scandal-plagued Clinton White House. When Republicans planned hearings on fund-raising abuses by the Democratic Party, hoping to create investigative gotcha moments, Davis tried to get the White House out front to deflate the stories, often disclosing embarrassing details first on terms more favorable to the president. No story was too big to get in front of, not even embarrassing revelations that Clinton had made fund-raising-related calls from the Oval Office or had confessed to a grand jury that he had an "inappropriate" relationship with intern Monica Lewinsky.

Davis relished putting out the bad news first, and with all the facts that would win credibility with jaded reporters. Not everyone inside the administration was a believer in his approach. But he mastered a rhythm that dumped the most damaging news the White House could muster routinely on Friday evenings or holidays when most Americans had already tuned out. By the time Republicans returned to work, their latest gotcha moment had been turned into old news by this strategy. "Why let someone else tell your bad news when you can tell it yourself, on your own terms," Davis would preach inside the White House. "It's gonna come out anyway."

Davis' performance in the midst of the Clinton pressure cooker impressed Rabinowitz enough to hire him to help defuse the Justice

Department probe against Motel 6. The Accor lawyer hoped Davis' connections inside the administration and his pre-emptive strategies could forestall Justice from taking formal action against the hotel that would aid the civil litigation. After joining the case, Rabinowitz and Davis disclosed to the Justice Department that the hotel had implemented a training program instructing all employees against discriminatory practices—well before the lawsuits had been filed. And they assured officials they had tried to stamp out any offending managers. Davis and Rabinowitz were confident Motel 6 had solved the issue but they needed a bold, fool-proof mechanism to convince the Justice Department. Davis contrived a risky strategy: ask the Rev. Jesse Jackson, the vaunted and outspoken civil rights leader, to run a series of stings (called blind testing) to see if Motel 6 could live up to its promise to treat black patrons fairly. Rabinowitz loved the idea, and Davis struck a deal with Jackson to hire his Rainbow Coalition to dispatch teams of black and white customers to Motel 6 locations across the country and see if the minority customers would be turned away or treated worse than whites. Jackson's report essentially validated that the discriminatory practices from years past had ended, and Accor was able to persuade the Justice Department to drop its investigation and not to intervene in the lawsuits.

Now a decade removed from that victory, Rabinowitz once again turned to Davis to help steer the Sofitel Hotel chain out of a minefield. This time, though, the case stretched across multiple continents and pitted one of the world's most powerful men against a chambermaid who emigrated from Guinea. Rabinowitz needed Davis to help thread the needle so that Accor could cooperate effectively with prosecutors without appearing to pick sides. Davis accepted, relishing a challenge with high stakes and unusual characters.

As Strauss-Kahn's lawyers worked feverishly the day after his arrest to try to get their client released on bail, Rabinowitz sent Davis to New York City to start interviewing employees. For many of Davis's past clients, his role was designed to be out front in the media. But this assignment required him to take a decidedly low-key role. The hotel wanted to lower its profile and appear a neutral party in a highly charged legal proceeding. And Davis assumed the role with remarkable discipline, resisting the temptation to go public even in moments when his own conscience ached and his passion for justice tugged at his heart. "It's not normally my nature to stay quiet when so much was at stake," he joked to a friend. "It's sort of ironic that most of my effort was to stay behind the scenes in this one."

As a result, Davis became one of the most influential players in the case whose name never surfaced in the media during the height of the drama. In fact, Davis only talked to two reporters during the crisis, both on background. And he only surfaced publicly around Christmas 2011, long after the criminal case had ended. That's when the Sofitel felt compelled to issue a rare public statement after some of its security video footage had been leaked by supporters of Strauss-Kahn, exposing the identities of some of the hotel's workers and raising concerns for their safety. Before that, Davis operated like a silent assassin, sniping budding legal and media crises before they could damage the Sofitel's reputation.

Everybody wanted something from the Sofitel—the prosecutors, the victim and her attorneys, and DSK's legal team. Rabinowitz gave Davis a simple rule for his mission: "Stay neutral on the issue of innocence and guilt. Be fair to everyone and do the right thing." Beyond that, Davis was on his own.

Davis worked to deliver just enough to each side to create a sense that the hotel was playing fairly with everyone. He had managed to straddle political and legal fulcrums throughout his career, and as such the lifelong Democrat could counsel Bill and Hillary Clinton one year and hitch a ride aboard Air Force One with his Yale fraternity brother George W. Bush in another. When Connecticut senator

Joe Lieberman stunningly left the Democratic Party in 2006 after losing the primary to an antiwar challenger, Davis helped him mount an unforgettable Independent campaign that against the odds won Lieberman another term in the Senate. Davis even relished writing a newspaper column called "Purple Nation" that found middle ground among Democrats and Republicans even as he held his own liberal ideals.

In many ways, Davis's approach for the Sofitel mirrored the triangulation strategy his old boss, Bill Clinton, implemented during the dark days of his presidency when the White House was caught between Republicans eager to investigate him and Democrats who felt abandoned by him after the 1994 election. Clinton's strategy was to stay between the factions, and not get cornered into any one camp. Davis would have the Sofitel do its own triangulation to avoid being squashed by the giant forces at work in the case. He wanted every player to know the Sofitel was firmly in the middle.

That's not to say Davis didn't have his moments to meddle. He was personally convinced (as was the hotel's security chief, John Sheehan) that something untoward happened in Suite 2806. Diallo's colleagues who encountered her in the moments just after the alleged attack were simply too compelling and the forensic evidence too consistent to believe otherwise. So when prosecutors seemed to drift away from Diallo due to her inconsistencies, Davis made several impassioned pleas, especially to the junior sex crimes prosecutor on Vance's team, Artie McConnell, to look beyond Diallo's flaws and stay focused on the substantial forensic evidence and outcry testimony. Davis even made calls at times to point out evidence the prosecution may have overlooked, such as the security key card records or a simple phrase in one hotel employee's recollections.

Davis's below-the-radar contacts extended outside the case to academia, as well. Shortly after prosecutors made public their concerns about inconsistencies in Diallo's testimony, the famed appellate attorney and Harvard law professor Alan Dershowitz wrote an opinion piece for *The Daily Beast* in early July suggesting the charges against Strauss-Kahn should be dropped. The Dershowitz piece created a wave, adding to a tide that was turning against the maid and in favor of freeing Strauss-Kahn. One afternoon in late July, Davis made an unsolicited call to Dershowitz at his Martha's Vineyard vacation spot, urging him to look more closely at the evidence. One of the stories Davis pointed Dershowitz to was a *Daily Beast* story that I had written that provided one of the most complete timelines of what occurred just before, during, and after the alleged incident in DSK's suite. The story included specific time stamps from hotel security card entry records as well as specific testimony from the outcry witnesses, and it helped answer some of the mysteries that had lingered about what Diallo did just before and after the alleged attack and why it took the Sofitel an hour to report the incident to police.

Dershowitz—usually not one to doubt his instincts or judgment—was swayed by Davis's factual presentation. In early August, weeks after advocating dismissal of the charges, Dershowitz called me out of the blue at my *Newsweek* desk. "I've changed my mind," he said. "I would certainly not rush to dismiss it. I would conduct further investigation." The Harvard lawyer had decided to take the matter one step further, choosing the DSK case as the topic for his fall legal ethics class in Boston. "This is going to be a great case to present to my students in legal ethics," he boasted, adding the case had shown "even an old guy like me can have his thinking changed by good reporting." Dershowitz made good on the promise, bringing some players in the legal case to his classroom to talk with the next generation of lawyers that fall.

Most on the prosecution team seemed to appreciate Davis's cooperation. He was to the point, quick to respond, and seemed interested only in the facts. To show his gratitude, Vance himself made a personal call to Davis after the charges were dismissed to thank him. But a few prosecutors began to chafe at Davis's subtle suggestions as the case neared the end, especially when the Washington lawyer urged prosecutors to come back a second time and interview all of the hotel witnesses who had contact with Diallo before deciding the fate of the case. The lead prosecutor, Joan Illuzzi, took particular umbrage, wondering aloud at one meeting with Davis why he and the hotel seemed to still be supporting Diallo after issues about her credibility emerged.

"Why are you so invested in seeing this go forward?" Illuzzi snapped. Davis insisted the hotel wasn't taking sides and simply wanted to make sure authorities looked at all the evidence. "Listen, Joan, I've spent my whole life fighting for the presumption of innocence, and that applies to DSK," Davis snapped back. "I've tried to stay in the middle of the road on this. And you're the one who seems to be taking too much of this personally, not me."

If the hotel's French owners had any motive for seeing the criminal case go forward, it could have been that a dismissal of the criminal charges might open the door for Strauss-Kahn's lawyers to attack the Sofitel for exposing their client to the housekeeper and her allegations. Strauss-Kahn could sue for defamation or negligence, or float a theory in the ravenous foreign press that Sofitel's French owners supported the current President Nikolas Sarkozy and conspired to set up Strauss-Kahn by preying on his sexual weaknesses. Davis and Rabinowitz were acutely aware of the pressures, but their intention was solely to stay neutral and focused on the facts. And they were amused by the threats from DSK's and Diallo's lawyers of potential lawsuits. In the end, they ultimately brokered a deal to turn over the hotel's evidence—everything from key card entry records to phone calls, security videotapes, and e-mails that had been given to prosecutors—to DSK's defense to signal the Sofitel had nothing to hide and was remaining neutral. Davis and Rabinowitz insisted, however, that if prosecutors and DSK's team wanted evidence from the hotel, they would have to issue a subpoena first so the hotel could say publicly it was compelled to produce the evidence and cooperated voluntarily. The prosecutors and Strauss-Kahn's lawyers complied by issuing the subpoenas.

The Sofitel produced the same evidence it gave prosecutors in May to Strauss-Kahn's lawyers in July, even though the case at that point appeared to be heading toward dismissal. At the time, it seemed the prudent decision was not to fight a subpoena. But after the case ended, Davis and his client would suffer the heartburn of watching confidential evidence they had turned over become leaked into public by Strauss-Kahn's defenders in France in an effort to weave wild conspiracies and alternate theories of the case.

Right after Thanksgiving 2011, DSK's team mounted a full offensive in the French press to discredit Diallo, the Sofitel, and the hotel workers who had supported her. Strauss-Kahn's earlier efforts to rehabilitate his image, including a French television interview, had backfired. So now it was time to try to lure the French press into reporting some of the conspiracy theories. The onslaught started with the publication of a book in France by author Michael Taubman entitled *DSK Affairs: The Counter-Investigation* that gave DSK's side of the story: Diallo invited the sexual encounter with a wanting look in her eyes and only became dismayed when she returned to the room afterward to discover her French lover hadn't left behind a big tip as thanks for a few minutes of oral sex.

A writer in America named Edward Jay Epstein would take the conspiracy theories to a new level with an article published around Thanksgiving in the normally staid *New York Review of Books* in which Epstein suggested Sofitel employees may have conspired with Sarkozy allies to set up Strauss-Kahn for a sexual encounter—a classic "honey trap" that the Frenchman couldn't resist—and to steal his IMF BlackBerry for incriminating evidence that would end the

Socialist Party leader's ambitions for the French presidency. To bolster his theory, Epstein cited the then previously unknown security videotape from the afternoon of May 14 purporting to show two security officials celebrating—Epstein claimed for three minutes—on a dock around the time police were called. The names of several hotel employees were published, essentially implicated in the conspiracy theory.

The footage had been given to DSK's lawyers by the hotel under the subpoena, and Davis and Rabinowitz were furious. So, too, were Accor officials in France. They considered it a leak of grand jury materials that had been provided in good faith. But worse yet, the hotel had reviewed the footage and the celebration had lasted just thirteen seconds, and not the three minutes Epstein reported.

Rabinowitz again dispatched Davis to New York to review the tapes and interview the security officials shown in the tape since they had not mentioned the celebration during the earlier interviews he conducted back in May. Neither could remember the exact reasons for the fleeting celebration, but they opined it probably had to do with sports, since they often acted that way when talking sports. And they conceded they probably were just blowing off steam after an hour-long effort to convince a reluctant Diallo that the right thing to do was to report her attack to police. Also, they were adamant that at the time of their celebration they had no idea who Strauss-Kahn really was or the power he wielded.

I confirmed the story with sources who had seen the tape and the *Beast* was first to report that the celebration was just a few seconds, and not three minutes long. I also included the security employees' explanation for their conduct.

Davis also contacted *The New York Review of Books* and showed the editor that the alleged celebration was just thirteen seconds long. He demanded a correction. It worked. On December 6, the magazine pulled back with a partial retraction.

The article entitled "What Really Happened to Strauss-Kahn," by Edward Jay Epstein, which appeared in our December 22, 2011, issue, contained a description of what "looked like" a "dance of celebration" by two employees of the Hotel Sofitel in New York City at approximately 1:35 PM on the day that Dominique Strauss-Kahn was arrested in connection with an alleged sexual assault. Security camera recordings have established that the episode, as described, lasted approximately thirteen seconds, not the three minutes mentioned in the article.

Davis felt like he had stamped out a conspiracy theory that had been based on virtually no facts. But he was wrong. DSK's team in France had just begun their assault. A couple of days later, the actual video footage showed up on French television and the story was revived. This time, Davis demanded to go public. For half a year, he had stayed away from the cameras and kept his name out of the story, a secret hand guiding the Sofitel legal/media strategy. He didn't want to stay silent any longer. He wanted to take the gloves off and fight the DSK machine. There were enormous risks. Davis had represented some fairly controversial clients in recent years, including two with egregious human rights records, Equatorial Guinea and the embassy of Ivory Coast. Davis had done so in hopes of facilitating conversations with the Obama administration that might lead to regime change in Ivory Coast or democracy in Equatorial Guinea. But his representation nonetheless stirred controversy that could be resurrected anew. And all the baggage of defending a philandering president was certain to flood into the public arena as fresh fodder for DSK's lawyers. But at this point Davis and his client weren't worried. They wanted to fight back. And they did, sending Davis onto NBC's *Today* show on December 9 to knock down the conspiracy theory. "The notion that this video is evidence that Accor is involved in some conspiracy is utter nonsense," Davis declared to NBC's Michael Isikoff.

The Sofitel had another reason for becoming more assertive in public, one that was much more secret. In the days leading up to the leak campaign, several Sofitel employees who were key witnesses supporting Nafi Diallo's account reported feeling intimidated and threatened by sudden visits—at night, at home, in parking garages—by private investigators hired by DSK to dig up dirt on Diallo.

One of Diallo's housekeeping supervisors was contacted, as was the room service attendant who had entered DSK's room just before Diallo and had assured the housekeeper the room was empty and okay to clean. The room service attendant's experience was particularly troubling. His wife called him at work to report that two or three investigators were sitting in her living room and had identified themselves as investigators for Accor. When he got home, he discovered the investigators were from DSK's defense team and ushered them out. Sofitel's lawyers protested to Strauss-Kahn's lawyer, Bill Taylor, who insisted there must have been a misunderstanding. All of DSK's investigators were instructed to use their true identity and affiliation, Taylor assured them, and they have nothing to hide as they did their job.

There was another incident, too. One of the employees in the security video footage that eventually leaked was approached by DSK investigators when he went to his car in a parking garage near the hotel. The men told him there was a story about to come out about him (the Epstein story on the security footage as it turned out) and they urged the Sofitel worker to tell them what had happened. He declined.

As tensions rose with DSK's side of the case, a much different relationship was blossoming with the maid's attorneys. As the alleged victim, Diallo and her lawyers didn't have the same subpoena powers to get information during the criminal case. And their civil case also was interrupted by a judicial stay almost as soon as it was filed in late summer because Strauss-Kahn was challenging whether U.S. courts had jurisdiction. The delay left Diallo's lawyers few ways to compel evidence be turned over to them in the early going. But Davis eventually found a way to communicate with them effectively as well, ensuring they had the information necessary to help their client.

For weeks, Davis sought his own elusive interview with Diallo, who hadn't formally talked to her employer since that afternoon May 14 when she reported in detail what happened to hotel security, and the police were summoned. So much had transpired in the courts since then, and Davis, Rabinowitz, and the hotel management had many follow-up questions they needed Diallo to answer to close out their own investigation. Furthermore, Davis relished his own chance to get in a room with Diallo and judge for himself whether she was a victim or a con artist.

Davis reached out to Diallo and Thompson when relations became strained over the issue of whether the hotel would keep paying her during her extended absence. Under the workmen's compensation policy, the hotel had a right to transfer her from salary to workmen's comp insurance, which paid slightly less than her salary. When the issue was first raised, Thompson's inclination was to threaten a fight, just as he had done with the prosecutors when they began to doubt his client. "I'll sue if you do that," Thompson told Davis when the issue of transferring her to workers' compensation first arose. Davis didn't take the bait. "Don't bother threatening me," Davis would respond. "If you don't let me interview her to be reassured she is telling a credible story about what happened in the hotel room, I'll just hang up and she'll be on workers' comp today."

Davis sought to break the ice with Thompson by finding some common ground—a decade earlier the two lawyers unwittingly had been on opposite sides of a high-profile discrimination case, though they hadn't met. Thompson had been representing a black woman named Sharon Simmons-Thomas, who claimed she was singled out because of her race and falsely detained and handcuffed by the Macy's department store in New York City for shoplifting. Thompson led the class-action lawsuit and eventually settled out of court. Davis was secretly brought in by Macy's, not to handle the courtroom work but instead to help devise a media strategy. His work led to a front-page *New York Times* story that showed the embattled Macy's security department in a more positive light. Once again, Davis had launched a preemptive strike for a client in the court of public opinion, validating his theory of legal crisis management.

For weeks after the alleged incident, Diallo continued to get full pay and benefits even though she was not working. She was staying in the protective custody of the NYPD in a safe house. And she did not want to return to work. Among her concerns was the lingering shoulder injury she claimed to have suffered during the alleged attack. Pressure was mounting inside the hotel management to either get Diallo to return to work (the hotel had offered her a job at a different one of its hotels) or move her to disability/workers' compensation, which would substantially reduce her income and benefits. Thompson was peeved at the mere suggestion that the hotel might bump Diallo from the payroll, seeing it as yet another victimization of his client. On the flip side, the hotel had not had access to Diallo since the first day of the attack, meaning Davis had not had his own chance to interview the key witness. After breaking the ice with Thompson, Davis did his best Monty Hall imitation and offered the lawyer two options. Behind Door No. 1, Thompson could keep his client away from an interview with Davis and she'd be bumped from salary and put on workers compensation. Behind Door No. 2, Diallo could consent to the interview and the hotel would keep paying her salary and benefits for the foreseeable future. Thompson took the second option, a decision that proved advantageous for more than just financial reasons. After a ninety-minute session in mid-July with Diallo, Davis left with the same original impression as prosecutors and the grand jury, convinced she had to be telling the truth about what happened inside Suite 2806. By that time, Davis already knew the details of the forensic evidence, security videos, and testimony of the other hotel employees. Diallo's account matched them closely.

"I just spent several hours with Nafi Diallo," Davis would tell a friend after the interview. "And I walked away convinced she is telling the truth that an unwelcomed sexual encounter occurred in that room. I know everything the hotel knows about it, even more than Nafi would know about the evidence, and her story mostly matches what the hotel investigators gathered. She comes off credible about what happened in the hotel room."

Davis concluded that Diallo's account—especially as given immediately after the incident to her Sofitel colleagues—could not have been contrived. The outcry witnesses, her housekeeping colleagues, and the security officers were adamant that Diallo's emotional response—the vomiting, the spitting, and the trembling—could not have been an act.

What about the fact that she lied to get into the country, even made up a story about an earlier rape? "She's not the first or last to lie to get into America for a better life for herself and her daughter," Davis would tell a friend after prosecutors disclosed her falsehoods in court in late June. "The important thing is there's no evidence she's lying about what happened in the room. Whether DSK was guilty or not, isn't for me to decide but a job for a jury," Davis added, using a refrain he would repeat time and again around the witnesses as well.

Davis wasn't making a determination on whether DSK was guilty or innocent. He simply needed to determine whether Diallo's claim about what happened was credible enough to justify keeping her on the payroll, and with health benefits, even though she wasn't returning to work. He felt he had done that, and he reported it to his client.

Soon, some trust developed between Davis and Thompson and his partner, Douglas Wigdor. Twenty years their senior, Davis became in some respects a sounding board, suggesting on more than one occasion that it might be prudent for Diallo's team to lower the temperature from the public attacks it had made on the prosecutors. Davis, after all, had seen from the other side just how offended the prosecutors felt after Thompson's courthouse press conference. They felt personally attacked and wanted an apology. Davis feared that emotion was influencing the prosecution's legal judgment about whether to proceed with the case, distracting from the facts and evidence. Little things like loss of trust can tip cases that are close calls, he knew.

As the signs grew that the case was slipping away on the criminal side, Davis also proved unwittingly instrumental in one of the more stunning steps taken by Diallo's legal team—the decision in late July by the housekeeper to shed the normal anonymity of an alleged sexual assault victim and go public with her name and her story. It was a Hail Mary effort aimed at turning public opinion back in the alleged victim's favor and to increase pressure on Vance's team not to drop the case.

Thompson's original instinct was to hold a press conference and have Diallo go public before the cameras, taking up an offer by the activist Rev. Al Sharpton to hold a rally in favor of the housekeeper. Thompson even had staked out a possible church as the location for the event. But realizing such a step was risky, Thompson and Wigdor reached out to others they trusted for advice. Davis was one, and they mentioned the idea of a Sharpton event when Davis came over to discuss a deal to interview their client. Davis advised that a press conference would end up becoming a ghastly media circus, exactly the wrong venue for a shy immigrant maid to tell her story calmly. When Thompson called me, I had a similar response.

If you're going to take the leap of going public, Davis advised, do it with all the facts and do it in an environment where the facts can be carefully absorbed. Find a respectable reporter in print who would have the luxury of putting out all the details and limit her coming-out to the interview. Thompson took the advice to heart, and soon the most dramatic public relations offensive of the case was being planned inside the conference room of Thompson's fifth-floor law offices in Manhattan.

While Davis could provide such helpful advice to any colleague who asked, he also knew it was important to keep some separation between the hotel and the maid's supporters. Thompson's attacks on prosecutors in late June and early July, in Davis's opinion, did not serve the best legal interests of the housekeeper. Davis had watched a similar episode unfold a decade earlier when a California civil attorney named William Ginsburg became the first lawyer to represent Monica Lewinsky in early 1998. A family friend, Ginsburg had little criminal experience when he was thrust into the role of brokering a deal between an intern who had an affair with Clinton and the Whitewater prosecutor Kenneth Starr, whose team was investigating whether the president had lied under oath in denying the relationship.

Ginsburg became an instant media celebrity, hitting the TV talk shows and talking to reporters continuously. The lawyer seemed to embrace the intoxicating glare of the media limelight. But the strategy ultimately put Ginsburg's client in a tougher spot, Davis felt, essentially cornering prosecutors and creating a hostile environment where Lewinsky herself might face legal troubles of her own for obstructing the investigation. Eventually, Lewinsky jettisoned Ginsburg for two old Washington legal hands, Plato Cacheris and Jacob Stein, who hardly held another press conference while working behind the scenes to repair Lewinsky's relationship with Starr's office. They secured a deal that removed her from legal harm by providing the testimony that prosecutors wanted from the twenty-something intern at the center of the jaw-dropping impeachment scandal. Davis could see some parallels in the cases, and hoped Thompson could suppress some of his concerns about the way his client had been treated and instead mount a campaign to repair her relations with Vance's office.

Davis also had another worry: he believed Thompson would try to file a civil lawsuit against Strauss-Kahn even before prosecutors had made their decision on whether to dismiss the criminal charges.

Davis thought such a move, just like the press conference, would prove unseemly from both a legal and a public relations viewpoint. Suing before the criminal case was over would only heighten the public's suspicion that this Guinean immigrant might be seeking money more than justice. Eventually, Davis's fears were realized. In early August, Thompson filed the suit. Two weeks later, Vance's team dismissed the charges.

Davis's interactions with Thompson seemed to have some impact in softening the maid's legal and public relations strategy, especially after Davis had gotten his own interview with Diallo in mid-July. Thompson dropped the press conference for his client in favor of the lengthy interviews. And while he continued a barrage of accusations in public letters and statements against Vance's team, Thompson privately tried to mend some fences with the prosecutors. In late July, for instance, Thompson personally apologized to Illuzzi if any of his attacks felt personal. By that time, however, prosecutors had been steamed for too long and were reconciled to dropping the charges.

Davis's behind-the-scenes work, however, continued. Because it served the Sofitel's interest to see its employee treated fairly, he wanted the prosecutors to focus on the evidence of the attack, rather than the maid's lies on her asylum application or her attorneys' accusations. Davis made two important forays with prosecutors as the criminal case began unraveling.

The first occurred leading into the long Fourth of July holiday weekend, right after Vance's team had filed in court the notification that accused Diallo of several lies during the investigation. There was one allegation from prosecutors in the court filing that the Sofitel lawyers were certain was wrong. Vance's team wrote in the June 20 notification:

> *The complainant told detectives and assistant district attorneys on numerous occasions that after being sexually assaulted*

by the defendant on May 14, 2011, in Suite 2806, she fled to an area of the main hallway of the hotel's 28th floor and waited there until she observed the defendant leave Suite 2806 and the 28th floor by entering an elevator. It was after this observation that she reported the incident to her supervisor, who arrived on the 28th floor a short time later. In the interim between the incident and her supervisor's arrival, she claimed to have remained in the same area of the main hallway on the 28th floor to which she had fled.

The complainant testified to this version of events when questioned in the grand jury about her actions following the incident in Suite 2806. The complainant has since admitted that this account was false and that after the incident in Suite 2806 she proceeded to clean a nearby room and then returned to Suite 2806 and began to clean that suite before she reported the incident to her supervisor.

Davis and Rabinowitz knew that this new allegation by prosecutors—the only lie authorities ever alleged Diallo made about the incident itself—had to be wrong. It was directly contradicted by the hotel door key records that showed Diallo's activities inside the hotel that day. And even worse, the two Sofitel lawyers knew prosecutors had made a mistake, going to court to undercut this part of their victim's account before they had even acquired and reviewed the key card records for the other room, 2820, that she supposedly cleaned after the attack. Had they gotten those records and went over them with Diallo before rushing to court, prosecutors would have known their new theory and their new allegation could not be true.

Diallo purportedly changed her story about the incident during the chaotic, emotionally charged interview session on Tuesday, June 28, a month and a half after the attack. She didn't have her normal

Fulani interpreter that day, and there was disagreement over the translations between prosecutors and Diallo and her lawyer.

Diallo would later tell me and Davis in separate interviews that she first mentioned Room 2820 during that June session with prosecutors because she believed prosecutors wanted to know what other rooms she cleaned that day. She is adamant she told them she had cleaned Room 2820 *before* being attacked by Strauss-Kahn and then only went back afterward to get the cleaning gear she had left behind.

The next day, Wednesday, June 29, Vance's office called the Sofitel and for the first time asked them to gather up the door key records showing Diallo's entries into Room 2820. John Sheehan, the hotel's security chief, obliged and put the records in an envelope to be picked up by the district attorney's investigators. But no one showed up to retrieve the records. And they sat idly in a bin in the Sofitel security office for three days.

Instead of picking up the records, Vance's team invited Strauss-Kahn's lawyers, Taylor and Brafman, to meet at 3 p.m. on June 29 and formally informed them about Diallo's credibility problems. They were told a Brady disclosure was forthcoming that would lay out each purported lie.

The prosecutors sent their Brady disclosure letter to Strauss-Kahn's lawyers and the court on Thursday, June 30, complete with the claim that Diallo had changed her story and apparently had gone to clean Room 2820 after the attack. The story leaked out that night, and the next morning, Friday July 1, Sofitel officials were stunned to read the claim. They knew that sitting in the envelope that was never picked up by prosecutors from Sheehan's security office was evidence that Diallo keyed Room 2820 on three occasions at 10:30 a.m., 11 a.m. and 11:30 a.m. before entering Strauss-Kahn's room at 12:06 p.m. And they knew the records showed Diallo only reentered the Room 2820 one last time at 12:26 p.m. for less than a minute before returning to

Strauss-Kahn's suite. She couldn't possibly have cleaned the room in one minute after the alleged attack. And *all* the evidence proved she had cleaned Room 2820 beforehand, most likely after the Room 2820 guest had checked out around 11:30 a.m.

Davis was flabbergasted by the mistake. He felt compelled to call Vance's office the Friday before Independence Day weekend, reaching out to the junior prosecutor McConnell. "Artie, you need to send someone over here to pick up those records. You're wrong about 2820. You're wrong and you'll see it."

McConnell asked Davis to fax over the records instead and soon prosecutors would understand their representation in court could not be accurate. They never corrected it, however. In public, prosecutors would defend their decision to file the Brady disclosure by saying it was Diallo's fault and that as soon as she changed or added to her story they felt obliged to divulge it in the court.

But Davis, and some of the more experienced sex crimes detectives and prosecutors in the D.A.'s Office, believed a mistake had been made. They knew the Brady letter to the court was now inaccurate. And they wondered aloud if the inflammatory relations with Thompson—and the personal anger of some of the prosecutors about having been hoodwinked by Diallo's bogus account of the rape in Guinea—had lured the office into skipping a key investigative step it might normally have taken.

"I could see how some might wonder in hindsight whether if the victim was white and from upper Manhattan with a lawyer who was cool and calm whether we might have gone, gotten the records and walked the victim through the key cards and refreshed her recollection before going to court," one player in the investigation would later concede. "I don't think that's fair or that we treated Nafi any differently, but I could see how some might ask that question."

Davis would make one last-ditch effort to get prosecutors to focus on the evidence. From the beginning, as the hotel lawyer who had interviewed the employees who had contact with Diallo on the day of the attack, he believed the most compelling evidence was the testimony of the outcry witnesses. Each had recounted Diallo's story in almost identical fashion, suggesting the housekeeper was extremely consistent in her recollections and retelling of what happened in Strauss-Kahn's room. Davis believed that should weigh heavily on the prosecutors' decision of whether to dismiss the case.

In late July, McConnell called and asked for permission to talk to just one hotel employee, Syed Haque, the room service attendant who had entered Strauss-Kahn's suite just before Diallo. Davis saw his opening. He invited—perhaps jawboned is a better description—McConnell to reinterview all the witnesses, from the security team to the housekeeping supervisors who first interviewed Diallo about the alleged incident.

Davis became hopeful when he got word that the lead prosecutor, Joan Illuzzi, was coming to the hotel to do the reinterviews with McConnell. But he would soon recognize prosecutors were there for a different mission than interviews.

NINE

Going Through the Motions

DURING THE FIRST WEEK in August, District Attorney Cyrus Vance's lead prosecutor on the Dominique Strauss-Kahn case, Joan Illuzzi, and the sex crimes prosecutor Artie McConnell went back to the Sofitel. Ostensibly, their mission was to reinterview the outcry witnesses that Diallo had spoken with immediately after the incident and to get any last information from witnesses before deciding the fate of the case.

But Illuzzi, a hard-nosed homicide prosecutor with few subtleties to her personality, soon left the hotel's staff with a clear impression that she had a different intention: to convince Diallo's hotel colleagues that the housekeeper had lied repeatedly and that dismissing the case was the only possible resolution.

"That was a complete waste of time. She already had made up her mind," the housekeeping floor supervisor Jessica Hollingsworth told Sofitel superiors after her meeting with prosecutors. "They weren't interested in what I had to say."

Syed Haque, the room service employee who had gone into Strauss-Kahn's suite moments before Diallo and had assured the housekeeper the suite was empty, walked away from his reinterview a bit shaken. He told his Sofitel superiors that the prosecutors seemed interested in just one question: whether he could have yelled louder when he walked into Suite 2806 the morning of May 14 to pick up Strauss-Kahn's breakfast tray. Syed felt like he was being blamed for failing to realize that Strauss-Kahn was still occupying the room, and giving Diallo the okay to enter.

Shortly before the interviews, Illuzzi and McConnell sat down at the Sofitel restaurant and bar with the hotel's security chief, John Sheehan, and its private attorney, Lanny Davis, to close the loop. Illuzzi sat across from Sheehan, while McConnell, who had bonded with Davis over the course of the investigation, sat across from the Washington lawyer. In fact, it was Davis who had instigated the gathering, inviting McConnell to come back one more time to make sure prosecutors had the benefit of all the information the hotel and its outcry witnesses had to offer.

It was still morning and the restaurant was mostly empty. The four sat in the back of the room at a corner table.

Illuzzi started by thanking Davis and Sheehan for the hotel's cooperation during the investigation, and she laid out her plan for talking to the employees. But Davis and Sheehan soon came to conclude that she really was just there to prepare them for a decision by Vance to dismiss the charges.

"Do you think there is substantial evidence that DSK's sexual encounter with Diallo—which DNA evidence proved was beyond dispute—was welcomed or unwelcomed?" Davis asked Illuzzi bluntly.

The veteran prosecutor put a pencil down on the table to make her point that there were two extremes in sexual assault cases. On one extreme, she said as she pointed to the tip of the pencil, there is "brutal rape." At the other end, there is pure consent. Davis was immediately struck by the presentation, wondering silently to himself whether there was any other type of rape except "brutal."

He interjected. "Joan, are you telling me that you don't believe some sort of unwelcomed sexual advance occurred in that room? Yes or no?"

"I have no doubt something unwelcome occurred," she answered, for a rare moment put on cross-examination by Davis. Sheehan and McConnell were mostly spectators at this point, letting them duke it out.

"Well, then, is there some sort of spectrum for unwelcomed sexual advances?" Davis asked, adding a touch of incredulity to his voice. "That seems to me to be a little like being half pregnant. I just don't see how a prosecutor investigating rape makes such a distinction. Why not let a jury decide?"

"Why are you so invested in this?" Illuzzi shot back. Davis and Sheehan both chimed in to correct her, insisting that the Sofitel wasn't invested in the outcome but simply in fully cooperating with prosecutors and making sure all of their employees, including Diallo, were treated fairly in the investigation.

Illuzzi tried to explain her thinking: Diallo's credibility problems—lying about an earlier rape in Guinea, lying on her asylum application, cheating on her taxes, and understating her income on her low-income housing application—would make it impossible for a jury to believe the housekeeper's account that the incident with Strauss-Kahn was a sexual assault by force. Vance's team had already made that conclusion. In fact, several in the District Attorney's Office had already begun the process of writing a dismissal brief for the court.

"Every time she came in contact with the law, she lied," Illuzzi told Sheehan and Davis. Davis felt like the prosecutors had taken Diallo's lies personally and he wondered if that was affecting their decisions.

At another point in the conversation, Illuzzi offered a boast about her prosecutorial record. "I've never lost a case," she told the men.

The Sofitel security chief and the lawyer found the comment inappropriate, an insinuation that Vance's team was more worried about preserving its conviction record than in fighting for a victim in what was a difficult, but still provable case in their minds. Davis, ever impassioned, eventually complained to Illuzzi's supervisor.

Daniel Alonso, Vance's number two, was well schooled in diplomacy, being a former federal prosecutor and the top deputy in New York City's most famous local prosecution office. So he tried to smooth things over about the comment, telling Davis that Illuzzi was simply proud of her decision making and wasn't suggesting won-loss records were a motive for any decision.

"She probably was just trying to point out she knows when the evidence supports a decision to prosecute and when it supports dismissing," Alonso told Davis. "I wouldn't read anything more into it."

At the coffee shop, Davis and Sheehan asked Illuzzi whether she believed Diallo had accepted money for sex.

"No," she answered.

Did prosecutors think Diallo had known Strauss-Kahn beforehand or had enough information that he would be in Suite 2806 that weekend that she could have schemed to set him up for a honey trap? Again, she answered no. Any chance the encounter was consensual? Illuzzi answered again, "No."

Then how could it be that Vance's office was even thinking about dismissing the charges, Davis and Sheehan wondered to themselves.

The meeting came to a polite end, but the hotel's employees were convinced that Vance's team was simply going through the motions with the interviews and that it had already made up its mind: the prosecutors' distrust of Diallo's truthfulness outweighed the substantial forensic evidence and the testimony of the outcry witnesses.

They soon would be proved right.

When the case began falling apart, not everyone on Vance's team or the Special Victims unit in the police department was ready to dismiss. Some wanted to keep investigating, to shore up the evidence, and to learn more about whether Strauss-Kahn had a pattern or history of preying on vulnerable women. Vance did not weigh in at first, instead allowing the debate to rage for weeks.

Occasionally, the office would hold roundtables to talk through the issues and debate the right course. They even held rounds of mock court to see how they might try to make a case with Diallo's credibility issues. Vance liked the idea of building consensus. And over time the senior prosecutors—who had concluded early on that Diallo would make a terrible witness—began to win the debate. They had met with Strauss-Kahn's lawyers to get a sense of what sort of defense Benjamin Brafman and Bill Taylor might level and they brought that knowledge into the room. Some even began parsing Diallo's every word, looking for the slightest hint of contradiction or inconsistency. The cumulative effect eventually secured a unanimous decision to dismiss the charges.

By the third week of August, a lengthy dismissal motion has been drafted, the handiwork of far too many chefs stirring the same pot. Even the office's public relations spokeswoman, Erin Duggan, not a lawyer by training, had been asked to weigh in. Vance's team was trying not only to address the legal issues to support dismissal but also the many allegations that had surfaced in the media from Diallo's outspoken lawyer Thompson. The team had reread his comments on the courthouse steps July 1, his allegations in the war of letters that followed over the next month, as well as his request to disqualify Vance's office from the case. And the prosecutors wanted to counter several of Thompson's public claims. In that respect, the motion to dismiss had become a document aimed just as much at the court of public opinion as it was for the court of law.

Several of the prosecutors had felt personally insulted by Thompson's attacks and had expected an apology. Thompson gave a partial one to Illuzzi at the July 28 meeting but it did not seem to erase the anger. The animus and distrust had remained so intense that at one point the prosecutors even debated internally whether in the final court motion they should credit Thompson for being the person who first came forward to divulge Diallo's prior false statements about the rape in Guinea and her asylum claims. To some, such debate inside the office seemed petty. Of course they needed to be honest with the court and divulge Thompson's role. And they ultimately did.

The draft motion to dismiss began to feel adrift, straying from its original mission to justify repeal of the criminal charges. Some of the drafts were approaching fifty to seventy pages long, far too much for a judge or a member of the public to consume. So Vance decided he needed a fresh set of eyes, someone who could cut through the clutter, crystallize the key points, and make the document readable to layman and lawyer alike.

Vance had remembered the offer of help that Linda Fairstein, the sex-crimes-prosecutor-turned-author, had made at the beginning of the case. She seemed perfectly suited to help focus the brief. After all she was a lawyer, a sex crimes expert, a wordsmith, and early on was suspicious of the case against DSK and the motives of the alleged victim when the prosecutors on the case seemed enamored with the star witness. She also was a trusted member of Vance's Kitchen Cabinet of outside advisers.

Fairstein had already begun her summer vacation on Martha's Vineyard, the place where the Kennedys and other political royalty spend their Augusts. Vance packed up some files and a draft of the brief and headed out toward Massachusetts and the vacation hamlet known as the summer colony of the rich and famous.

Vance had two goals. First, he wanted to tap Fairstein's sex crimes expertise and her writing prowess to make the most compelling, concise case for dismissal in the court brief. And secondly, he wanted to pay a quick visit to his predecessor, Robert Morgenthau, to keep the legendary former Manhattan district attorney in his camp. Both were at the Vineyard, making a one-day trip worth the price of two.

On the morning of August 17, Fairstein picked Vance up from the small airport and they went to her vacation home. He explained to her that he was concerned about the reaction a dismissal might generate among victims' advocates groups, a key constituency for Vance's election win two years earlier. He planned to reach out to the victims' advocacy community after the decision became public to help further manage their reaction.

Fairstein told him he shouldn't be afraid to "put the facts out there" and explain to the public how Diallo's own words and changes in her story were the real reason for the undoing of the case.

For hours on the back deck of her vacation home, Fairstein and Vance wrote and rewrote the brief, trying to synthesize the most important legal and public relations points and accentuate the storyline.

The brief was structured like a chapter in a good book, and written with an unusual dose of literary flair. The proposition of the story line is made clear right from the start. Yes, there's no doubt a rushed sexual encounter occurred in the hotel room between Strauss-Kahn and Diallo. But the problem is the case had become a he-said-she-said as to the issue of whether it was an attack by force.

"It is clear that proof of two critical elements—force and lack of consent—would rest solely on the testimony of the complaining witness at trial," the brief ultimately declared.

"Undeniably then, for a trial jury to find the defendant guilty, it must be persuaded beyond a reasonable doubt that the complainant is credible. Indeed, the case rises and falls on her testimony," it added. The prosecutors initially found Diallo credible "but evidence gathered in our post-indictment investigation severely undermined her reliability as a witness," the brief explains.

"The nature and number of the complainant's falsehoods leave us unable to credit her version of events beyond a reasonable doubt, whatever the truth may be about the encounter between the complainant and the defendant. If we do not believe her beyond a reasonable doubt, we cannot ask a jury to do so," the brief declared.

The story line is simple. We believed the victim at first, but further investigation found so many lies we could no longer ask jurors to believe her story.

Now a good author always assumes the questions a reader might be conjuring as they are reading, and he or she moves quickly to answer them before they become a distraction.

And Vance's final motion to dismiss does just that.

Are prosecutors saying that the only way a sexual assault case can be brought in Manhattan is if the victim is credible beyond a reasonable doubt?

"That an individual has lied in the past or committed criminal acts does not necessarily render them unbelievable to us as prosecutors, or keep us from putting them on the witness stand at trial," the brief answered.

Haven't you been unfair to this poor immigrant housekeeper because she accused one of the world's most powerful men? Wasn't she subjected to a critical examination that most sex assault victims never get? Don't many immigrants lie to get into the United States?

"This is not a case where undue scrutiny or a heightened standard is being imposed on a complainant," the brief countered. "Instead, we are confronted with a situation in which it has become increasingly clear that the complainant's credibility cannot withstand the most basic evaluation. In short, the complainant has provided shifting and inconsistent versions of the events surrounding the alleged assault."

Well then, wasn't your original indictment a rush to judgment? Shouldn't you have done more investigating before dragging us all along on this legal roller coaster?

"At the time of the indictment, all available evidence satisfied us that the complainant was reliable," the brief insisted, adding that there were "no red flags" during the early going of the case.

The rest of the brief relates a narrative of the lies Diallo told and how the substantial physical and outcry evidence alone can't prove the sexual encounter was forced.

"All of these falsehoods would, of course, need to be disclosed to a jury at trial, and their cumulative effect would be devastating," the brief concluded, resorting several times to language that appears more literary than legal.

Fairstein's contribution was helpful. In some ways it helped push the legal brief into a form seldom seen in court, a concise and compelling narrative that goes well beyond the legal basis for dismissal. It was exactly what Vance had hoped for. And he could head back to Manhattan with a document about half the original size.

In the afternoon, Vance borrowed Fairstein's car to go over to Morgenthau's vacation home. He told Fairstein beforehand he wanted to brief his predecessor on the decision to dismiss, making sure he remained a supporter of what was certain to be a contentious decision. It was the second time the two lawyers had met in the last six weeks.

In early July, Vance had met with Morgenthau in New York City, shortly after prosecutors first divulged problems with Diallo's testimony. At the time, Vance was being buffeted from two directions. On one side, DSK's defenders were claiming the sudden problems with the case were evidence he had rushed to judgment in seeking an indictment. On the other side, Diallo's supporters were accusing prosecutors of abandoning a victim over unrelated lies in an asylum application.

Amidst the white-hot debate, the ninety-one-year-old, still sprightly Morgenthau took the extraordinary step of helping out his protégé one more time, issuing a public statement in early July suggesting Vance's team's actions were consistent with the way Morgenthau would have run the office if he were still in charge.

In New York legal circles, it was the equivalent of having the blessing of the pope.

"The most important attribute I looked for in hiring junior prosecutors was a strong ethical sense. The recent actions from the District Attorney's Office show me that these attributes are alive and well," Morgenthau declared, reminding readers subtly that Vance started as a junior prosecutor on the Morgenthau team years earlier.

"Prosecutors from my former office were never supposed to be hired guns; seeking convictions or cherry-picking easy cases. We sought justice in every case, no matter how big or how small. And, in my opinion, the Manhattan District Attorney and his staff upheld this proud tradition through their conduct in the past week," he added.

To some inside and outside the office, the two outreaches to Morgenthau in July and August were viewed as a sign of weakness, and further evidence Vance was still trapped in the vapor trail of his legendary predecessor. "Does a champion skater on the night of their Gold Medal performance bring their coach onto the ice to skate with them?" one senior member of Vance's team would ask me later. "We've got to cut the umbilical cord if we're ever going to blaze our own path."

To others, the visit was a sign that Vance was maturing in the job, recognizing that after a controversial case was decided on the laws and merits, the job of Manhattan district attorney also involves politics and the need to build consensus in the community when controversy strikes. "He knew people needed to be educated about the facts in this case in order to come to grips with what he decided, so why not ask your rabbis and the respected voices of the legal community to help sell that?" another Vance adviser explained.

Officially, Vance's office steadfastly refused to talk about anything having to do with the trip to Martha's Vineyard. In fact, when I filed a request under New York's Freedom of Information Law for records related to his contacts with Fairstein and Morgenthau, it was turned down on the grounds that Vance enjoys "executive privilege" like a president, an absolute right to get confidential legal advice.

"The executive privilege and the deliberative materials exceptions are designed 'to permit people within an agency to exchange public opinions, advice and criticisms freely and frankly without the chilling prospect of public disclosure,'" the January 4, 2012, letter from Assistant District Attorney Maureen T. O'Connor read, rejecting my request.

I'm still appealing that decision as this book heads to press, eager to test Vance's commitment to transparency, especially when he made the rare decision to take the case materials and issues outside his office to third parties like Fairstein and Morgenthau.

Whatever the resolution of that FOI case, O'Connor's letter was notable for another reason: she misspelled the defendant's name throughout as "Dominique Strauss Khan." As in Genghis Khan, the marauder. Some might interpret it as a Freudian slip. But in fact, the letter accentuates something everyone in Vance's office has stressed to me since the case ended: they quickly put the DSK case out of sight and out of mind and moved on to other issues.

Vance returned to Fairstein's home late in the afternoon. He had a final mission, one completely unrelated to the case. Fairstein's husband, the New York lawyer Justin Feldman, had been in declining health for about two years. And he was so ill that morning he couldn't join them on the deck. Vance knew this might be his last chance to spend time with Feldman, so he insisted on going into the house and socializing. He had a flight to catch back to New York, but he didn't care. This was more important. Fairstein and Feldman were inseparable, and their Martha's Vineyard vacation home was their pride and joy. Vance spent an hour inside reminiscing. No shop talk. Just the banter of good friends savoring what would ultimately be a final visit. Feldman died just five weeks later. To Fairstein, the episode spoke volumes about Vance's sincerity and compassion, a private side hidden from public view by the intense, relentless glare of the media spotlight on the Manhattan District Attorney's Office. Whatever struggles and tribulations Vance faced in the case, he could set them aside to comfort two old friends.

Vance returned to Manhattan from Martha's Vineyard, nearly ready to pull the trigger on a decision that had lingered for weeks. He and his top deputy, Daniel Alonso, reviewed the latest draft, tightening some sections, tweaking important legal points, and adding a few late-breaking details. On occasion, the prosecutors inserted footnotes and phrases to push back against Thompson's many diatribes of the last month, especially the July 1 one on the courthouse steps that most angered Alonso.

Thompson all but accused Vance's office that day of abandoning and sabotaging the victim. He also alleged that Vance's team ignored evidence of a tear in her pantyhose, a shoulder injury, and bruising on her vagina that he claimed proved a sexual assault had occurred.

Prosecutors had for weeks mostly accepted the "redness" found on Diallo's vagina during the hospital exam as proof of attempted rape. But then Strauss-Kahn's lawyers got an expert who questioned whether the seeming bruising was caused by something else, like an irritation, infection, or earlier sexual encounter. Vance's team got their own outside expert who came down in the middle. Inside the District Attorneys Office, some had come to call Thompson's press conference the "vagina moment" and decided in a footnote to cast doubt on it as proof of an assault.

The expert summoned by prosecutors "opined that although it was possible for the redness to have been caused by the defendant's grabbing the complainant in the manner that she had described, it was not likely caused by such an act," the prosecutors wrote in the motion.

The shoulder injury? There was an answer from another medical expert. "This expert has concluded that, to a reasonable degree of medical certainty, the injury, if it was an injury at all, was likely caused by repeated overhead use of the upper extremity," the brief answered.

And as for the tear in the stockings, prosecutors believed in the beginning that it—coupled with Strauss-Kahn's skin cells on the stocking—proved he had tried to go inside Diallo's panties. But in the motion, it was reinterpreted to "defects in the pantyhose" that might have had nothing to do the incident.

Nearly every piece of proof Thompson cited on the courthouse steps—much of which the prosecutors themselves had accepted as proof of guilt in the beginning—was reinterpreted in the motion with the tone and viewpoint of a defense lawyer. In fact, the motion read a lot like Bill Taylor's private presentation to Vance's office a month earlier.

There was another issue prosecutors wanted to address: the possible financial motive of the victim.

Thompson had asserted that Vance's office had leaked the tape recording of the prison call between Diallo and Amara Tarawally, and only later learned that the suggestion that Diallo had raised the issue of Strauss-Kahn's wealth was inaccurate. He believed it had created a false picture of his client as a gold digger. "All of this stuff that they leaked to *The New York Times* was designed to discredit this woman," Thompson charged from the courthouse steps.

Alonso himself was unhappy with the leak, which had occurred before prosecutors had a full transcript of the recording. And prosecutors knew the *New York Times* account wasn't quite accurate. But rather than give a full accounting of what was on the tape, they used a sleight-of-hand reference in a footnote to make it look like the office stood by the leak.

"The call was translated and certified as true and accurate by two Fulani-English translators," the footnote read. "While differing in their precise word-for-word transcriptions of the call, both translations are materially similar in their discussion of making money with the assistance of a civil lawyer."

The footnote is technically accurate but it fails to divulge a key fact that might have changed the public's mind: it was Tarawally who raised the issue of Strauss-Kahn's wealth, not Diallo, according to those who have listened to the tape.

Vance's team also couldn't resist inserting into the motion a shot at one of Thompson's most controversial decisions: filing a lawsuit against Strauss-Kahn. They decided in the footnote to contrast that decision with Diallo's earlier claims she had no financial motive in the case.

"On Aug. 8, 2011, the complainant filed a civil suit against the defendant, seeking unspecified monetary damages," the motion noted. In the court of law, the lawsuit had no bearing on a decision to dismiss. In fact, the prosecutors had conceded elsewhere in their motion that there was "nothing wrong with seeking recovery from a defendant." But Vance's team couldn't resist the temptation to suggest to the court of public opinion and the news media that Thompson's decision to sue could be used as evidence to impeach his client.

Some legal experts I talked with found the whole round of footnotes in the motion "petty," but nonetheless insightful as to the amount of bad blood that had developed between the prosecution and the victim.

Vance's team also wanted to make sure it addressed criticism from the other side of the case as well. The prosecutors were clearly still sensitive about an argument that Strauss-Kahn's lawyers had made behind closed doors: that Vance's office had rushed to remand the Frenchman without bail and secure an indictment in just five days while ignoring evidence of innocence.

Taylor had pointedly made the case in his private meeting in July that prosecutors had not considered that the defendant's actions on the day of the attack—the leisurely lunch with his daughter, the call from the airport to the hotel, his apparent stated willingness to talk to police at first—failed to exhibit the guilty conscience of a person who thought he had committed a crime. Vance's team wanted to push back on the rush to judgment argument more specifically.

"Pre-indictment investigation indicated that the defendant had left the hotel in a hurried manner, but it was not known at the time where the defendant went immediately after his departure from the hotel," the prosecutors wrote in the motion, trying to justify their early actions.

In a footnote, the prosecutors added a supposed second defense: "Not until the June 6, 2011 arraignment did the defense reveal that the defendant's precise location in the time period between his departure from the hotel and arrival at John F. Kennedy Airport was a Manhattan restaurant located at Sixth Avenue between 51st and 52nd Streets."

To Strauss-Kahn's experienced lawyers and to many others in the legal profession, the argument was laughable.

Since when was it left to the defense to ascertain a defendant's whereabouts on the day of the crime? Isn't that the job of police and prosecutors before they indict? A simple check of the defendant's credit card and phone records could have uncovered the restaurant stop. Or just a quick read of the newspapers would have found it, since on May 16 numerous news organizations had already reported the lunch between Strauss-Kahn and his daughter.

But perhaps most disturbing to insiders was the fact that the passage was blatantly misleading to the court.

During the very first court hearing forty-eight hours after Strauss-Kahn's arrest, defense lawyer Brafman told the entire courtroom that his client had gone from the hotel to a nearby restaurant for lunch. "The record will reflect he was in the vicinity of the hotel for several hours before and after checking out," Brafman declared in court May 16. "The reason he was rushing is because he had a luncheon appointment with a person. . . . The theory that he ran out of the hotel and ran to the airport, running away is simply not true."

Okay, so Brafman didn't hand the prosecutors the exact location on Sixth Avenue that first day, but it is implausible the prosecutors could argue with a straight face that they were unable to determine Strauss-Kahn's whereabouts for a whole month afterward. And it was just as implausible to suggest it as a defense against any charges they had rushed to judgment.

Of course, the public and the judge at the dismissal hearing (who was different from the judge that first day) would not have enough detailed knowledge to spot the hyperbole. But to those on the inside of the case, the weak effort at defending the early rush to judgment actually exposed anew the sloppy investigative work, and the inexperience witnessed at the beginning of the case.

Despite what some saw as hyperbole and flaws in the document, Vance declared himself satisfied with the motion to dismiss. So on Monday evening, August 22, five days after Vance's writing and editing session with Fairstein, the prosecutors submitted the request to the court to dismiss all charges against Dominique Strauss-Kahn.

There was only one last task before Vance's office could jettison a case that had consumed the office and its resources for three unforgiving months: the prosecutors had to inform Diallo and her lawyers.

Thompson received a call Monday evening asking him to bring Diallo to the District Attorney's Office at 10 a.m. Thompson already suspected bad news, but he obliged the request to appear in person. He, Wigdor, and Diallo sat quietly in an office that Tuesday morning. There was little suspense, except for how the prosecutors would deliver the news.

Suddenly, there was a brief knock on the door and the prosecution's three main players streamed in: Illuzzi, the lead prosecutor, McConnell, the sex crimes prosecutor, and Ann Prunty, the violent crimes prosecutor who had yelled at Diallo during the contentious June 9 interrogation and then threw the housekeeper out of the office in front of her teenage daughter. Though they played important roles editing the final motion to dismiss, neither Vance nor Alonso showed up.

The prosecutors had stern expressions on their faces, and only Illuzzi spoke. "Nafi, you have not told us the truth about everything. You have lied," she started.

Diallo spoke up. "How did I lie?"

"Nafi, you have lied, and we're going to dismiss the case," Illuzzi shot back.

"How did I—" Diallo started again. But there was no time for any more objections. Not even for Thompson, who didn't even get a chance to speak.

The prosecutors just turned their backs and walked out of the room. The door shut. The entire episode, the final salvo in a tumultuous case that upended world history, took less than forty-five seconds.

And as she had done so many times before—sometimes in genuine anguish, and other times to embellish fake stories—Nafi Diallo began to cry.

TEN

DSK's Story: The Conspiracy of Theories

No one, except maybe his defense lawyers, really knows Dominique Strauss-Kahn's complete version of events or his official defense for his behavior on the weekend of May 14, 2011. Thus far, he's never been forced to testify under oath about what happened between him and Nafissatou Diallo. Likewise, he was never questioned by detectives about what occurred inside Sofitel Hotel Suite 2806 during the four-plus hours that he was in police custody before he asked to see his lawyer. And his own public comments since the case was dismissed have been tantalizingly vague, filtered through friendly interviewers in France like his biographer or a TV anchor who is friends with his wife.

The truth is Strauss-Kahn's own story is still shrouded in mystery. He hasn't answered the key factual questions or even been given a forum yet to challenge in court some of the specifics of Diallo's account. That time may eventually arrive if Strauss-Kahn is ordered to stand civil trial in New York City in the lawsuit filed by his accuser. But in the absence of that court proceeding or a true *60 Minutes* tell-all, the media has done its best to offer a rousing stew of anonymous alibis and conspiracy theories from Strauss-Kahn's defenders:

Private security officials at the Sofitel worked to set up DSK to attack the housekeeper, then celebrated with glee when they persuaded the reluctant housekeeper to let them call police.

Diallo stole Strauss-Kahn's cell phone after a consensual sexual encounter and gave it to his French presidential rival Nicolas Sarkozy's supporters so it could be mined for embarrassing details.

A secretive French intelligence agent in Room 2820 worked with Diallo to set up a honey trap, backed by elements of the Sofitel's parent company, Accor, that were aligned with Sarkozy.

Russian intelligence set up a trap to compromise Strauss-Kahn and steal his IMF BlackBerry, because Russian leader Vladimir Putin opposed DSK's approach at the IMF for the global financial crisis.

Such stories have multiplied in the aftermath of the case, distributed by a media eager and willing to accept theory as a substitute for fact. And to be fair to the news profession, Strauss-Kahn himself has helped fan the flames with his own vague responses and tantalizing sound bites.

"A trap, it's possible. A conspiracy, we'll see," Strauss-Kahn declared when asked whether he believed he was set up. He made that comment during his first interview about the Sofitel incident back in September after he was freed from bail in the United States and the criminal charges were dropped. The French politician returned home to Paris and chose to tell his story to Claire Chazal, the popular TF1 weekend anchor and friend of DSK's wife, Anne Sinclair. During the interview, Strauss-Kahn offered a simple defense, insisting he had a consensual sexual encounter with Diallo that was "stupid" but involved "neither violence, nor coercion, nor aggression, nor any criminal act.

"What happened was a relationship that was not only inappropriate, but more than that, an error. An error with regard to my wife, to my children, to my friends. But also an error with regard to the French people, who had placed in me their hope for change," Strauss-Kahn said.

Neither Strauss-Kahn's televised equivalent of an apology to his fellow citizens nor the conspiracy theories floated by his supporters in the media have done much to repair the former IMF chief's reputation in France. (Ironically, Sinclair's popularity has soared with her stand-by-her-man routine, leading her to be chosen France's most popular woman at the end of 2011 and landing her a job as editor of the new *Huffington Post* edition in Paris in early 2012.)

In fact, there is strong evidence that the theories and alibis may actually have been counterproductive for Strauss-Kahn. He and his supporters seem to have offered multiple, and at times implausible, explanations for his conduct judging by the many anonymous media leaks. Put another way, his friends' and supporters' various conspiracy theories and alibis ultimately boomerang to DSK, even if he or his lawyers don't share a complete belief in them. A quick sweep of media clips identifies as many as a half dozen versions of Strauss-Kahn's possible defense and alibi, all attributed to anonymous supporters.

The first sympathetic alibi emerged on the weekend he was arrested, suggesting Strauss-Kahn couldn't have had sex with the housekeeper because he was having lunch with his daughter at a Manhattan restaurant. Then, when word surfaced that DNA evidence may have been retrieved from the scene and from Diallo's housekeeping uniform, a theory of consensual sex was offered. Later, it was suggested that Diallo had consented to sex but then became angry and reported the incident because Strauss-Kahn didn't leave money behind to pay her. And there's been a bevy of theories suggesting Diallo was part of a honey trap conspiracy with Sarkozy backers and Sofitel officials to catch Strauss-Kahn in an embarrassing situation and possibly unearth incriminating information from his IMF BlackBerry.

The problem with conspiracy theories, though, is they suffer from an absence of facts and often try to weave a yarn out of the unknowns. And good lawyers like the two hired by Strauss-Kahn, Benjamin Brafman and William Taylor, don't like unsubstantiated theories or alibis floating around in the courts of public opinion or law. They know such uncorroborated stories and wild speculation can taint a client's credibility if they can't be backed up. Good lawyers don't harbor conspiracy theories, only questions that need to be answered, maybe under oath or through cross-examination. And so they often wince when someone, in the absence of the answers, constructs a theory that sounds like a premature defense for their client.

One famous theory floated on Strauss-Kahn's behalf illustrates the potential for causing heartburn for the defense. It surfaced around Thanksgiving 2011, about three months after the criminal charges were dropped. That's when writer Edward Jay Epstein, viewed in many circles as sympathetic to Strauss-Kahn, published his story in the respected *New York Review of Books* that raised the possibility that Diallo or Sofitel employees may have conspired to steal Strauss-Kahn's IMF BlackBerry in search of incriminating evidence of affairs or other wrongdoing that could sink his presidential ambitions.

Epstein doesn't quite articulate the full-blown theory, instead leading the reader to the inevitable conclusion through a series of tantalizing facts and half-facts. First, Epstein reports that Strauss-Kahn had received a text message the morning of the alleged Sofitel incident from a friend temporarily working as a researcher at the Paris offices of Sarkozy's political party. The text warned that Strauss-Kahn's phone might have been "hacked" and that one private email from it may have ended up with Sarkozy's partisans. Strauss-Kahn was so shaken he called his wife to hire a computer expert to sweep his electronic devices for bugs or malware when he returned to Paris.

Epstein then notes that Strauss-Kahn mysteriously lost the phone that day and that "the missing phone's GPS circuitry was disabled at 12:51 p.m.," about thirty-eight minutes after his encounter with Diallo ended. "This stopped the phone from sending out signals identifying its location," Epstein claims, opining that such a disabling would have "required technical knowledge about how the BlackBerry worked."

Epstein suggests that around the time the phone's GPS circuitry was disabled, Sofitel hotel security "might" have contacted parent company officials in Paris who were close to Sarkozy to alert them that Strauss-Kahn was about to be arrested. To put the icing on the conspiracy cake, Epstein reported that two Sofitel security officials were later caught on security videotape celebrating for three minutes.

Readers are inevitably left thinking that Diallo, or her colleagues in Sofitel security, must have lifted Strauss-Kahn's cell phone at the hotel, disabled it, and then turned it over to Strauss-Kahn's enemies in the Sarkozy camp for exploitation of its messages. "Whatever happened to his phone, and the content on it, his political prospects were effectively ended by the events of that day," Epstein concludes.

But such conspiracy theories carry risks for the people they were intended to support, let alone the defense lawyers who might end up in court trying to distance themselves from unprovable supposition. First, Epstein ended up making a major factual error. The "celebration" by the security officials was thirteen seconds, not three minutes. That error forced *The New York Review of Books* to issue a high-profile retraction that undercut the whole article.

Second, the first known call from a Sofitel official to France isn't for nearly an hour *after* the phone stopped working. Sofitel security chief John Sheehan called the on-call supervisor of Sofitel's parent, Accor, in France around 1:40 p.m. The phone stopped transmitting at 12:51 p.m.

As for Sarkozy administration involvement in a honey trap conspiracy, the earliest known contact occurred shortly before midnight Paris time. That's when an official from the Sofitel's parent company, Accor, security chief René-Georges Querry, learns about the incident from a subordinate and then notifies Ange Mancini, a top intelligence adviser to the French president. That occurs around 5:45 p.m. New York time, or about an hour after Strauss-Kahn was already pulled off the Air France jet by police.

Perhaps most importantly, the DSK defense team's own fact gathering pointed toward a different likelihood. Strauss-Kahn made his last call on the phone at 12:15 p.m., after the sexual incident is believed to have occurred with Diallo inside Suite 2806, and the housekeeper is believed to have fled to a nearby hallway on the twenty-eighth floor of the hotel. That makes it hard for her or the security guards to steal it, unless it was left behind in the hotel room after he checked out. On that point, Strauss-Kahn's lawyers also noticed in the hotel security videotape footage that Strauss-Kahn can be seen departing the Sofitel at around 12:29 p.m., and he appears to grab a small, BlackBerry-like phone from his jacket pocket and put it to his ear briefly as a bellhop flags a taxi for him to take him to the restaurant where he planned to meet his daughter. That image leaves a strong implication that Strauss-Kahn may have still had his phone with him when he left the hotel, though he did not make another call on the device.

The lawyers also determined that the phone's tracking signal indicate it was moving away from the hotel before its GPS transponder stopped transmitting, suggesting the phone likely left the Sofitel when Strauss-Kahn did. In fact, Strauss-Kahn didn't notice the phone missing until after lunch. And when he finally did, his first instinct was to call his daughter Camille, and ask her to return to the restaurant to check if he left it on the table or a seat.

Finally, a cell phone can stop transmitting its GPS location for a much simpler reason than the high-tech disabling suggested by Epstein: if the battery runs out, if someone shuts off the phone or takes out the battery, or if the phone is put into "airplane mode," a common practice among frequent world travelers before boarding a flight.

The cumulative evidence leads Strauss-Kahn's lawyers to consider a much more plausible theory about the missing BlackBerry: it fell out of their client's coat during the cab ride to see his daughter. It then shut off either because the battery was worn down or because the person who found it shut it off or removed the battery to hawk it on the street.

Good lawyers don't weave uncorroborated conspiracy theories, and they certainly don't offer them up lightly in public. Instead, they prefer to create lists of unanswered questions and then use the legal process—subpoenas, depositions, testimony under oath, private investigators, and the like—to find answers and ascertain facts that can best help their client.

Shortly before the Thanksgiving holiday 2011, Strauss-Kahn's private investigators stepped up their efforts to get such answers, scouring anew the West African immigrant neighborhoods in the Bronx and Harlem where Diallo lived, trying to learn more about her finances, and her friendships and dealings with men. The investigators also zeroed in on Diallo's colleagues at the Sofitel, especially those who encountered her in the immediate aftermath of the alleged incident, the outcry witnesses. Some of the Sofitel employees reported to their superiors and the hotel's lawyers that they felt intimidated by the approaches that occurred around Thanksgiving 2011.

Sofitel officials found the approaches to their employees to be too aggressive and instructed their lawyers to call Taylor and complain that the tactics bordered on witness intimidation. Taylor assured the Sofitel lawyers that there was no intent to mislead or intimidate the witnesses, and that the investigators were just trying to get answers to unsettled questions in the case.

Strauss-Kahn's legal team has its own share of unanswered questions. It certainly will want to know why Diallo went back to Suite 2806 as soon as Strauss-Kahn left it, and why she stopped momentarily in Room 2820 around the corner even though she had already cleaned it. They'd also like to know who the guest in Room 2820 was and whether he had any connections to Sarkozy. Likewise, they'll almost certainly want to know from Diallo and her hotel colleagues whether they disturbed any evidence in Suite 2806 during the twenty-five minutes from 12:26 p.m to 12:51 when five separate Sofitel employees went through the alleged crime scene, well before police arrived.

The defense lawyers also have some suspicions and questions about what happened inside Strauss-Kahn's suite before he arrived that night of May 13. Three Sofitel employees entered the suite separately during the 120 minutes before DSK checked into the room—one from housekeeping, another from room service, and a third purportedly to "turn down" the bed even though the guest hadn't arrived.

Why so much activity in the early evening, long after rooms should already be cleaned? Was it because they wanted to make sure the room was perfect for such a big-name VIP? That's what the hotel believes. Or is there a more sinister reason, like placing a secret audio or video recorder to catch DSK in a compromising situation? The lawyers may ask such questions to hotel witnesses under oath when the time comes. It doesn't mean they believe in or plan to offer any such theory about the room being bugged. They just need the answers.

Similarly, DSK's lawyers are certain to focus some of their questions on Brian Yearwood, the Sofitel's engineering chief who functioned as the on-call hotel manager that weekend. He also appeared in the video security tape "celebration" made public by Epstein's article and by a later leak of the footage in France. Strauss-Kahn's lawyers will almost certainly want to know why Yearwood was brought to the twenty-eight floor to interview Diallo after the alleged attack since he was not a security official. Sofitel officials say Yearwood was called by a security officer, Derrick May, and asked to join the interview because Yearwood was acting hotel manager at the time. Strauss-Kahn's lawyers will want to ask their own questions, though.

Likewise, they'll want to know why Yearwood remained behind on the twenty-eighth floor after Diallo, her housekeeping supervisor, and the security officer left Suite 2806 to go to the security office, where they eventually reported the alleged attack to police. The defense lawyers' biggest question may be why Yearwood keyed the door to Suite 2806—now clearly a crime scene—and entered it again at 12:52 p.m. when the others had already left. Did he remove something? Did he touch anything? Did anything seem out of place? The defense lawyers will want to know. And they'll also want to ask Yearwood not only about his brief celebration caught on camera but also his other activities in the ninety minutes after he left the twenty-eighth floor since video cameras caught him meeting various people and making various phone calls during that time.

None of this means Yearwood did anything wrong at all. In fact, he's offered plausible explanations for all of his activities during his interviews with Sofitel officials. For instance, Yearwood told his supervisors he keyed the door one last time at 12:52 p.m. just to make sure that the Sofitel workers hadn't left anything behind and that he had not touched anything in the room. Still, if the civil case goes forward, Strauss-Kahn's lawyers are prepared to zero in on this hotel official because he was front and center during the critical first two hours.

The police detectives and prosecutors won't be spared questions, either. Why wasn't their client taken for a forensic exam sooner? Why did prosecutors raise the Tristane Banon case in France during the initial effort to keep Strauss-Kahn imprisoned without bail and then never followed up with their own investigation in France if the incident was so critical as to mention it before the first judge? Why was

Diallo allowed to see three photos of Strauss-Kahn on the Internet and TV before she made her official identification of her alleged attacker in a police lineup? Why wasn't Diallo's background, finances, and asylum claims, especially the claim about an earlier rape in Guinea, not investigated sooner and more aggressively?

Of couse, of all the witnesses, Diallo will face the biggest barrage of questions from DSK's lawyers if the civil case proceeds—everything from why she lied on her taxes, apartment application, and asylum application to the nature of her relationships with the men in her life and her finances—at least to the limit allowed by the judge.

Strauss-Kahn's defense team almost immediately hired private detectives from Guidepost Solutions, a respected investigations firm of former federal and local law enforcement experts who could find out what was in the detectives' notebooks, mine Diallo's neighborhood for embarrassing details, and locate any evidence of French/Sarkozy involvement. These private detectives spent part of the summer interviewing witnesses in the West African communities in Harlem and the Bronx, to develop a portrait of Diallo as a woman who was willing to do what it took to get to the United States and then make extra money to support herself and her daughter. Such folks who try to make money on the side are often known as "earners" in their community.

The defense gathered evidence and accounts of Diallo socializing, accepting gifts, and being courted by male friends, particularly at the restaurant where she worked before she became a housekeeper. Diallo's relationship with a now incarcerated illegal immigrant, Amara Tarawally, could be used by the defense to build the "earner" storyline. Tarawally has been convicted on drug charges and told *The Daily Beast* over the summer he befriended Diallo in New York City where he sold handbags. He described her as his "fiancée."

Diallo told me during the *Newsweek* interview that the two were *just* friends and that she received six or seven handbags from Tarawally, but insisted she did not know he and his friends were using her checking account to deposit and withdraw large sums of money, perhaps $40,000 or more. The housekeeper said she cut off her friendship with Tarawally after her lawyer told her about the transactions. Defense lawyers may try to argue Diallo accepted handbags, calling cards, phones, or other benefits in return for allowing the money to move through her accounts. They also have questions about two cash deposits into her account in December 2010 and April 2011 that they believe Diallo made herself.

Creating the backdrop that Diallo was focused on making money will allow the defense to suggest to a civil jury that Diallo's interest was in cashing in on her encounter with Strauss-Kahn, at least after the fact. In that respect, the Tarawally call from prison could become critical evidence.

Painting a financial motive for a jury, whether or not true, might allow the defense to interpret some of the physical evidence in a new light. For instance, Diallo's return to Strauss-Kahn's suite after he checked out around 12:26 p.m.—about ten minutes after the alleged attack—seems uncharacteristic for a victim. Diallo told me she went back to the suite because she wasn't even certain she wanted to report the attack, fearful she might be fired for walking in on a VIP client. She said she wanted to start to clean the room but was shaken by the sexual attack and didn't know where to start. But Taylor and Brafman might press a different question: Did Diallo go back to the crime scene to see if Strauss-Kahn had left any money behind for her, a suggestion Diallo and her lawyers steadfastly dismiss.

Nearly every statement the housekeeper has made or is purported to have made about what happened in the room will be scrutinized by Strauss-Kahn's legal team, highlighting even the slightest of inconsistencies or potential for embellishment.

For instance, a passage in the notes of a hospital worker who examined Diallo that first night raised questions for the defense about whether Diallo is a trained, theatrical liar. The hospital employee noted that Diallo was "tearful" as she retold the incident "in narrative fashion, paused while she was describing" being forced to perform oral sex. Defense lawyers wonder whether the narrative nature—the pausing and the tears—are all the work of a person with a history of rehearsing false stories. In fact, the hospital worker's description of a theatrical telling matches in many respects the way prosecutors and detectives claim Diallo told them the bogus story of the earlier rape in Guinea during her debriefing.

On the flip side, Strauss-Kahn likely will face a deposition and be summoned to testify if the civil case goes to trial. And he'll face an excruciating cross-examination from Diallo's lawyers about his own conduct with other women and his every action in Suite 2806 that weekend. That's because civil defendants can be compelled to testify, especially when the threat of prosecution no longer exists and the Fifth Amendment right to avoid self-incrimination is negated.

The lead-up to a civil trial—if a judge proceeds with the case and there is no settlement—will provide a feast to the tabloids and the media at large. But it also will help resolve some of the unsettled questions of evidence, alibis, and behavior left unanswered by District Attorney Cyrus Vance's short-lived prosecution. And for the first time, DSK will likely be compelled to tell his version of events under oath before a watching world.

Ironically, it's a tribute to Brafman and Taylor's legal acumen that Strauss-Kahn was never required to declare his defense in the court of law before the criminal case was dismissed. Their carefully executed strategy after getting Strauss-Kahn freed on bail was focused on rattling Vance's prosecutors in private, creating reasonable doubt without ever having to offer an official alibi or defense in a court filing. And they succeeded.

Brafman and Taylor sensed weaknesses in the case almost immediately, stunned by the sloppy law enforcement and prosecutorial work they saw on the first weekend of the arrest. They noticed right away that detectives had failed to question their client when they had the chance, inexplicably delayed a police lineup for twenty-four hours until after the alleged victim saw other pictures of DSK that might taint a lineup identification, and failed to bring Strauss-Kahn for a forensic body exam for a full day after his arrest.

They also sensed indecision and division within the prosecutorial ranks that first weekend when prosecutors first discussed with them the idea of bail for Strauss-Kahn on that Sunday afternoon and then backed off it, blaming superiors "on the eighth floor." And during Strauss-Kahn's first court appearance on the Monday after his arrest, the defense lawyers witnessed prosecutors so unprepared and so in a rush to seek an indictment that they provided inaccurate information to the judge, such as claiming Strauss-Kahn didn't own a home in the United States. (In fact, he and his wife owned a $4 million mansion in Washington, D.C.) The prosecutors also suggested he was in a hurry to leave the hotel to flee on a flight. (In fact, the flight had been booked days earlier and Strauss-Kahn even stopped for lunch with his daughter before heading to the airport.)

So Taylor and Brafman developed a strategy early on: stay mostly quiet in public, use the Guidepost detectives to find the facts that the prosecutors failed to obtain about the victim and her motives, identify overlooked flaws in the evidence, and then undermine the case behind the scenes, taking advantage of Brafman's long-earned access to the District Attorney's Office in Manhattan.

Once armed with a bevy of facts, Brafman and Taylor would whisper into the ears of prosecutors, who by mid-June were overtly on the fence about moving forward with the case. Over several weeks, the two lawyers in private conversations with Vance's team highlighted certain inconsistencies in Diallo's stories that detectives likely missed.

Taylor and Brafman got at least two opportunities to privately make the case to Vance's team that the charges should be dismissed. The most compelling came in July during an in-person presentation from Taylor entitled, "Reasons to Dismiss." It was designed to give prosecutors a taste of what they might face if the case went to court against the high-profile legal defense team. With precision and specificity, Taylor rattled off the holes in the evidence, the inconsistencies in Diallo's various statements about what happened in the room and afterward, and the behavior of their client in the aftermath that would suggest he was *not* acting like a criminal.

Taylor's presentation was unnerving to the prosecutors, and forced them to check several aspects of their case. Among the weaknesses and concerns Taylor cited:

- Diallo's mouth either suffered no trauma or wasn't checked fully in the hospital for trauma consistent with a violent, forced oral sex attack. This fact was ultimately noted in the dismissal motion.
- Redness detected on Diallo's vagina at the hospital was unlikely to have been caused by Strauss-Kahn's alleged grab of the hand and was more consistent with another cause such as a prior sexual event, an infection, irritation, or friction from clothing. Vance's team got its own outside expert to review the same question. That expert rendered an opinion similar to Taylor's that the redness—once thought to be key evidence that Strauss-Kahn tried to rape her—"was a very nonspecific finding that could be attributed to a host of causes other than trauma, including any type of friction, irritation or inflammation," prosecutorial records show.
- Diallo had made comments recorded by a Sexual Assault Forensic Examiner (SAFE) who interviewed her at the hospital that suggested the housekeeper had remained in the hotel suite after the alleged attack. The attacker got dressed and left

the room, and "said nothing to her during the incident," the hospital notes said, purporting to quote Diallo. In her interview with police and her account to *Newsweek*, Diallo recalled several statements Strauss-Kahn made during the alleged attack and insisted she had fled immediately after the oral sex ended. Authorities went back and interviewed the hospital examiner after the conflict in the notes. The SAFE examiner told prosecutors it was possible the notation was mistaken or conflated.

- Diallo had alleged she either was dragged or pushed down the hallway where she was attacked, yet no rug burns, bruising, or abrasions were found on her body that were consistent with this sort of a violent attack.
- Diallo's friend Blake Diallo, the Harlem coffee shop manager, was quoted in the foreign media as claiming she told him she had been making the bed when Strauss-Kahn attacked her and that he was so violent that she had suffered visible "black and blue bruises" and abrasions on her body. "The scars are noticeable on her body," Blake Diallo was quoted as telling one outlet. Taylor argued those outcry statements were inconsistent with her testimony and the forensic exam of her body, which found no such bruises, just redness to her vagina and pain to one of her shoulders. In an interview with *Newsweek*, Blake Diallo said he had been misquoted in those early reports and that the maid had simply told him the first time she called that "somebody tried to rape me" and that police and doctors at the hospital were "checking for evidence."
- Diallo may have misled detectives, prosecutors, and the grand jury when she claimed she hid in the hallway until being found by a housekeeping supervisor. She later changed her story, admitting she went into nearby Room 2820 after the alleged

attack to pick up her cleaning gear and then returned to Strauss-Kahn's suite to begin cleaning it before encountering a housekeeping supervisor in the hallway and reporting the alleged attack.

- Diallo had proven herself to be a "very good liar," Taylor told the prosecutors. He noted she had made false claims on her taxes, her subsidized housing application, and her application for asylum. She also convinced prosecutors, with a tearful recounting, that she had been gang-raped by soldiers in Guinea in what turned out to be a fictional attack contrived by an immigration adviser.
- Strauss-Kahn's own actions in the immediate aftermath of the alleged attack "don't support consciousness of guilt," Taylor argued, because he called his daughter immediately after the incident, went to lunch calmly with her, and called the hotel seeking help finding his lost cell phone. He also acknowledged to the hotel that he was at JFK International Airport waiting to fly to Paris. "A guilty man doesn't call the scene of the alleged crime and tell them where he's located, does he?" Taylor asked the prosecutors to consider.

Just a few weeks before the dismissal, Strauss-Kahn's lawyers dropped one last bombshell on the prosecutors, divulging that Thompson and Wigdor had approached them in mid-June, less than a week after Diallo admitted to prosecutors her first lies, to discuss a possible civil settlement. The two sides discussed setting up a process (including the names of potential mediators) that might lead to Strauss-Kahn making a monetary payment to Diallo to settle any civil charges. Those initial discussions were covered by a nondisclosure agreement signed by both sides, but Brafman and Taylor knew such agreements weren't enforceable in a criminal case.

By late July, the two defense lawyers and their investigators had uncovered their own evidence suggesting Diallo might have developed a financial motive, at least after the incident, and that she also associated with people with possible criminal backgrounds, such as Tarawally. And they had seen Diallo's lawyer, Thompson, quoted as saying flatly his client had had no financial motive in the case. Taylor and Brafman decided Thompson's public comments freed them from their commitment to the previous nondisclosure agreement with Diallo's lawyers. Their need to keep the civil confidentiality agreement was outweighed by their obligation as defense attorneys to alert prosecutors to additional evidence of a possible financial motive. So they divulged to Vance's office the existence of the earlier talks about a possible civil settlement that had occurred back in June. At that time, Thompson and Wigdor were only interested in setting up a process through a mediator to govern settlement talks while Brafman and Taylor were seeking an estimate for how much Diallo might be seeking in money. No matter the specifics, the revelations once again caught prosecutors off guard. And on August 5, prosecutor Joan Illuzzi belatedly sent Thompson a letter demanding he turn over any correspondence or records about the settlement discussions. Thompson saw it as an unwarranted intrusion on his attorney-client privilege, and he never complied.

Strauss-Kahn's lawyers had fanned the flames as best they could behind the scenes without talking much in public. But they weren't sure at the time how much impact their private overtures with Vance's office had made. When the final motion to dismiss was filed a month later, however, they could see the fruit of their handiwork. Many of the inconsistencies and concerns they had raised in private showed up in the prosecutors' court brief, ranging from challenges to the physical evidence to inconsistencies in the alleged victim's various accounts. And they saw evidence that Vance's office belatedly investigated questions the defense had raised. Poking holes in an accuser's credibility and prosecutors' evidence, however, was just part of Taylor and Brafman's mission. They also needed to create a timeline of their client's stay at the Sofitel from independent evidence and witness testimony and to reconstruct from their client's own statements and recollections what had happened during the entire weekend of May 14, 2011.

From that reconstruction, there were warning signs that Strauss-Kahn's insatiable appetite for sex would lead him astray nearly the second he waltzed into the Sofitel and checked into his room around 7:30 p.m. on Friday night, May 13, 2011. As is the hotel's tradition for VIP clients, a female concierge named Marie took Strauss-Kahn to his room on the twenty-eighth floor. He was predictably flirtatious as the VIP concierge showed him around the suite, with its large living room, two bathrooms, and spacious bedroom. After that concierge left, Strauss-Kahn remembered the beautiful young blonde with the French accent named Vivian who had checked him into the hotel at the registration desk. So he phoned her at the front desk less than a half hour after first arriving at the Sofitel and invited her to his room to share a bottle of wine. She demurred. But both women would later report his advances to their superiors and to prosecutors.

By 10 p.m. that night, Strauss-Kahn was out on the town, meeting with a forty-something French-born businesswoman who worked in New York and with whom he had been having a relationship. The two went to dinner and returned to the Sofitel in the wee hours of the morning on May 14. The security camera outside the hotel captures the two exiting a dark sedan together at around 1:46 a.m. Strauss-Kahn enters the hotel first, while the stunning-looking and clearly younger blonde remains outside for a few seconds. She finally enters the hotel and heads straight for the elevator, while Strauss-Kahn stops by the concierge desk before joining the woman in the elevator. Strauss-Kahn's camp acknowledges the two had a consensual relationship, one of many he has had outside his marriage over the last two decades.

The hotel cameras capture the woman exiting the elevators and heading out of the hotel just before 4 a.m. She pauses in the lobby for a second, and the cameras catch a brief glimpse of a beautiful silk scarf, which was not evident when she entered hours earlier. She's also carrying a shopping bag, perhaps containing accoutrements and gifts from her famous French lover after a night of romance.

The next morning, Strauss-Kahn ordered breakfast for room delivery, which arrived at around 10 a.m., and he spent the morning checking email and text messages, reading and making calls on his IMF BlackBerry. He was due back in Paris the next day for critical global debt talks with German chancellor Angela Merkel. The last highlight of his whirlwind stop in New York would be lunch with his daughter Camille a few blocks from the hotel.

It was one of those messages on his BlackBerry that morning, purportedly from an acquaintance working inside Sarkozy's rival political party, that alerted Strauss-Kahn that his email or phones might have been hacked. Concerned about being bugged, Strauss-Kahn phoned his wife back in France at 10:07 a.m. to ask her to arrange for a computer expert to be available when he returned home to sweep his devices for bugs or malware. With his bags packed, he then jumped in the shower around noon, preparing for his luncheon date with his daughter.

The incident with Diallo occurred between 12:06 p.m. and 12:13 p.m., after which Strauss-Kahn immediately called his daughter to indicate he might be late for lunch. He eventually left the hotel at around 12:28 p.m. Three hours later he called the hotel as he neared the airport, fearful he left his phone behind.

Strauss-Kahn's lawyers saw in that timeline significant evidence to build a defense. It is clear that Strauss-Kahn had come to the Sofitel for a weekend of leisurely sex and flirtation, which might lead him to accept one last sexual favor from a housekeeper before he left town to return to work. Strauss-Kahn said as much himself in an interview with his biographer, Michael Taubman, that was published as part of a book in France released over the 2011 holidays entitled *DSK Affairs: The Counter-Investigation.* "The flesh is weak. Dominique Strauss-Kahn saw a proposition. The situation amuses him. Rarely in his life has he refused the possibility of a moment of pleasure. He does not resist the temptation of fellatio," Taubman wrote.

The calls to his daughter immediately after the incident and then later to the hotel to find his missing cell phone don't seem to the defense lawyers to be acts of a man with a guilty conscience, but rather evidence of the mind-set of a man completely comfortable with having had casual oral sex with a housekeeper whom he had known for less than a minute. The lawyers also have an explanation for why Strauss-Kahn may have moved his encounter with Diallo from the bedroom, where it purportedly started, to a narrow hallway near the back bathroom: he was fearful he would be seen through the open curtains of the bedroom window. The unknown question is how jurors in a civil lawsuit in Diallo's own backyard of the Bronx will interpret the same evidence if the case ever reaches trial.

Strauss-Kahn's interviews with the French TV anchorwoman and Taubman—the only public descriptions he has given about what happened in Sofitel Suite 2806 on May 14, 2011—clearly create a defense which suggests that DSK believes the incident was nonviolent and consensual and that Diallo did not seem "the least terrified" by her encounter. In fact, he claims, she gave him a suggestive look that he interpreted as an invitation for sex.

But there is one part in the Taubman recounting that could come back to haunt DSK and his lawyers if the Diallo lawsuit proceeds to trial. In one passage, Strauss-Kahn appears to admit that Diallo tried to flee the room.

> *Exiting the bathroom in Adam's clothes, the managing director of the IMF finds himself face to face with Nafissatou Diallo whom he sees for the first time. The young Guinean appears*

surprised, but not at all terrified. DSK is not prudish. He does not take umbrage at the incongruous presence of the housekeeper in a presidential suite that is still occupied. Nafissatou Diallo, crossing the room, heads toward the exit. But she hardly hurries.

If an accurate account of what DSK said, it would appear to corroborate what Diallo told prosecutors and me: that she tried to leave the room before Strauss-Kahn closed the door. Such an admission by a powerful world leader could very well be interpreted by a jury as evidence that he forced the poor, immigrant housekeeper to submit to a sexual encounter.

For Taylor, who had stuck by DSK's side through the earlier sex scandal at the IMF involving a female subordinate, the weekend romp at the Sofitel had a familiar ring to it. Taylor had long ago heard the legends about DSK's sex soirees, his penchant for swinging, and his notorious womanizing around the globe. And while Taylor could quickly devise a potent, credible defense to the criminal charges in New York, many inside Strauss-Kahn's inner circle also fully appreciated that his "sexual liberation" had reached a plateau of reckless abandon and excess, even by permissive French standards. The incident in Suite 2806 was almost certain to tank Strauss-Kahn's political aspirations for president, and open the door for old allegations to be aired in a new, hypersensitive media environment.

Strauss-Kahn admitted as much himself in his interview with Taubman. "Nothing would have happened if I hadn't had those consensual but stupid relations with Nafissatou Diallo. That day, I opened the door to all the other affairs," he is quoted as saying.

In the best-case scenario, Taylor knew that DSK's defense in the court of public opinion was that he had engaged in casual consensual sex with an immigrant housekeeper who had just a few years earlier escaped poverty and sexual oppression in Guinea. And Strauss-Kahn was willing to accept a quickie, seven-minute sexual favor from a complete stranger just a few months from launching his campaign, raising inevitable questions about whether his drive for instant sexual gratification was more powerful than his sense of duty to lead a nation with a permanent seat on the United Nations Security Council.

After nearly a week in Rikers Island, two months of house arrest in New York, and a humiliating return to a France disgusted at the squandering of his political prowess, it seemed that Strauss-Kahn himself also appreciated at least the political consequences of his conduct on May 14. "I missed my rendezvous with the French people," he conceded in his first TV interview.

In that same interview, Strauss-Kahn also poked fun at the long-running rumors and controversy his sexual encounters had produced, insisting he had always behaved with "lightness" around women. That comment did not sit well in France, where rumors of his overseas liaisons, his nightclub swinging, and love-'em-and-leave-'em affairs had festered for decades.

And it provided further motivation for Diallo's lawyers to cull through numerous tips they had received about alleged sexual conquests by Strauss-Kahn—both forced and consensual—from women around the world that ranged from airline attendants to Brazilian grandmothers. Attorneys Thompson and Wigdor tried to interview or corroborate a half dozen of the accounts in preparation for the lawsuit, hoping to establish a pattern of boorish behavior showing that Strauss-Kahn preys on vulnerable young women in their workplace and in some cases proceeded with sexual advances over the objections of the women. In other words, he takes what he wants and interprets a woman's "no" to mean a sexually inviting "yes."

At least three credible sexual or romantic encounters have surfaced in full public view since Diallo first aired her allegations and

DSK was arrested. They range from a young student of Strauss-Kahn's in the 1990s to a subordinate female employee at the IMF, and a journalist who interviewed him. All purportedly occurred since Strauss-Kahn married his current wife, Anne Sinclair, in the early 1990s.

Early in summer 2011, Diallo's lawyer Thompson received information from France that Strauss-Kahn had had an affair in 1997 with a twenty-three-year-old student named Marie-Victorine M'Bissa in Sarcelles, France, where Strauss-Kahn taught a class and served as mayor. Thompson's investigators in France located the woman's father, a Congolese immigrant, who told them a tale of how his daughter attempted suicide when DSK broke off the affair.

"My daughter attempted suicide. Before I found her dying, I found a note: 'Call the number.' It was that of Mr. Strauss-Kahn. I called the rescue service . . . who took her to the hospital in Gonesse where she was resuscitated," André M'Bissa wrote in a signed affidavit he gave Thompson's investigators. "The first deputy [mayor] François Pupponi was already there." The father had even kept, all these years later, a handwritten letter, which began "Dear Papa," that his daughter wrote the day she purportedly attempted to kill herself. The anguish of losing a relationship with an older man was palpable in the letter.

"When you read this letter, I will be gone. I will finally know peace of mind," the young woman purportedly penned in a rough English translation of the note that the father gave Thompson's investigators. "I have to tell you that you are not responsible for my departure. As a father I believe that you have done what you could to protect me.

> *I am tired. I am worn out pretending to be happy when inside of me, I feel like a dead bird. I am empty. I don't feel any more pain or sadness. I am cold, that's all. I had a great life and I don't regret anything. Only, today I don't have a taste for anything, so I have decided to leave. I only ask that you do me a*

last favor. I want you to say to Dominique that he made me very happy and that I wish him to be happy, that life is generous with him.

And I ask you to tell him that it's because I think that he hates me, and that is unbearable for me. I don't know what happened and for what reason. Tell him that if I wounded him . . . I never wanted to hurt him—how could I have?

I would have accepted everything of him, the secrecy, the waiting, everything. Yes, I accepted it and if it were to do over, I would begin it again. Not because he is a well known politician. But, quite simply, he is the only man who has succeeded in changing my life.

The letter, if real, also offered an insight into DSK's modus operandi in seducing the young student the first time.

Do you know what he said to me that day? That from the time he arrived and that he had seen me, he had known that he could not let me leave without being sure he would see me again. A single look had been enough: fate.

The idea that Strauss-Kahn could deduce from a single look from a woman that she wanted to have a relationship with him became a recurring theme among his accusers, and perhaps provides evidence of a pattern of conduct. For instance, Taubman wrote in his book that Strauss-Kahn confided to him that Nafi Diallo "looks him straight in the eye, looks ostentatiously at his genitals" and the only conclusion that Strauss-Kahn can draw is that the "flesh is weak" and there is a "proposition" for sex. (Diallo, of course, strongly disputes his account.)

Whatever the similarities in the approach, M'Bissa's purported letter also makes clear she was a willing participant, and that it is the ending of the relationship that thrust her into a despair so great that she was willing to consider taking her life.

"All that I can tell you is that his voice, when he looks at me, makes me beautiful and happy to be alive. Hearing his voice gave me the desire to live, bewitched me. I didn't need to see him; I hear his voice and I was happy for whole weeks at a time. That voice changed my life. Today when I hear it on the TV or the radio, I have tears in my eyes and I cannot manage," the purported letter states.

André M'Bissa gave Thompson's team in France his daughter's phone numbers in the United States, where she now lived. And Thompson interviewed the woman, pressing for details about how Strauss-Kahn had seduced her or whether he was rough or violent during their encounters. Several news outlets in the United States and Europe also pursued the young woman, spurred by rumors back in France from DSK's political enemies.

Eventually, Marie-Victorine M'Bissa went public with her story, her photo gracing the cover of the Swiss magazine *L'illustré* in late July. In that article, the woman agreed only to be named Marie-Victorine M. But eventually, in follow-up TV interviews, she used her full name. In the course of the interviews, M'Bissa offers a second portrait that could prove useful to Diallo in the civil case: Strauss-Kahn is a rough and physical lover, consistent with the housekeeper's account of being shoved down the hall and pinned against the wall.

"When I read the first articles in the American press containing, for example, the detail that he was supposed to have taken his presumed victim from behind, that encouraged me to believe this woman," M'Bissa told the Swiss magazine, describing Strauss-Kahn as a man with a "big sexual appetite" who perhaps "went a little too far" with Diallo.

"Frankly, I think that there was a relation between the two, a forced relation. I don't know if it was about a rape. This is a man who is physical, so it's altogether possible that he grabbed this woman in a brusque or brutal manner," she offered.

The M'Bissa story, a footnote in the criminal case, could surface prominently in the civil case, both in building a modus operandi for Strauss-Kahn's sexual conquests and raising questions about witness intimidation. Late in the summer, André M'Bissa alleged that political associates who support Strauss-Kahn came to him after his daughter went public and asked him to help silence the woman. The lawyers Thompson hired to help him investigate in France have sought an investigation into possible witness intimidation in that country.

M'Bissa's account, especially about Strauss-Kahn's rough, physical nature, has some similarities to the most infamous of his disputed sexual encounters—the one in 2003 with the young journalist Tristane Banon.

Banon is the daughter of a French socialite and politician named Anne Mansouret, who alleges she, too, was an earlier lover of Strauss-Kahn. Mansouret disclosed after DSK's arrest in America that she herself had engaged in "brutal" but consensual sex with the French leader.

Banon alleges that Strauss-Kahn attempted to rape her when she went to a Left Bank flat in Paris to interview him in February 2003 for a book she hoped to write. Then just twenty-three, Banon alleges Strauss-Kahn acted like a "rutting chimpanzee" as he grabbed her breasts, they fell to the floor, and he tried to open her jeans and bra. Banon alleges she managed to fight off Strauss-Kahn and flee the apartment. But she chose not to file charges at the time. Four years later, she first went public with her allegations in an unusual French TV appearance in which she didn't use her name or DSK's but described the incident.

It wasn't until after Diallo's case emerged in 2011 in New York that Banon decided to formally file a criminal complaint against Strauss-Kahn in France, a move that forced a formal judicial investigation. At first, Strauss-Kahn dismissed Banon's allegations as "imaginary" and filed a libel lawsuit against her. But Banon remained undeterred, and her lawyer even flew to New York in July 2011 to offer to assist prosecutors in the Diallo case, an offer that Vance's team did not pursue aggressively.

Banon and Strauss-Kahn met for the first time in eight years in September 2011 when they both appeared at the same office to be interviewed by French authorities separately. In his formal police interview, Strauss-Kahn reversed course and acknowledged he tried to forcibly kiss Banon and grab her. But he insisted he let her go as soon as she objected.

"I tried to take her in my arms. I tried to kiss her on the mouth. She pushed me away firmly. She said to me, in essence, 'What's wrong with you?' I right away released my grip. She collected her things and left the apartment furious," Strauss-Kahn said, according to an excerpt of his police testimony released by his French lawyers.

A month later, French authorities concluded the investigation with an announcement that both Banon and Strauss-Kahn claimed was in their favor. The authorities concluded there was not enough evidence to sustain a charge of attempted rape, though the evidence supported "facts that can be qualified as sexual assault." The problem, French authorities concluded, was that the statute of limitations for a sexual assault that had occurred in 2003 would have expired in 2006, long before Banon came forward. So the case was ended. Strauss-Kahn declared he had been exonerated; Banon crowed that authorities had believed her story and would have pursued charges if the statute of limitations hadn't expired. And both seemed to move on. Banon doesn't intend to sue DSK to prolong the controversy.

The impact to Strauss-Kahn's reputation, however, was severe.

Newspapers seemed to focus on the fact that he admitted grabbing the young woman and forcing an unwanted kiss. And after his TV interview and the resolution of the Banon case, public polls showed the toll. Only 4 percent of those surveyed in France in a poll after his September TV interview felt he had helped his image, while 56 percent were unchanged in their opinion and 31 percent believed his reputation had worsened. Likewise, a poll in *Elle* magazine found that only 17 percent of French women believed Strauss-Kahn was innocent. Those aren't the numbers of a French politician on the rise, and they demonstrated that Strauss-Kahn has a long way to go before he can claim rehabilitation in the political sense.

The third sexual escapade to tarnish Strauss-Kahn's reputation occurred in 2008 in Washington, D.C. That's when the IMF was forced to open a formal investigation into his affair with Hungarian economist Piroska Nagy, a married subordinate at the international finance agency. According to the people familiar with the investigation and the final report of the internal probe, Strauss-Kahn had just started his job in fall 2007 as the IMF's managing director when he met Nagy at a presentation by division heads. Blond, bespectacled, and elegant at fifty years old, Nagy clearly caught Strauss-Kahn's fancy, and soon he began to romance her with overtures via his secretary and increasingly sexually suggestive emails. She apparently reciprocated.

Both players "acknowlege . . . a two-week-long exchange of consensual and very personal messages occurred," the internal report concluded. "Both parties initiated those communications." By that time, Strauss-Kahn was married to Sinclair for about seventeen years, and his expertise in global economics was center stage in the financial crisis and his stock rising toward a possible run at the French presidency.

The prospects of future political promise, however, did not seem to inhibit Strauss-Kahn's sexual appetite. During a January 2008 trip to Davos, Nagy and Strauss-Kahn engaged in a "consensual physical relationship of a short duration," the internal probe found.

Nagy broke it off after her husband discovered the affair, the report says. When DSK learned that the husband had found out, he hired Taylor as a personal lawyer in the matter and a public relations firm to seek advice. But he left officials inside the IMF blind to the threat that the affair soon could be exposed and cause adverse publicity for the agency, according to the internal findings. In short, Strauss-Kahn worried only about his own reputation, not the agency's, the report concluded.

In spring 2008, Nagy took advantage of a severance package and left the IMF and the awkwardness of her now strained relationship with Strauss-Kahn. She told investigators she left voluntarily, but only after her lawyer had contacted Strauss-Kahn's lawyer and learned that the IMF boss "would feel more comfortable if she left," the report found. She took a job instead with the European Bank for Reconstruction and Development.

Strauss-Kahn admitted during the internal investigation that "he made both a personal mistake and business mistake" in pursuing the subordinate. His apology in 2008 would sound eerily similar to the one he would give three years later in France in the aftermath of the Diallo incident at the Sofitel.

For the IMF, the incident became a sort of Clarence Thomas–Anita Hill moment—a clarion call to examine anew what constituted sexual harassment in the workplace. The investigation found that Strauss-Kahn played no role in Nagy's departure or in arranging the severance package, and that he did not abuse the power of his position or violate the IMF's code of conduct.

But in a moment of reflection, the final report opined whether that code should have been toughened to hold DSK to "a higher standard of conduct than staff, given the prominence and reputational consequences of his activities."

Nagy herself also weighed in with a private letter to the IMF in which she suggested there was an element of coercion to her affair. "I was damned if I did and damned if I didn't," she wrote in a letter to the investigators that was uncovered by *The New York Times.* Nagy also described Strauss-Kahn in the letter as "a man with a problem that may make him ill-equipped to lead an institution where women work under his command."

The details of the three separate sexual encounters beyond Diallo's allegation are harbingers of the challenges Strauss-Kahn's lawyer will face if forced to defend him in the civil lawsuit. It's unclear yet how much about the previous affairs or accusations will be admissible. But already, a portrait has been painted in the court of public opinion that leaves an unfavorable impression of the potential civil defendant, even if you rely solely on his own words. He is a married man willing to seek outside sexual conquests with little discretion for the intended targets: a young Congolese immigrant student, a young woman his daughter's age, the daughter of a former lover, a subordinate at work, and an immigrant hotel housekeeper from Guinea.

And contrary to his insistence that all of his relationships with woman involve "lightness," there's consistent evidence suggesting coercion and physical aggression in the story lines of the women who preceded Diallo.

Whether alleging consensual or forced encounters, the women have consistently raised issues of physical force, brutality, and aggression that bear some similarities to Diallo's own account. Vance's prosecutors never fully developed that body of evidence as a potential factor in deciding to drop the charges. But Diallo's lawyer may get the chance to make the case in civil court that Strauss-Kahn was a serial sexual Lothario whose political and economic power and choice of subordinate women may have negated the consent of his targets of lust.

ELEVEN

Lessons for Tomorrow's Lawyers

THE THEATER-STYLE, FLUORESCENT-LIT classroom at Harvard University's law school was virtually silent on a crisp fall afternoon in Boston. And why not? It's not every day that law students get the chance to see one of America's most famous defense lawyers assume the role of prosecutor. There, in the pit of the classroom, Alan Dershowitz was in effect holding court as one of Manhattan district attorney Cyrus Vance's bulldogs, making the prosecution's closing arguments to jurors in the sexual assault trial against Dominique Strauss-Kahn that never was. Dershowitz was convinced he could secure a guilty conviction, even with the victim's credibility problems. And he was intent on teaching his students a lesson on how a courageous prosecutor could divert a jury from the weaknesses of his star witness to focus on the evidence of a sexual attack and the preposterous defense of an elitist Frenchman.

It was a tall assignment, and a role quite frankly that Dershowitz himself might never have imagined assuming. After all, the youngest legal scholar ever to be named a Harvard law professor, Dershowitz was known to take the side of high-profile defendants such as televangelist Jim Bakker, football star O. J. Simpson, boxer Mike Tyson, and publishing heiress Patty Hearst. And his appellate work that overturned Claus von Bulow's conviction for murdering his wife was the stuff of legal legend, reserved for books and movies.

So, true to character, Dershowitz had initially sided with Strauss-Kahn's defense when Vance's prosecutors filed documents in court June 30 identifying their concerns with housekeeper Nafissatou Diallo's credibility.

"Prosecutors of sex cases need to do some major housecleaning—not only in District Attorney Cyrus Vance's office in Manhattan but also in prosecutors' offices all across the country," Dershowitz wrote in a widely quoted op-ed on *The Daily Beast* on July 1, the day after prosecutors stunned the world with their bombshell court filing. Dershowitz concluded in his column that the New York prosecution team had "messed up in speaking to the press, publicly vouching for the truth of the woman's account and for her character" when inevitable questions about her motives and skeletons in her closet were certain to surface.

"I believe there's been a Nancy Grace aspect to this case," he added, referring to the TV legal commentator known for a "they're-all-guilty-as-hell" attitude. "The prosecution presented its case in public as if there were no doubt about the alleged victim's credibility or the complete guilt of the alleged offender."

Dershowitz held that view for much of July. Then, while on vacation in Martha's Vineyard, he took a call from a friend, the Sofitel lawyer Lanny Davis. And he began to rethink the case. Davis had chafed at Dershowitz's column for some time. But fresh from interviewing Diallo himself in late July for the first time, the always impassioned Washington lawyer felt compelled to reach out to Dershowitz and try to change his mind. Over the years, the two had sat alongside each other as fellow legal commentators on CNN and elsewhere. They respected each other, enough to even challenge in private each other's publicly held views on cases from time to time. Davis was convinced after lobbing hard questions at Diallo during a two-hour interview on July 18 that the housekeeper was mostly telling the truth about what happened in Strauss-Kahn's hotel suite back in May. And after carefully reviewing the evidence from the hotel—especially the time stamps on the hotel security logs and the outcry witness testimony of Diallo's hotel colleagues—he was certain prosecutors were mistaken in some of their claims that Diallo had changed her story. He saw problems with the investigative work and understood the communication gaps that a shy Guinean immigrant might face when confronted by New York's grittiest prosecutors in the pressure cooker of a court case with international consequences. "Alan, you have to look at the timeline and what the outcry witnesses told us," Davis implored on the phone, citing some of the work *Newsweek* and *The Daily Beast* had published earlier in the summer about the substantial, nonpublic evidence in the case.

"Many rape victims have credibility issues. But what does it say to future rape victims if a case with *this* much physical evidence and credible outcry witnesses gets dropped because the victim lied about how she got in the country and other personal issues? Please take another look," Davis pleaded.

Dershowitz obliged. And soon, he had reversed his thinking: the decision on whether Strauss-Kahn was guilty or innocent shouldn't rest with prosecutors, but with a jury.

Soon after, Dershowitz called me up at *Newsweek* to describe his change of heart. He had read *Newsweek*'s and *The Daily Beast*'s stories on the evidence and timeline in the case, and he now believed it would be a rush to judgment for prosecutors to throw out the case. He was willing to go on the record saying so. (He did an interview with me in early August.)

And he wanted to do one better. For weeks he had been looking for a fresh subject for his fall legal ethics class at Harvard. He had already assigned students to read the book on the mistakes made by the prosecutors who charged Duke University lacrosse team players with rape in a case that ultimately was withdrawn. But the Strauss-Kahn case had something different, something more compelling to challenge the minds of America's next generation of lawyers: a decision by the prosecutors not to prosecute.

"The decision not to prosecute is often a less visible decision and less focused on by the media," Dershowitz explained to me, calling the court filing written by Vance's prosecution team that dismissed the charges against Strauss-Kahn the "perfect teaching vehicle" for showing his students the enormous forces inside and outside the courtroom that can buffet a prosecutor in the twenty-first century. Now he had a theme for the fall semester: how would you, America's future lawyers, handle the DSK prosecution? It was timely. It was sensational. It posed lots of ethical questions, from wrestling with a victim's credibility issues to allowing leaks and media attention to shape the case. And it was the perfect twenty-first-century case for soon-to-be-lawyers to wrestle with the questions of balancing the court of public opinion's voracious appetite for instant answers with the court of law's more methodical pursuit of justice.

"This case provided very, very important lessons for students on how prosecutors make decisions, on how they are influenced by the media, and how they are influenced by class and race and ethnicity," Dershowitz explained to me. "All of the big issues of ethics come into play in a case where a very prominent defendant is accused by a worker from another country." Dershowitz readied the fall curriculum. The class had some students who were volunteering at immigration clinics, and they were already sympathetic to the plight of immigrants and familiar with the lies and embellishments someone like Diallo might use to gain entry into the United States. The majority of students also were generally distrustful of the tactics prosecutors use to prepare witnesses and to present evidence to win over jurors, so the students seemed to admire Vance's team and its decision to disclose problems with its victim. And, finally, the students held a general disdain for elitism in the judicial system and the perception that the wealthy and the powerful have better odds of winning. The combination of values made for a perfectly turbulent debate, the type Dershowitz relishes. He watched as his students' opinions swung wildly from one extreme to the other over the course of several weeks as they reviewed different documents and heard from different players.

When the fall semester started, the class was evenly divided on whether prosecutors should have tried Strauss-Kahn. After reading the *Newsweek* articles, many of the students switched their opinions and believed Vance erred and that he should have proceeded with the criminal charges. After reading the prosecutors' brief laying out the concerns with Diallo's credibility, several students swung back to the notion that dismissing the case was the right decision. It was exactly the legal and emotional seesaw that Dershowitz wanted his students to ride. "It was a perfect way to confuse them and make clear the world is a complicated case in which single-minded ideologies don't answer hard questions," he told me later.

As he often does, Dershowitz arranged for a special guest appearance in his classroom. Kenneth Thompson, the housekeeper's outspoken lawyer, spent one afternoon in October with the law students explaining his reasons for taking the steps he did. Thompson was candid. He had made a mistake by trusting the prosecutors and going to the Lake George judicial conference and leaving Diallo to be interviewed alone. But the housekeeper had done most of her previous interviews without a lawyer present and "I never thought they would turn on her because I trusted them to do the right thing," Thompson explained. He was adamant that prosecutors had let his client down and that there was plenty of evidence to convict.

To back up his argument, Thompson related to the students his own tale from fourteen years earlier when, as a young federal prosecutor, he was forced to deal with similar questions about the veracity of a high-profile sexual assault victim named Abner Louima.

Louima was a Haitian immigrant who alleged in 1997 that NYPD officers sodomized him with a bathroom plunger while he was in custody, a case that fanned racial tensions across New York City during Rudolph Giuliani's tenure as mayor.

While riding in the back of a detective's car with Louima one evening, Thompson related, he leaned over and asked the victim about his most sensational claim: that the police officers who attacked him declared it was "Giuliani time," an incendiary allusion to the mayor's new law and order program.

"Tell me Ab, did the cops really say it was 'Giuliani time'?" Thompson asked.

"No, my friends told me to say that so that people would believe what happened to me," Louima confided in Thompson's recounting of the conversation.

Thompson was forced to disclose the stunning lie, but he and the rest of the prosecution team managed to take the case to trial and win with a tarnished victim—a story he used repeatedly behind the scenes to pressure prosecutors in the DSK case to stand by Diallo despite her credibility problems.

Thompson's point, which lingered with the class, was emphatic: it is still possible to secure a conviction in a sexual assault case even when the victim has lied, as long as the forensic evidence and other testimony validate the allegations. The students were riveted by the opportunity to hear an insider's take, and they peppered Thompson with pointed questions.

It's never a good idea to file a lawsuit before a criminal case is over, so why did you violate that rule? You knew asking a court to remove Vance from the case in the summer would alienate the prosecutors, so why did you do it? The harsh comments outside the courthouse on July 1 only seemed to antagonize the prosecutors. Do you think they really helped your client's case?

Lawyers usually don't let their clients create multiple accounts of their story so why did you let Diallo do the *Newsweek* and ABC interviews?

Thompson answered each and every question.

"I never, ever thought for a second that the prosecutors would turn on her and try to make her the defendant," Thompson explained. "She was the victim but they stopped treating her that way. It was unreal, and it was unfair."

The courthouse press gaggle? The early lawsuit? The request to remove Vance from the case? The media interviews? Thompson offered an explanation that opened the students' eyes: he had concluded much earlier than was publicly known that Vance's prosecutors weren't going to proceed with the criminal case. As soon as Assistant District Attorney Joan Illuzzi told him on June 9 that no one with "half a brain" would put Diallo on the witness stand, Thompson realized the case was essentially over. The prosecutors' rushed effort to run to court and disclose problems with her prior statements to prosecutors and detectives—some of which were still in dispute or not yet fully investigated—only confirmed Thompson's and his partner, Douglas Wigdor's, fears that prosecutors were looking for a way out. And when the erroneous leak was given to *The New York Times* about the prison phone call—a leak that painted Diallo as a gold digger—Thompson saw the beginnings of a political campaign by the prosecutors to prepare the public for dismissing the charges.

Faced with those odds, Thompson consciously chose to defend his client's reputation at all costs, seeing it as the only way to preserve his client's legal interests, he told the students. His hope was to counter the public perception of his client as a gold-digging liar, refocus the public on the substantial evidence that proved a sexual attack, and create enough public pressure from the hotel workers' union, victims' advocates, the immigrant community, and other key voting blocs to sway Vance's political instincts.

If nothing else, the public relations onslaught would at least help correct the public's perceptions for the civil case. Thompson had decided that suing Strauss-Kahn was Diallo's best chance for justice, and that he would bring that case in the Bronx, where the large West African immigrant population and blue-collar mind-set would be more sympathetic to Diallo, less trustful of any decision made in Manhattan, and more disdainful of a sixty-two-year-old Frenchman who believed housekeepers were willing to throw themselves at him for sex.

When prosecutors began leaking stories in mid-July that they were still investigating the case and hadn't made a decision—a leak Thompson believed was contrived to create the perception that Vance was being fair to the end—the housekeeper's attorney decided to call Vance's bluff. Thompson's team arranged for the French lawyer representing journalist Tristane Banon to come to the United States and offer her cooperation. Banon had alleged Strauss-Kahn tried to sexually assault her, and most importantly for Thompson, there were similarities between her account of Strauss-Kahn's behavior and that described by Diallo.

Though Vance's prosecutors had cited Banon's allegations early on in their effort to keep Strauss-Kahn from making bail, they had never followed up and investigated her claims and whether they provided a basis for alleging Strauss-Kahn had a modus operandi for preying on vulnerable young women in their work environment. So Thompson alerted reporters to stand outside Vance's office the day he brought Banon's lawyer to New York. The newspapers and TV stations had a field day—both in the United States and in France. And Vance's office was forced to state publicly it would belatedly look at Banon's allegations. Thompson didn't hold much faith that would happen. But he was at least glad to expose how little investigative work Vance's team had really done and how ill-prepared in his mind it was for deciding the fate of the criminal case. Even the timing for Diallo's lawsuit against Strauss-Kahn—dismissed as a stunt because it was filed just a few days before the criminal charges were dismissed—was carefully planned to protect Diallo's legal interests. Thompson said he and Wigdor were concerned that Strauss-Kahn would flee the United States as soon as the criminal charges were dropped. And then it would be difficult, if not impossible, to serve him in France with the lawsuit papers. So they filed early, less worried about the public perception and more concerned about ensuring legal service of the suit.

Thompson's candid session with the students came off something like an episode of Bravo TV's popular and long-running show *Actors Studio*, unmasking the unexpected personal tale of an actor everybody thought they knew. The only difference was that Alan Dershowitz played the role of facilitator, not James Lipton.

Many of the students may have entered class that day thinking Thompson's tactics in the final days of the criminal case seemed like the handiwork of a lawyer who let his emotions overtake his client's interests. But they left satisfied that there was an alternate story: Thompson had executed a carefully devised plan—albeit a desperate Hail Mary plan—to try to repair his client's tarnished reputation in the court of public opinion, save the criminal case if possible, and preserve her best chance for getting justice with a civil lawsuit.

"Thompson was up against it quite clearly, and he knew the odds were heavily stacked against him," Dershowitz explained to me afterward. "The students understood what he did had to be viewed in the context of taking desperate measures to save what at that time seemed like an unsalvageable case. The decision [to dismiss] had already been made at the highest levels. And the students recognized that Ken was trying to change minds, at least trying to salvage a civil lawsuit afterwards."

More importantly, Dershowitz hoped, the students had learned that the practice of law isn't always a clear, simple proposition of what you see is what you get. And some old adages in the profession are worth challenging, he would argue.

"When it comes to issues of criminal law, there are no rules of tactics," he told the students.

"Never put your client on the stand? Always put your client before the jury? It depends. Likewise, never ask a question you don't know the answer to? That's ridiculous. Your client is about to be convicted, and there is no chance of winning except if you get the right answer? Then you take your 30 percent or 40 percent chance, and you ask the question."

Well into the semester now, Dershowitz felt confident he had challenged his students to think differently. Whatever assumptions they started with had clearly been altered. But the gargantuan legal lesson still lay ahead: proving that Strauss-Kahn could be convicted even if jurors doubted the housekeeper's credibility. To make the point, Dershowitz would assume the role of prosecutor himself.

While Thompson's words were still ringing in his students' ears, Dershowitz arranged to give the closing arguments at Strauss-Kahn's trial. Before he started, though, he needed to set a few predicates for his students, now acting as the jurors. First, Thompson had tried zealously to bolster Diallo's credibility as the accuser. Dershowitz told his students he would do no such thing at the trial. In fact, he would tell the jury they had every right to doubt the accuser. Secondly, Dershowitz would seek to get entered into evidence a picture of Strauss-Kahn's naked body, possibly from the police forensic exam after his arrest. If that failed, Dershowitz would have to help jurors picture in their imagination a naked sixty-two-year-old DSK—overweight and slightly hunched, his chest sunken and his skin sagging from the natural progression of age. That image, Dershowitz told the students, would have to be emblazoned in the consciousness of the jury during the trial so that it could be summoned during closing arguments. Finally, the various accounts DSK's supporters and lawyers gave—publicly in court and anonymously in the media—need to be presented during the trial to show Strauss-Kahn had played a game of "multiple-choice defense."

With those ground rules established, Dershowitz took center stage in the theaterlike classroom and held court.

"Ladies and gentlemen of the jury," he started, "we have enough evidence to convict this man beyond a reasonable doubt even if you don't believe the accuser. In fact, we are prepared to concede that based on statements she's made in other contexts, you would be within your right to have some suspicions about her credibility."

The classroom was silent, with students hanging on every word.

"What we are asking you to do is to look at all the facts in the case and decide based on all the facts whether she is, in fact, telling the truth about this one instance, mainly that she was sexually assaulted in that hotel room," Dershowitz bellowed in his usual impassioned courtroom voice. "In coming to that conclusion, we ask that you not only look at her account but at what the alternative accounts might be.

"Ladies and gentleman, you have seen the photograph of Dominique Strauss-Kahn naked. Now I just want you to imagine for a second him walking out of the shower, stark naked, and this young woman who you see before you, an attractive young woman, looks at him."

Finally, there are a few giggles from the jurors' box. Then another hush.

"Now the theory of the defense is that she looked at him and could not resist her lustful temptations to have seven minutes of oral sex with this man. She simply couldn't control herself," he continued, a touch of sarcasm in his voice.

"She didn't do it for pay because if she did, you would have heard in the media or this courtroom the theory that this was a financial transaction. She didn't do it because she was forced to, if you believed the defense. She did it because she wanted to. And why would she want to? The only reason she would want to, according to the defense, is that she was so lustfully driven by this beautiful sixty-two-year-old, white-haired, overweight man's presence that she couldn't resist his chops."

Dershowitz elicited a healthy dose of laughter with that last line, a sign that the student jurors were beginning to buy into the absurdity of DSK's defense. Now, the legal scholar wanted to remind them of the forensic evidence pointing to a sexual encounter that was forced, unplanned, and uncomfortable from the victim's point of view.

"She must have been really enticed by this man's beauty because she was willing to have this sexual encounter in just seven minutes, with her maid's uniform still on. Remember that's where we found his DNA, on her uniform top. And it doesn't appear she arrived planning on such an encounter, either. There's no nightie or sexy lingerie. In fact, she wore two pantyhose that day, hardly the attire of a woman looking for casual sex in a hotel room.

"And so we don't forget, let me remind you also where this all happened. He's rented a $3,000-a-night suite, one worthy of a honeymoon. It's got a big bed and a glorious living room. But that's not where this all went down. In fact, this sexual encounter seems to occur in the most inglorious of places. She was prostrate on the floor, her back pressed to a wall in a narrow hallway near a bathroom, right where we found that DNA. And when this encounter ends, how does the woman the defense says couldn't control her sexual desires show her appreciation? By spitting his semen on the floor and running out of the room."

The giggles and laughter are now yielding to a slow-boiling anger.

"Now ladies and gentleman of the jury, if you believe that story you should acquit. But if you don't believe that—if you say to yourself that there is no plausible basis for that account—then you have to seriously consider the prosecution's account: mainly that she was forced to submit to his sexual advances.

"When you then look at that and put that in the context of the timeline that morning, the semen stains on her dress, his DNA on her crotch, the sickened, disgusted way she acted in the immediate aftermath when she encountered the outcry witnesses, I'm confident you will conclude beyond a reasonable doubt that he sexually assaulted her.

"And you can do so whether or not you believe she is a woman who is generally credible in the other aspects of her life, whether or not this is a woman who has previously lied about other important matters in her life. Yes, she lied to get into the country. But so have many other immigrants seeking a better life. And yes, she told the prosecutors a bogus story about an earlier rape in her homeland because that is what her immigration adviser instructed her to memorize. We'll concede that," Dershowitz said.

"But let's not forget what tales our defendant and his surrogates have tried to get us believe—even before his current account at this trial. At first, they said it couldn't have happened because he was out at lunch with his daughter. But that got thrown out as soon as we found his DNA mixed with her saliva in the room and on her dress. Then there were the various theories of a conspiracy, the old honey trap scenario. Maybe it was his rival for the French presidency. Or the guy staying next door to him in Room 2820. Or the French intelligence agents whom he believed bugged and then took his IMF cell phone.

"Nope, never mind. Today, the man the world knows as DSK, a globe-trotting economist and potential heir to the French presidency, wants you to believe it was just a maid who couldn't control her sexual urges and just threw herself at an aging, overweight man.

"Now back in law school we had a name for this. We called it the 'multiple-choice defense.' And he's been playing it. You don't like this defense? Don't worry, I got another one for you. You know how it goes. I didn't borrow the cup. But if I borrowed the cup, it was broken. And if I broke it, it was returned.

"The good news is such games are transparent. And I know you can see right through it. We're asking you to look at the totality of the evidence and the circumstances in this case and to return a just verdict that reflects the truth of what happened in Suite 2806 on May 14, 2011. And I believe if you do, you will vote to convict this man of sexual assault."

Dershowitz had offered the argument that Vance's prosecutors acknowledged they couldn't, or were unwilling to, devise in weeks of deliberations after they learned of their alleged victim's flaws. No one can be certain how a jury would rule. But Dershowitz had shown that a credible case—one meeting the burden to overcome reasonable doubt—could at least be presented to a jury.

In the days that followed, the Harvard legal scholar would try to wrap up his takeaways from the Strauss-Kahn case. Dershowitz had his own impressions of Vance and the competence of the Manhattan District Attorney's Office in general from his dealings in other cases. In fact, right as the DSK case was playing out, Dershowitz was working for the defense of a woman accused of killing her autistic son where a key piece of forensic evidence, a vial of blood, was lost by Vance's office.

So where did Vance's team go wrong with Strauss-Kahn? Dershowitz faulted the prosecutors on two counts.

First, Dershowitz told me he believed that "Vance essentially did not think the strategy through. He accepted a general rule that you can't win a sexual assault case unless you believe the victim, and I believe that is a flawed analysis."

Second, the prosecutors "failed to understand that because he was DSK he had to put on a defense to clear his name. He had to put on a defense in the media and the court. And his defense would have sunk him. Then it would become a case of who is more likely to be lying. And jurors would ultimately see he's much more likely to be lying even if she is a liar on other counts," he said.

If that is the Monday-morning analysis of the prosecution, what are the takeaways for defense lawyers and their clients, his students wondered.

Dershowitz wouldn't disappoint, delivering a classic reply.

"If you're a criminal, pick your victims carefully," the Harvard law professor advised. "If this had been an articulate upper-class victim, the prosecution would have gone forward. Secondly, pick good lawyers. DSK picked two of the best and they knew exactly how to navigate the courts, the prosecutors, and the media."

There's a pause now, maybe for dramatic effect or maybe because Dershowitz knows his last takeaway is also his most tart.

"Finally, pick a jurisdiction where there is a relatively new DA who listens to his staff too much and who is very, very concerned about reelection and believes that a case like this is largely political and has little to do with the law," Dershowitz argued, suggesting witnesses with credibility problems like Diallo are used all the time to convict.

"An experienced prosecutor would also know prosecutors often put on police witnesses who are lying and accomplice witnesses who copped a plea and tell a story that may not be the whole truth. It's well known some bought prosecution witnesses not only sing, they compose. And many of these cases result in convictions."

And with that, the gavel bangs down on his court of lessons.

TWELVE

Making Sense of the Madness in Manhattan

One of my earliest journalism mentors taught me a trick to be a better interviewer. "Always look around the office, the home, the surroundings of the person you are interviewing and you'll learn something about that subject that will speak volumes about the story you are pursuing," he would say. The advice has stuck with me all these years later.

So when I went up to Manhattan over the Christmas season 2011 to interview a key player in the case, I landed on the eighth floor (as the line prosecutors call it) of Cyrus Vance's office. The person I had come to interview opened our session with a predictable spiel. "You know it's been months now and I've put it out of my mind," the interviewee said, insisting that the D.A.'s Office had moved past the DSK case. There were new strategies, new cases, and new crimes to pursue. "We're looking forward, and don't have time to look back."

I was listening politely, as my eyes wandered the room. On a credenza, I noticed a pile of papers that looked instantly recognizable as a "clips" report of news stories. I strained my neck ever so slightly, hoping not to appear too nosy. The pile included stories and editorials about the DSK case. On top were an editorial from *The New York Times* and a story from *The Wall Street Journal.* The case hadn't faded too much, yet, I thought.

"In the end we ended up okay in the editorials," the interviewee interjected, catching me red-handed at my peeking.

The moment was worth savoring, though. It essentially provided confirmation of a truism about the practice of law in the twenty-first century: prosecutors are as cognizant about what is being said in the media and the court of public opinion as they are in the court of law. The days of the legendary defense lawyer Brendan Sullivan's rule that lawyers should never talk to the press are long gone. And the Dominique Strauss-Kahn case, perhaps more than anything, demonstrates just how far that pendulum has swung in the era of 24/7 TV reports, bloggers, wire service bulletins, and niche Web news sites.

In fact, there's a good case to be made that all sides in this drama engaged more aggressively in the court of public opinion—with the anonymous leaks, the war-of-words press conferences, the exchange of letters, the interviews, the thinly veiled conspiracy theories—than they did in practice of good law and solid investigation. And in so doing, they may have yanked the case from the normal, deliberative path required by the system of justice our Founding Fathers envisioned when they demanded the power to prosecute be balanced with the assurance of due process.

Prosecutors are under a constant media microscope today, and their fortunes in the courtroom can be changed by a media report, right or wrong. The jury pool can be tainted, the activists who help make or break reelection campaigns can be set into motion, or witnesses can be scared away or compelled to come forward as a result of media coverage. It's always been that way, but the proliferation of media outlets and an increasingly breathless pursuit of stories has poisoned the well in ways few could have imagined a decade or two ago. And prosecutors have awkwardly tried to compensate for this changing dynamic.

In New York City, the grand-daddy of the media madness, the pressures are even more immense. For thirty-five years, Robert Morgenthau, a throwback from an earlier era of lawmen, reigned as the Manhattan district attorney. His opinions and judgments were seldom challenged and the office enjoyed a general assumption that it was acting fairly even as evidence was mounting in the courts that police and prosecutors weren't always doing a top-notch job.

The end of the Morgenthau era and the start of Vance's tenure inevitably created a period of intense scrutiny and uncertainty. Vance's personality isn't as stage-grabbing as his predecessor, and his style is a bit cautious, like that of his late, diplomatic father, the former secretary of state Cyrus Vance Sr. The public, in Manhattan at least, still harbors suspicions about whether Vance can stand on his own two legs or whether he simply rode into office on the coattails of Morgenthau's endorsement.

Vance has spent considerable time in office trying to make the case for why he should remain D.A. in the next election. In fact, on the Tuesday after DSK was arrested, he spent his morning attending a reelection fund-raiser with defense lawyers. It's just one of many signs that this prosecutor and his staff have politics on their minds. The lesser verdict in the Cop Rape Trial, which had been the New York media's crime fancy before the DSK arrest, added to the pressures in spring and summer 2011 for Vance to show that his office could deliver on the next big case.

It was that dynamic that the legal tempest of the Dominique Strauss-Kahn case confronted. And there was ample evidence that first weekend that police and prosecutors weren't up to the task, both missing basic investigative steps and overreaching to show they could go toe-to-toe with the biggest-name defendant to come their way in a long time.

First there were the missteps: not questioning Strauss-Kahn during those first four-plus hours in custody before he invoked his right to counsel, failing to take him for a forensic exam for more than a day, delaying the police lineup until *after* Nafi Diallo had seen his photo elsewhere three times. Some mistakes weren't that consequential in the end because prosecutors ended up with DNA evidence to prove the sexual encounter occurred. But there were signs that police and prosecutors weren't on top of their game for a case that required it.

Strauss-Kahn's arrest and first court appearance provide provocative evidence that prosecutors seemed to be playing to the media, too. The perp walk in front of the cameras that Sunday night still makes many uneasy today. And the prosecutor's ham-handed effort to compare DSK to the fugitive movie director Roman Polanski earned the slap-down it got from the judge. It wasn't necessary, and seemed aimed more at the court of public opinion than the court of law.

Prosecutors went into court that Monday with bad information, too, falsely claiming Strauss-Kahn didn't have any ties to the United States, a key factor for determining bail status, when in fact he and his wife owned a $4 million mansion in Washington, D.C. They also turned down DSK's lawyers' reasonable request to delay indictment—waiving the five-day rule and installing a bail package—an offer that could have slowed down the process so that all sides would have more time to evaluate the evidence and the victim's credibility. And their argument that a speedy indictment and imprisonment was the only way to ensure DSK wouldn't flee to France also was proven wrong. Four days later, Strauss-Kahn was released into a protective custody arrangement that worked for months.

The evidence also suggests Strauss-Kahn's lawyers weren't the only ones seeking to slow the madness. Lisa Friel, then the sex crimes unit chief inside Vance's office, clearly wanted to slow down the grand jury process so she'd have more time to debrief the victim and ask the hard questions to ensure her credibility and story were solid.

As it turned out, she got just less than forty minutes with Diallo before taking her into the grand jury that first week.

Likewise, one of Vance's own Kitchen Cabinet advisers, the former sex crimes prosecutor and author, Linda Fairstein, pulled the district attorney aside that first week to caution him about the importance of debriefing the witness thoroughly and checking for other motives. She even offered her services, sensing there was tension in the relationship between the senior managers in the office and Friel, their top sex crimes expert. Vance passed on the opportunity.

Within a few days of Fairstein's caution, Friel was removed from the case. In her place, two respected violent crimes prosecutors were assigned. Both were courtroom bulldogs with impeccable credentials and winning records. But neither had the experience, the training, or the temperament to deal with a complicated immigrant housekeeper and her assertive lawyer. The necessary investigative work to check Diallo's finances and her stories of how she was gang-raped in Guinea and got into the country seemingly fell by the wayside in the early going. The prosecutors seemed enamored with the victim, and mesmerized by her ability to weave a false tale with tears and emotions. Ironically, or perhaps tragically, it took Diallo's second lawyer, Kenneth Thompson, to discover the credibility issues and voluntarily bring them to the attention of Vance's office.

The revelations seemed to spawn a sense of panic in Vance's office, perhaps driven by embarrassment. Prosecutors were soon shouting at Diallo, creating an instant rift in the bond of trust that sex crimes prosecutors normally build with their victims, who often have legal and credibility issues like Diallo. With little time to think through the evidence after first learning of the problems, one prosecutor declared on June 9 she'd never put Diallo at the stand. Another kicked Diallo out of the office like a defendant, humiliating the housekeeper in front of her teenage daughter.

The prosecutors' lack of investigative thoroughness continued.

They don't even follow a basic step and get the hotel records when Diallo appears to change her story and admits she returned briefly to Room 2820 in the aftermath of the attack. They instead run to court and disclose an apparent change of story, undercutting their case. It's only afterward that they get the records and recognize that the story they had just told the court was implausible. Diallo couldn't have cleaned 2820 after the incident. She had cleaned it *before* and then stopped back for a few seconds just to pick up her supplies. Given the language barriers in dealing with the victim, there clearly was some miscommunication.

Longtime legal watchers are left wondering whether a well-to-do white woman from the Upper East Side might have been treated differently from this immigrant housekeeper from Guinea with a lawyer who seemed to irritate the prosecutors. Isn't the normal investigative process when a conflict in a story arises to check the evidence and review it before running to court? And even if Vance's prosecutors didn't feel they owed it to the victim to check the hotel records, they owed it to the courts to get it right.

Office politics and personal feelings only further impacted a case already suffering from subpar work. The prosecutors and Thompson seemed to almost relish trading barbs in private and in public, letting their own personality clashes escalate to a point that the interests of Diallo seem to take a backseat. There were moments where either side could have deescalated the growing feud. But neither did: Instead they fought over petty issues, like vacations and doctor's appointments and perceived slights.

One excellent example, because it involves Vance himself, can help demonstrate the missed opportunities. When Thompson demanded his first meeting with Vance in mid-June, it was designed to be a clear-the-air session. Relations had not spun out of control yet. Thompson brought a handful of grievances into the room, one of them emanating from a *New York Times* article that divulged that a top prosecutor in the office was married to one of DSK's defense lawyers and had to recuse herself from the case to avoid a conflict of interest.

Thompson and his partner simply wanted to know exactly when the recusal occurred and how it had been done. Vance said he didn't know but would get back to them. He never did, allowing the issue to fester even though there was clear proof the prosecutor in question, Karen Agnifilo, had stepped aside in the case within minutes of her husband's firm being hired by DSK. I know, I have a copy of the email, from 10:45 p.m. that first night of the case.

Vance could have easily assuaged the concerns and lowered the temperature. But he passed. Instead, his office engaged in antagonizing leaks to the media. They wrongly claimed Thompson kept his client away from prosecutors for nineteen days when in fact Diallo showed up at the office during that time only to find a scheduling problem with the translator. The leak of the audiotapes proved to be character-crushing, and it ended all goodwill. It led Thompson to conclude the case would be thrown out. He felt a need to defend his client's reputation. And he escalated, first with the courthouse press conference on July 1 and then a series of letters and motions that barely disguised the sense of abandonment Diallo and he felt.

Vance's prosecutors may look you in the eye today and say on the record that none of this tit-for-tat influenced their decision to dismiss the case. But there is evidence to the contrary. One need only to look at the final motion to dismiss to find subtle barbs and adjective-laden phrases slipped in footnotes or passages solely to counter Thompson's personal attacks. (Prosecutors admitted to me in post-case interviews that was their intention, in fact.)

There's a good case to be made, in fact, that the prosecutors spent much of the last seven weeks of the case acting more like politicians than arbiters of the truth. There was plenty more that could have been investigated. Instead, Vance's team seemed preoccupied, asking Fairstein to go on television in July and spin favorably for him and visiting with Morgenthau to get him to issue a publicity statement supporting the handling of case. And then Vance took his final motion, a legal document, to Martha's Vineyard to have it polished by the accomplished author Fairstein.

These aren't the normal actions of everyday lawyers and prosecutors; they're the handiwork of a team gauging the political winds and hoping to win the public relations battle. Even innocent bystanders, like the outcry witnesses at the Sofitel, who by every account tried to do the right thing, were sucked into feeling that they had their arms twisted or their well-intentioned efforts insulted when prosecutors came back to interview them one last time.

Vance's office may insist all of these events can be, and should be, interpreted more favorably. The prosecutors made all the decisions by the book and simply wanted to build consensus in the community, they insist. And Vance's team will argue (as they tried with me) that the personal vitriol with Thompson, the anger at being lied to so convincingly by Diallo, and the sensational media coverage had no bearing on the outcome.

To counter those statements, I offer a personal but powerful experience. It came from an exit interview I did on background with one of the key players on the prosecution team in late August.

"If Ken Thompson had just apologized early on, we might have been able to bring this case. We might have trusted her and trusted him," the prosecutor said, in a moment of candor that ricocheted through the humid August air.

Could it be that the dismissal of the Strauss-Kahn case turned on the mere animosity that developed between the prosecution team and the outspoken lawyer-advocate for the victim? I wondered, so I followed up, sending an email back to the source recounting the comment to see if the prosecutor really meant what was said.

The prosecutor responded with a clarification, without much distinction.

"If SHE had come clean earlier, there could have been a way we believed her, if we did," the prosecutor wrote back. "His apology, early or late, would not have affected our decision on the merits, though it would have made interacting with him a lot easier."

The comeback rang hollow. "Could have been a way we believed her"? Would have made interacting with Thompson easier? These don't seem to be relevant factors for a case that was supposed to be decided on the merits of the law and facts. They're factors seemingly better suited for personal or public relations spats.

There seems to be ample evidence, in hindsight, to render a verdict that Vance's office committed some missteps. Any prosecution office that in a span of just twelve weeks goes from insisting to a court that its case and victim are compelling to arguing that they are unreliable and not provable has missed some important investigative steps. It's even more stunning when the core evidence of forensics and outcry witnesses hasn't changed at all. The rush to indict Strauss-Kahn within five days and keep him held without bail looks, in retrospect, to be the work of an inexperienced D.A. thrust onto the biggest stage while still unprepared. And when the victim begins unraveling, that same inexperience seems to prompt an overreaction in the other direction.

One overarching sentiment I picked up in my exit interviews was how personally offended prosecutors felt at having been lied to by Diallo and criticized so publicly by Thompson. They volunteered stories about apologies received, and neglected. And when they spoke of the decision to dismiss, it often focused less on how jurors might view the case and more on how the prosecutors themselves viewed guilt and innocence. In fact, Vance himself offered some rare, personal insights five months after the end of the case during a law firm forum in January 2012 that escaped much notice.

"I determined that I was no longer convinced beyond a reasonable doubt that I knew what happened—not that something didn't happen, but whether we, as an office, knew beyond a reasonable doubt what happened," Vance told the crowd. "We did not have that quantum of confidence."

The frequent "I's" and "we's" and "me's" in the prosecutors' dialogue with lawyers, witnesses, and outsiders in the final weeks of the case, and afterward, troubled some veterans of the legal system like Lanny Davis. There was a sense that prosecutors were substituting their own opinions on guilt and innocence for a jury's judgment. And it left Davis, for instance, wondering aloud to prosecutors why they wouldn't let a jury decide.

To be fair, Diallo's credibility issues would have made a final call on whether to proceed to trial or dismiss the charges a tough decision. It could have gone either way. In this case, though, personal and political factors seemed to tip the balance. The best evidence comes from the prosecutors' own writing. In the beginning, all the substantial evidence from the forensics and outcry witnesses was interpreted in the court filings and police documents in the worst light to the defendant, with little scrutiny to the victim's potential flaws and motives. And then just a few weeks later, the same exact and unchanged evidence was interpreted in the most favorable light to the defendant.

"The moral of this case is that DSK got indicted after hiring two great lawyers and facing six zealous prosecutors, and he got freed by eight defense lawyers, the same two great ones he hired and the six who had flip-flopped in the prosecutor's office," Alan Dershowitz would tell me in a classic sound bite afterward.

Vance's comments in January also implicitly nodded to another factor in the case: the rush to indict DSK within New York's legally mandated five-day deadline after arrest. "We could benefit, I think, from slightly more extended timetables," Vance would concede at the legal forum. Of course, there was no mention of the fact that his line prosecutors initially contemplated a bail package that would have extended the deadline, but were overruled by the eighth floor. And in the end, Vance doesn't seem sure how much slowing down the case at the beginning might have helped. "There is no single thing that can change the complicated dynamic of determining who's telling the truth between two strangers," he told the law firm audience.

No Monday-morning quarterbacking would be complete without an analysis of the accuser and her lawyer. Nafi Diallo is an immigrant with a complicated life story. Those complications include an imperfect grasp of the English language, a fear of losing her job, a belief rooted in her Guinean experience that reporting a sex crime might lead to personal harm, and the knowledge that she had contrived a story to ensure she and her daughter could stay in America and have a better life. To add to the complexity, she lives in a vibrant world in the Bronx and Harlem where story embellishment, fast-talking criminals, and distrust of Muslim women working in hotels are simply part of the cultural fabric inside a community of hard-working immigrants.

All of these influenced her early actions and the outcomes in the case. Yet none exempts Diallo from her obligation, upon setting foot in the United States, to know and abide by the laws and mores in this land. She had an obligation to tell the truth. And on that front, there is ample evidence she didn't do so with prosecutors as it related to her past. There's also evidence that she knew she had made a mistake—most likely driven by her fear of losing her job or being forced to return to Guinea—and tried to get right with prosecutors by coming forward within a few short weeks.

In the end, her lies about her past complicate the case but don't necessarily gut it. As for the prosecutors' assertion that Diallo also lied about what happened in the immediate aftermath of the incident in Sofitel Suite 2806 on May 14, 2011, there's a preponderance of evidence to the contrary. When my colleagues and I at *Newsweek* interviewed her in mid-July—right in the middle of the drama—she gave a complete accounting of what went on in the room and afterward. While there were clear limitations in her grasp of English, there were no hesitations or ambiguities. The more specifically we went over the evidence with her, the more precise and complete her answers were. And her account to *Newsweek* about the occurrences in the room and the aftermath appears to match the final version that prosecutors settled on in their dismissal motion. If Diallo could give an accurate, complete account to a group of reporters well versed in the evidence, why then did prosecutors feel like they got three separate versions of what went on in the room and the aftermath? The answer to that question may rest more on the failures and investigative shortcomings of the prosecutors. They hadn't gathered all the evidence they needed and also overlooked some incongruities in their initial theory of the crime. And so they missed some important questions and evidence early on. And Diallo, being illiterate and dependent on Fulani translators during interrogations, only seemed to answer the questions they asked. When prosecutors—already panicked by Diallo's lies about her past in Guinea—finally discovered the shortcomings in their theory of the case, there's strong evidence that they chose to blame Diallo, accusing her of concocting three separate stories. In fact, Diallo only appeared to have one story to tell about what happened in the room. And it was remarkably consistent with the forensic evidence and the outcry witnesses' testimony. The problem was the detectives and prosecutors didn't extract the full story from their evidence or their victim in the beginning.

And then there's Kenneth Thompson, the prosecutor-turned-passionate-lawyer who enters late but unmistakably stirs the case as Diallo's second attorney. There are three unmistakable impacts from his involvement. First, he discovers Diallo's earlier misstatements and falsehoods and immediately brings them to prosecutors' attention. It was the right thing to do and it is clear he never expected the blowback that followed from Vance's office. If he did, he wouldn't have left Diallo alone for the June 9 interview, a move he readily concedes was a mistake. Second, there's little doubt his aggressive style in defending his client's honor and reputation, once they came under assault, grated on the prosecutors and likely changed the dynamics in the final six weeks of the case. And third, he and his partner quickly pivoted in the face of a crumbling criminal case to try to stake out a second avenue for Diallo to seek justice through the civil courts.

To many watching the drama in real time, Thompson's actions appeared to be emotionally driven public relations antics. Some even questioned whether he was best serving his client's interests. But one of the benefits of putting the DSK case into slow motion afterward is that a new story line emerges. The students in Dershowitz's Harvard law class started their interrogation of Thompson with many of the same suppositions as legal observers. But over the course of two hours of Q&A they came to realize that Thompson had concluded far earlier than was visible in public, perhaps as early as June 9, that prosecutors were likely to drop the case. And what the public didn't know then was that Thompson and his partner had devised a clear, albeit desperate, strategy that was aimed at creating public and private pressure to get Vance's office to reconsider its thinking. When a series of leaks and allegations from Vance's office sullied Diallo's reputation, in some cases unfairly, Thompson then adapted the strategy to try to rehabilitate Diallo's public standing so she could at least seek justice through a lawsuit. In the end, there was a method to the madness. Legal experts can debate whether Thompson made the correct decisions, but at least there is a different paradigm for evaluating that strategy.

That doesn't mean Thompson won't continue to face tough scrutiny. As this book was heading to publication, a rift was developing between Thompson and Diallo's family, as some relatives and friends around the housekeeper questioned whether he should continue on the case. One of the legitimate questions that likely will be raised is whether any of Thompson's public comments could be used by Strauss-Kahn's lawyers to waive Diallo's attorney-client or medical privacy privileges under the law if the civil case proceeds. Thompson mentioned her hospital records at the July 1 press conference. He talked in public about some of his private conversations with his client. And his statements denying that his client had any financial motive opened the door for Strauss-Kahn's lawyers to abandon their confidentiality agreement and disclose their earlier settlement talks with Thompson to the prosecutors.

There is an early verdict that Thompson was a zealous, impassioned defender of an immigrant chambermaid who few others were willing to defend when things went sour. His desperation strategy also can be seen in a new light, thanks to his Harvard visit. What remains to be judged as the drama rolls forward in civil court is the merits of his legal decisions. And only time can reveal that verdict.

The main players in this case undeniably had a witting co-conspirator: the news media. DSK was branded "Le Perp" and "Le Perv," who preyed on a housekeeper during the first weekend's headlines. And implausibly, by the eighth weekend, he was suddenly the victim of a conniving, lying, money-grubbing housekeeper who was herself branded a "prostitute" in a thinly, anonymously sourced tabloid story. Conspiracy theories, thinly sourced leaks, and opinions masquerading as facts poisoned the public well of knowledge, often creating an unnecessarily vitriolic and misleading discourse.

Even the "Gray Lady" fell prey to shoddy journalism in my estimation. *The New York Times* rushed out a single, anonymous-sourced story from a "well-placed law enforcement source" that led the public to believe Diallo had raised the issue of cashing in on DSK's wealth while talking with a prison inmate. The allegation, with hedges like "words to the effect," was clearly going to change Diallo's fortunes forever. Yet there is little evidence the *Times* tried to reach the two people on the call who knew what they had said (Diallo and Amara

Tarawally) or that the newspaper was even willing to give them enough time reasonably to respond. The drive for a scoop seems to have prevailed. And there's ample evidence that the *Times*'s scoop was wrong on some facts, and misleading on others, to the great detriment of Diallo's reputation.

A month after the devastating story, Diallo and Thompson got to hear the now infamous tape of the prison exchange, spoken in Diallo's native Fulani tongue. They say it clearly shows that Tarawally raised the issue of DSK's wealth and that Diallo demurred, saying it was an issue for her lawyer, not her. If an accurate account, that's a big difference in meaning from what the *Times* story led us all to believe.

Until the tape is released publicly, if ever, we won't know the truth for sure. But the mere fact that there are significant doubts about the accuracy of the *Times*'s report all these months later provides prima facie proof that the *Times* violated the old adage, "Get it first, but get it right." It's clearly in the position of having gotten it first, and hoping it was right, or at least that it was not too wrong. And that isn't good journalism.

My reporting also shows that the most likely office that could have leaked the tape—the district attorney's—was in the midst of its own debate and uncertainty about the victim. The bosses in the office had decided the night of the leak to disclose publicly in court that Diallo had severe issues of credibility. But they did *not* want to disclose the tape because they did not have a full transcript of the Fulani conversation. All they had at the time was a "digest" giving the general sense of the conversation. That means whoever leaked the account to the *Times* may have had a motive, perhaps to tip the debate inside the D.A.'s Office toward dismissing a case that the prosecutors had soured on. A single anonymous source with a hidden agenda is exactly the reason journalism on most days insists on a two-source rule along with fair comment and balance.

Beyond the performance of prosecutors, lawyers, witnesses, and reporters, there are two remaining questions left open by the way the criminal case ended so abruptly. And we may only know the answers if the civil trial is allowed to proceed.

The first is, what happened in Sofitel Suite 2806 between 12:06 and 12:13 p.m.? And second, could a more courageous prosecutor have secured a conviction?

No one disputes that a rushed sexual encounter occurred. The forensics are irrefutable. The question is how to decide who is telling the truth. Strauss-Kahn would have us believe Diallo invited his advance with the look in her eyes. Diallo is adamant she did not consent, and tried to flee and fight.

I think the biggest fact to emerge *since* the dismissal comes in a little noticed passage of biographer Michael Taubman's book that tells DSK's side of the story. If you read it quickly, you might miss it. But Taubman states that Strauss-Kahn told him flatly that Diallo tried to leave the room at first, though she didn't appear to be in a hurry.

The instinct to leave—one DSK purports to have acknowledged—would seem to support her account that the event was nonconsensual, and that she had tried to get away before Strauss-Kahn closed the door. The relatively short period of time that elapsed and the location where the oral sex occurred also seem to support a nonconsensual encounter. The sex didn't happen in the suite's glorious bedroom, with its large comfortable bed, which would have provided a more comfortable venue for casual but consensual sex. It happened in a narrow hallway near a bathroom.

Diallo doesn't seem to have come dressed for casual sex, either. She's wearing two pairs of pantyhose that day. And Strauss-Kahn's DNA from his hands are on the inside of Diallo's panties, suggesting he was going for more than just consensual oral sex. Finally, Diallo doesn't seem to act like a willing lover immediately afterward. She spits his semen on the floor, runs from the room, and hides in a hallway. And her actions with the outcry witnesses—though they certainly could be the work of a trained, theatrical liar—seem to match the classic behavior of a sex assault victim with low self-esteem. She feels guilty and even worries that she might be fired for walking in on a VIP. She is reluctant to report the incident to police at first and needs coaxing. She has physical effects afterward, like the urge to vomit and trembling.

It is possible that Diallo may have been more deferential in that room than she has let on. I saw clear signs of her shyness, discomfort, and deference around men during my three-hour interview with her. Perhaps her voice was softer when she objected to Strauss-Kahn. Maybe she didn't run from the room the first time but tried to walk slowly, as DSK is quoted as telling the author, Taubman. Perhaps at some point she finally gave in and let Strauss-Kahn finish his business, which would explain the lack of signs of mouth trauma or a more physical struggle inside the room.

But if DSK is to be believed—that Diallo tried to leave the room at first—it would seem to establish an instinct to flee that could convince jurors that one of the world's most powerful men took advantage of an illiterate, immigrant housekeeper fearful of losing her job if she spoke up. The question of whether Strauss-Kahn has acted this way before also lends weight to a conclusion that what happened in the room was a nonconsensual event. DSK was comfortable having an affair with a young Congolese student (if her account proves true) as well as a subordinate at the IMF. And by his own admission to French authorities he tried to force himself on the young journalist Tristane Banon—the daughter of a former lover and a woman his daughter's age—at least to get a kiss.

Many of the women who have come forward—both those who alleged consensual or forced sexual encounters with him—also describe Strauss-Kahn as extremely physical in his sexual behavior. "Brutal," a "crazed man," a "rutting chimpanzee" are just some of the descriptions. It's uncertain how much information about these prior activities would be admitted into a U.S. court of law, even in a civil case where there is greater latitude for evidence of prior conduct. But in the court of public opinion, they clearly lend credence to Diallo's account of events.

A civil trial may help answer the many outstanding questions and force DSK to offer his own defense in detail under a blistering cross-examination by Diallo's lawyers rather than the friendly French journalists who have talked with him so far.

The backdrop of the other women's claims isn't the only thing complicating Strauss-Kahn's efforts at rehabilitating his political standing in France. In late March, he was formally informed he may be charged with "aggravated pimping" back home in connection with an investigation into an alleged prostitution ring that was centered at the ritzy Carlton hotel in Lille, France, but may have reached as far away as Washington, D.C. DSK was released on bail of 100,000 euros. DSK's French lawyers acknowledge that he participated in libertine sex soirees at hotels, but did not believe he was engaged with prostitutes. While prostitution isn't illegal in France, profiting from it would be a crime. Prosecutors are investigating whether Strauss-Kahn was habitually involved in facilitating and profiting from the alleged prostitution ring. Whatever the outcome, the entire Carlton Affair—as it has become known in France—only furthers the portrait of a man as a sex addict who may have preyed on women in the workplace.

In the interim, we are all left wondering whether a different prosecution team—one more experienced in sexual assault cases and less obsessed with personality and politics—could have proceeded to trial and won. I'm not one to venture a guess. But to help answer that lingering question, I've offered you Dershowitz's closing argument to his law class in Harvard. I did so for two reasons. Dershowitz is seldom arguing *for* prosecution. He's your classic defense lawyer. And secondly, he takes a position that Vance would not—that it is possible to have a victim whom the jury distrusts and still secure a sexual assault conviction if you are willing to address the flaws up front and the rest of your evidence is solid.

Dershowitz's hypothetical closing argument and his entire semester of teaching on the case challenged the brightest members of the next generation of lawyers to look at the case in a light few could see when the events were occurring in real time. And in that respect, it provides the ultimate armchair quarterback's lesson.

In the end, the only certain loser in this case may be justice itself.

I'm grateful to all the players in the case who lent so much of their time to me to explore the deeper issues of the drama that many of us veterans of the case have come to call the "Madness in Manhattan." Each side let me inside their world with graciousness, trust, and candor. And none of the observations in this chapter are designed to pick sides, pick fights, or to impugn. Rather, they are designed to extract, posthumously, lessons from a legal drama that played out at the speed of light, on a high-pressure stage with extraordinary complications. Like most of journalism, this book is a first attempt at cataloguing history. It is certain to be amplified and augmented by future developments.

If there is one personal takeaway I could leave behind—for young reporters, future prosecutors, and future defense lawyers—it would be this. All of us in professions who engage the courts of law and public opinion must be better prepared and more sensitive to the enormous complexities that can lead to rushes of judgment, either at the beginning, the middle, or the end of any legal proceeding. Jurisprudence—at least as the wise men John Adams and Thomas Jefferson and John Jay envisioned it three centuries ago—is poorly suited for the instant gratification demands of the twenty-first century. It requires patience and thoroughness and a naturally contested process to mete out justice. And that may be the most important lesson any of us can take from the anatomy of this scandal.

INDEX